Transforming Treatment
New Pathways to Lifesaving Care with Data and AI

Ryan Bauer

Dedication

For my sister Alisha and my brother Corey, I could not have done this without the two of you!

Contents

Preface

Over the past three years, I have conducted market research on patients diagnosed with and undergoing treatment for a rare disease. My analysis revealed a surprising and intriguing pattern: these groups of rare disease patients often share common traits. These shared characteristics include, but are not limited to:

- Residing in similar types of locations (e.g., suburban areas)
- Watching the same television channels at similar times
- Making similar purchases around the same time

While some social, economic, geographic, and environmental overlap was expected, one behavioral trait consistently stood out: media consumption. This insight is particularly valuable given the challenges in educating the public about rare diseases. While we don't currently understand why rare disease patients have shared traits, we could, over time, if we are able to expand my analysis further, first to first better understand rare disease patients, and second, to be able to reach potential patients, before disease symptoms start.

The Importance of Early Diagnosis

Rare diseases often take more than five years to diagnose correctly, and many individuals never receive a proper diagnosis or treatment. This delay can have severe consequences:

- Significant and sometimes fatal health events
- Lack of access to appropriate clinical care and treatments
- Missed opportunities for slowing disease progression
- Limited access to services, peer support, and research opportunities

Early diagnosis is crucial. For example, newborn screening for Severe Combined Immunodeficiency (SCID) has increased the five-year survival rate from 73% to 87%. Moreover, a study by the EveryLife Foundation for Rare Diseases found that early diagnosis could save up to $500,000 per patient. Educating the public, healthcare professionals, policymakers, and the media about rare diseases is crucial for raising awareness, promoting early diagnosis, and advocating for better support and resources. But how can this be done in a way that is effective and efficient in the age of information overload and in the attention economy, where advertisers and influencers are competing for consumers' attention, and that competition is loud and crowded?

Challenges in Rare Disease Awareness

Several factors contribute to the lack of public awareness and understanding of rare diseases:

- Misconceptions and stigma
- Discrimination against affected individuals
- Limited education among healthcare professionals, policymakers, and the media

Raising awareness is crucial for promoting early diagnosis and advocating for better support and resources. If we can know, with a degree of accuracy, the media consumption habits of individuals with potentially rare diseases we can more efficiently and cost-effectively provide media placements that educate the public, driving earlier diagnosis.

A Data-Driven Approach to Education and Early Detection

My working theory proposes a new approach to rare disease detection, diagnosis, and treatment:

1. Analyze behavioral patterns of rare disease patients who have been granted access to their data
2. Identify common media consumption habits among potential rare disease patients
3. Use this information to provide targeted media placements for public education
4. Drive earlier diagnosis through more efficient and cost-effective awareness campaigns

This approach could revolutionize rare disease education and potentially save lives by enabling earlier interventions. That's why there is a tremendous benefit to delivering disease state education to the public in a more effective manner, primarily by giving patients and providers an earlier window for diagnosis. Early diagnosis also allows people to access the best clinical care and treatment and can help slow the progression of a disease, in part by helping people access services, peer support, and research and clinical trials.

The Changing Landscape of Rare Disease Research

Despite historical challenges in funding and attention from researchers and pharmaceutical companies, the outlook for rare disease treatment is improving:

- Increased federal funding
- Advancements in biotech and medical research
- Growth in markets for clinical trials, drug repurposing, and orphan drug development

The most promising areas are genomics and precision medicine. With 72% of rare diseases having genetic origins, the potential for tailored therapies based on gene targeting is immense.

This work is both exciting and hopeful. By leveraging data methodologies and artificial intelligence, we can develop innovative approaches to healthcare challenges. This analysis provides a framework for bringing new ideas in rare disease detection and treatment to life, potentially improving outcomes for countless patients worldwide. This could very well change rare disease education, and it represents an opportunity to save lives. Having developed systems for my own work provided a template for continued work and this book. My hope is that the information provided here brings your own innovative ideas in healthcare to life!

Chapter 1:
Introduction

In the bustling emergency department of City General Hospital, Dr. Sarah Chen faced a puzzling case. Jake, a 45-year-old man, had been admitted with symptoms that did not quite add up: fatigue, mild fever, and a nagging cough. Initial tests were inconclusive, and Jake's condition was steadily worsening.

As Dr. Chen pored over Jake's medical records, a notification popped up on her tablet. The hospital's new data analytics system had flagged a pattern: in the past week, it had detected a 40% increase in patients from Jake's neighborhood presenting with similar symptoms. Moreover, it had cross-referenced environmental data and noted a recent chemical spill in a nearby industrial plant.

Armed with this crucial information, Dr. Chen quickly ordered specialized tests. Within hours, Jake was diagnosed with chemical pneumonitis, a condition caused by inhaling irritants. Thanks to the rapid, data-driven diagnosis, Jake received targeted treatment immediately, potentially saving his life and those of others in his community.

This scenario, while fictional, illustrates a very real and growing trend in healthcare: the power of data to transform patient outcomes. In an era where information is abundant, but time is scarce, the ability to collect, analyze, and act upon data can make the difference between life and death, between a costly, prolonged hospital stay and a swift, accurate diagnosis and treatment.

In this book, we will explore how the vast seas of data generated in modern healthcare settings can be harnessed to improve patient care, streamline operations, and tackle some of the most pressing challenges facing healthcare systems around the world.

From artificial intelligence assisting in diagnoses to predictive analytics preventing hospital readmissions, from personalized treatment plans based on genetic data to population health management informed by social determinants of health – the applications of data in healthcare are as diverse as they are impactful.

As we delve into the transformative potential of data in healthcare, we will also confront the challenges and ethical considerations that come with it. How do we balance the need for comprehensive data with patient privacy? How can we ensure that data-driven healthcare does not exacerbate existing health disparities?

Whether you are a healthcare professional looking to stay ahead of the curve, a data scientist interested in one of the most consequential applications of your field, a policymaker grappling with healthcare reform, or simply someone curious about the future of medicine, this book offers insights into how data is reshaping the healthcare landscape.

In the annals of medical history, few developments have promised to revolutionize healthcare as profoundly as Artificial Intelligence (AI). We stand at the cusp of a new era in medicine, where intelligent machines work alongside human expertise to diagnose diseases, personalize treatments, streamline operations, and push the boundaries of medical research. This book aims to be your comprehensive guide through this rapidly evolving landscape.

Purpose of the Book

The primary purpose of this book is to provide a thorough, accessible, and forward-looking exploration of AI's role in healthcare. Whether you're a healthcare professional seeking to understand how AI will impact your practice, a technologist interested in the applications of AI in medicine, a policymaker grappling with the implications of these technologies, or simply a curious reader, this book offers valuable insights into the intersection of AI and healthcare.

Our goal is to demystify AI technologies and their applications in healthcare, shedding light on how these innovations are transforming the field. We will explore the current state and potential of AI across various aspects of medicine, highlighting its impact on diagnosis, treatment, and patient care. Additionally, we aim to discuss the ethical, regulatory, and societal implications of AI in healthcare, addressing concerns related to privacy, accountability, and access. By providing a balanced view, we will examine both the promises and challenges of AI in medicine, offering insights into how it can shape the future of healthcare while acknowledging the complexities it brings.

Scope of the Book

This book takes a comprehensive approach to examining AI in healthcare. We begin by tracing the evolution of AI in medicine, from early expert systems to today's sophisticated machine learning algorithms. We then delve into the foundational aspects of healthcare data and analytics before exploring specific applications of AI across clinical practice, patient care, medical research, and healthcare operations.

Key areas covered include:

- The fundamentals of healthcare data and its role in AI
- AI applications in diagnosis, treatment, and patient care
- The impact of AI on medical research and drug discovery
- How AI is optimizing healthcare operations and resource management
- Ethical considerations and the regulatory landscape surrounding AI in healthcare
- Global perspectives on AI adoption in different healthcare systems
- Future trends and preparing for an AI-driven healthcare ecosystem

Throughout the book, we ground our discussions in real-world examples and case studies, providing concrete illustrations of how AI is already transforming healthcare and what we might expect in the future.

Relevance in Today's Healthcare Landscape

The relevance of AI in healthcare has never been more apparent. As healthcare systems worldwide grapple with challenges such as aging populations, rising costs, staff shortages, and the need for more personalized care, AI offers potential solutions that could reshape how we approach these issues.

The COVID-19 pandemic has further underscored the importance of AI in healthcare, from accelerating vaccine development to predicting outbreak hotspots and optimizing resource allocation in overwhelmed hospitals. As we move forward, AI is poised to play an increasingly crucial role in making healthcare more efficient, effective, and equitable.

Moreover, as patients become more engaged in their own health management and as healthcare moves increasingly towards precision medicine, AI will be instrumental in analyzing the vast amounts of data generated and in providing personalized insights and recommendations.

However, the integration of AI into healthcare also raises important questions about data privacy, algorithmic bias, the changing roles of healthcare professionals, and how to ensure that the benefits of AI are distributed equitably. This book aims to address these crucial issues alongside the technological advancements.

A Journey into the Future of Medicine

As you read this book, you'll embark on a journey into the future of medicine. You'll explore how AI is already changing healthcare and imagine how it might transform medical practice in the years to come. You'll grapple with complex ethical questions and consider how we can shape the development of AI in healthcare to best serve humanity.

Whether AI in healthcare is a familiar topic or entirely new to you, this book is designed to deepen your understanding, challenge your assumptions, and inspire you to think critically about the role of AI in shaping the future of medicine.

As we stand on the brink of this AI-driven transformation in healthcare, it's crucial to approach the future with both excitement for the possibilities and a commitment to responsible development and implementation. It is our hope that this book will equip you with the knowledge and insights to participate in and contribute to this important dialogue.

In the chapters that follow, we'll break down complex concepts into accessible language, explore real-world case studies, and look ahead to the future of data-driven healthcare. By the end of this journey, you'll have a comprehensive understanding of how data is being used to improve healthcare outcomes and the tools to think critically about its applications and implications.

So, let's begin our exploration of this exciting frontier, where bits and bytes are becoming as crucial to patient care as stethoscopes and scalpels. Welcome to the future of healthcare – a future shaped by the power of data.

Chapter 2:

The Evolution: From Expert Systems to Machine Learning

AI's integration into healthcare spans over six decades, evolving from rule-based systems to today's machine learning models capable of analyzing complex medical data and predicting outcomes. This chapter traces that journey, highlighting milestones, breakthroughs, and persistent challenges that shape current AI capabilities and limitations.

Understanding this history offers essential context:

1. It clarifies how today's AI tools emerged and where they still fall short.
2. It reveals the cyclical nature of progress—returning to old ideas with new technologies.
3. It frames ethical and practical concerns still relevant today.
4. It helps forecast AI's future role in medicine.

Throughout this evolution, AI in healthcare has moved from specialized tools mimicking expert knowledge to systems capable of discovering patterns beyond human perception—navigating cycles of hype and skepticism. By the chapter's end, readers will grasp how far AI has come and what lies ahead.

Early Expert Systems in Medicine (1960s–1980s)

The first wave of medical AI centered on expert systems designed to replicate clinical reasoning through rule-based logic.

DENDRAL (1965): Although created for chemistry, DENDRAL's success in molecular analysis proved AI's potential for solving complex scientific problems, laying groundwork for medical applications.

MYCIN (1970s): A landmark system that diagnosed blood

infections and recommended treatments. It managed uncertainty, explained its reasoning, and separated logic from knowledge. Despite outperforming junior doctors in tests, MYCIN was never deployed due to ethical, legal, and technical constraints.

INTERNIST-I (1970s): Aimed to assist general internal medicine diagnoses with an expansive knowledge base and scoring system. Its broad scope revealed the computational limits of early AI when handling the complexity of general diagnosis.

CASNET (1960s): Innovated by modeling disease causality for glaucoma diagnosis and treatment. It pioneered multilevel representations of disease progression, influencing future AI approaches.

Challenges and Limitations of Early Expert Systems

While these early systems showed promise, they faced several significant challenges:

1. **Knowledge Acquisition Bottleneck**: Encoding human expertise into rules was time-consuming and difficult to scale.
2. **Brittleness**: Systems often perform poorly when faced with scenarios outside their specific knowledge base.
3. **Difficulty Handling Uncertainty**: Despite attempts like MYCIN's certainty factors, truly representing the uncertainties inherent in medical reasoning proved challenging.
4. **Limited Adaptability**: These systems couldn't learn from new data or experiences; they could only be updated through manual revision of their rule bases.
5. **Computational Limitations**: The hardware of the time limited the complexity and speed of these systems.

Legacy and Impact

Despite their limitations, these early expert systems were crucial in demonstrating the potential of AI in healthcare. They sparked important discussions about the role of computers in medical decision-making and laid the groundwork for future developments.

Key contributions included:

- Demonstrating that certain medical decision-making processes could be modeled computationally
- Highlighting the importance of managing uncertainty in medical reasoning
- Raising awareness of the potential for AI to assist in complex diagnostic tasks
- Stimulating research into knowledge representation and reasoning under uncertainty

Before we explore deep learning's healthcare applications, let's understand its basic structure. Deep learning uses artificial neural networks—computing systems inspired by the human brain's network of neurons. These networks contain multiple 'layers' of processing units, with each layer extracting increasingly complex features from data. For example, when analyzing a medical image, early layers might detect simple edges and shapes, while deeper layers identify complex patterns that could indicate disease. This layered approach allows deep learning to discover subtle patterns in healthcare data that might escape human notice.

Deep learning emerged in the 2010s as a revolutionary force in healthcare AI, fundamentally transforming how we process and analyze medical information. This advanced subset of machine learning, built on multi-layered neural networks, excels at handling the complex, high-dimensional data prevalent in healthcare environments.

The revolution was fueled by a convergence of critical factors: explosive growth in computational power through specialized GPUs and AI hardware; unprecedented access to vast healthcare datasets from electronic records and digital imaging; algorithmic breakthroughs like convolutional neural networks that revolutionized medical image analysis; and democratized access through open-source frameworks such as TensorFlow and PyTorch. Together, these developments created the perfect conditions for deep learning to flourish in medical applications.

This technological renaissance has produced remarkable advancements—

AI systems now detect subtle patterns in radiological images, extract meaningful insights from unstructured clinical notes, predict patient deterioration before obvious symptoms appear, and accelerate drug discovery. What makes deep learning particularly transformative in healthcare is its ability to continuously improve with more data, progressively enhancing its accuracy and utility in supporting clinical decision-making.

Major Applications of Deep Learning in Healthcare

1. Medical Imaging Analysis

Deep learning has revolutionized medical imaging analysis, achieving human-level performance or better in many tasks:

- In 2016, a deep learning algorithm developed by researchers at Google achieved dermatologist-level performance in classifying skin lesions, including malignant melanomas.
- In 2018, an AI system developed by DeepMind demonstrated the ability to diagnose over 50 types of eye diseases from OCT scans, matching the performance of top specialists.
- CNN-based systems have shown remarkable accuracy in detecting lung nodules on chest X-rays, brain tumors on MRI scans, and breast cancer on mammograms.

2. Natural Language Processing in Healthcare

Deep learning has significantly improved the ability to extract meaningful information from unstructured medical text:

- Systems have been developed to automatically extract relevant information from clinical notes, radiology reports, and medical literature.
- NLP-powered chatbots and virtual assistants are being used for initial patient triage and providing basic health information.
- Deep learning models have shown promise in automatically coding medical diagnoses and procedures from clinical text.

3. Predictive Analytics and Personalized Medicine

Deep learning models can integrate diverse data types to make predictions and personalize care:

- Models have been developed to predict patient outcomes, hospital readmissions, and disease progression with higher accuracy than traditional methods.
- In 2019, a deep learning model developed by Google Health demonstrated the ability to predict acute kidney injury up to 48 hours in advance.
- Deep learning is being applied to genomic data to predict drug responses and identify novel drug targets.

4. Drug Discovery and Development

Deep learning is accelerating various stages of the drug discovery and development process:

- In 2020, DeepMind's AlphaFold made a major breakthrough in the protein folding problem, with significant implications for drug discovery.
- Deep learning models are being used to predict the properties of potential drug compounds, potentially speeding up the drug discovery process.
- AI systems are being employed to design novel molecules with desired properties for pharmaceutical applications.

Looking ahead, we can expect to see continued advancements in the capabilities of deep learning in healthcare, alongside efforts to address its challenges and ethical implications. The integration of deep learning with other technologies, such as the Internet of Medical Things (IoMT) and robotics, promises to further transform healthcare delivery and research.

These milestones illustrate the rapid pace of advancement in AI healthcare applications, particularly in the last decade. They showcase the transition from narrow, rule-based systems to more flexible and powerful machine learning approaches, and finally to the current era of deep learning with its remarkable capabilities in handling complex healthcare data.

Each of these breakthroughs has opened new possibilities for improving patient care, enhancing diagnostic accuracy, accelerating medical research, and optimizing healthcare operations. However, they have also raised important questions about the integration of AI into clinical practice, the regulatory frameworks needed to ensure patient safety and the ethical implications of increasingly autonomous AI systems in healthcare.

As deep learning and AI continue to evolve, they have the potential to significantly enhance diagnostic accuracy, treatment personalization, and operational efficiency in healthcare. However, realizing this potential will require ongoing collaboration between AI researchers, healthcare professionals, ethicists, and policymakers to ensure that these powerful technologies are developed and deployed in ways that are safe, effective, and aligned with human values.

Challenges and Ethical Considerations

Despite its promise, the application of deep learning in healthcare faces several challenges:

1. **Explainability and Interpretability**: Many deep learning models operate as "black boxes," making it difficult to understand and explain their decision-making processes. This is particularly problematic in healthcare, where understanding the rationale behind decisions is crucial.
2. **Data Privacy and Security**: Deep learning models often require large amounts of sensitive health data, raising concerns about data privacy and security.
3. **Bias and Fairness**: Deep learning models can perpetuate or even amplify biases present in their training data, potentially leading to unfair or discriminatory outcomes.
4. **Regulatory Challenges**: The rapid pace of AI development is outstripping the ability of regulatory frameworks to keep up, raising questions about how to ensure the safety and efficacy of

AI-based healthcare solutions.

5. **Integration with Clinical Workflows**: There remain significant challenges in integrating deep learning tools into existing clinical workflows and gaining acceptance from healthcare professionals.

As AI in healthcare continues to evolve, addressing these challenges will be crucial for realizing the full potential of these technologies. Many of these challenges are interconnected and require interdisciplinary approaches to solve. For instance, improving data quality can enhance model performance, which in turn can increase user acceptance. Similarly, addressing ethical concerns can facilitate regulatory approval and boost public trust.

Moving forward, it will be essential to:

1. Develop robust, diverse, and unbiased datasets while ensuring privacy and security.
2. Advance techniques for interpretable and explainable AI.
3. Design AI systems that augment rather than replace healthcare professionals.
4. Establish clear regulatory frameworks and ethical guidelines for AI in healthcare.
5. Invest in education and training to prepare the healthcare workforce for the AI era.
6. Foster interdisciplinary collaboration between healthcare professionals, AI researchers, ethicists, and policymakers.

By acknowledging and actively working to address these challenges, we can help ensure that the evolution of AI in healthcare continues to progress in a direction that ultimately benefits patients and improves the overall quality of healthcare delivery.

As we'll see in the next section, the limitations of these rule-based systems would eventually lead to new approaches, particularly the rise of machine learning techniques that could learn from data rather than relying solely on pre-programmed rules

Current State of AI in Healthcare

As we progress through the mid-2020s, healthcare AI stands at a transformative juncture. Having evolved from basic rule-based systems to sophisticated machine learning models, AI now permeates multiple facets of healthcare delivery and research.

In clinical settings, AI's impact is increasingly evident. Diagnostic support has advanced remarkably, with deep learning models analyzing medical images across specialties with accuracy rivaling or exceeding human experts in specific tasks. Meanwhile, AI-powered clinical decision support systems embedded within electronic health records provide real-time insights, flagging high-risk patients and offering evidence-based recommendations. These capabilities extend to personalized medicine, where AI helps tailor treatments to individual patients based on their unique genetic profiles and predicted treatment responses.

The research landscape has been equally transformed. AI accelerates drug development from initial target identification through optimization, with AI-designed candidates now entering clinical trials. In genomics, breakthroughs like AlphaFold have revolutionized protein structure prediction, while machine learning uncovers new insights from vast genomic datasets.

Beyond clinical care, AI optimizes healthcare operations through intelligent resource management and streamlined administrative processes. Patient engagement has evolved through AI-powered remote monitoring solutions and virtual health assistants that provide initial triage and information. In public health, AI models predict disease outbreaks and analyze population trends, capabilities accelerated by the COVID-19 pandemic.

Despite these advances, significant challenges persist. Healthcare organizations struggle with fully integrating AI into routine clinical practice. Regulatory frameworks continue evolving to balance innovation with safety. Ethical considerations around fairness, transparency, and privacy demand ongoing attention. Data quality and interoperability limitations constrain AI's potential, while workforce adaptation requires cultivating AI literacy across healthcare professionals.

As these challenges are addressed, AI's role in healthcare will likely expand, driving improvements in patient outcomes, operational efficiency, and medical discovery.

Looking ahead, we can anticipate:

- Continued improvements in the accuracy and capabilities of AI systems
- Greater integration of AI into routine clinical workflows
- Expansion of AI applications in personalized medicine and precision health
- Increased focus on explainable AI to address the "black box" problem
- Growing emphasis on ethical AI development and deployment
- Evolution of regulatory frameworks to keep pace with technological advancements

The journey of AI in healthcare, from early expert systems to today's sophisticated machine learning models, has been one of remarkable progress and persistent challenges. As we look to the future, it's clear that AI will play an increasingly important role in shaping the healthcare landscape. By learning from the past, addressing current challenges, and thoughtfully navigating ethical considerations, we can work towards a future where AI enhances and extends human capabilities in healthcare, ultimately leading to better health outcomes for all.

As we've seen, AI in healthcare has evolved from basic rule-based systems to sophisticated machine learning models. However, these advanced AI capabilities are only as effective as the data that powers them. In the next chapter, we'll explore the critical foundation of all healthcare AI applications: the diverse, complex data ecosystem that captures everything from clinical observations to genomic sequences. Understanding these data fundamentals is essential for appreciating how modern AI systems can extract meaningful insights that transform patient care.

Chapter 3:

Fundamentals of Healthcare Data

In the era of digital health and AI, data drives modern healthcare. Every patient interaction generates valuable data that, when properly managed and analyzed, can transform care, optimize operations, and advance medical research. This chapter explores healthcare data, covering its types, sources, collection methods, and challenges. We examine clinical, administrative, -omics, and patient-generated data, highlighting their complexity and potential.

Data quality and standardization are essential, as healthcare decisions directly impact lives. Efforts to improve data accuracy, consistency, and interoperability are crucial for ensuring reliable, actionable insights. Privacy and security concerns are paramount, with a focus on regulatory frameworks and ethical challenges in safeguarding sensitive health data while enabling its beneficial use. Interoperability remains a challenge, but AI-driven approaches show promise in enhancing data exchange.

Healthcare's "big data" presents unique opportunities and risks, shaping care delivery and research. Lastly, we discuss the data foundations needed for AI applications in healthcare, emphasizing the importance of diverse, high-quality datasets to build effective, ethical AI systems. At the heart of all data is the patient or caregiver, whose health improvement is the ultimate goal. Understanding healthcare data lays the foundation for enhancing care, fueling discovery, and improving lives.

Types of Healthcare Data

Healthcare data comes in many forms, each serving different purposes and offering unique insights into patient health, healthcare delivery, and population health trends. Understanding these different types of data is crucial for leveraging them effectively in AI applications. Let's explore the main categories of healthcare data.

➤ Clinical Data

Clinical data forms the foundation of healthcare information systems. At its core are Electronic Health Records (EHRs), comprehensive digital files that paint a complete picture of a patient's health journey. Within these records, clinicians can access everything from basic demographics to detailed medical histories. They contain crucial information about diagnoses that guide treatment decisions, medication records that prevent dangerous interactions, and personalized treatment plans that chart the path forward. EHRs also track preventive care like immunizations, flag potentially life-threatening allergies, store visual data through radiology images, and compile laboratory results that reveal the invisible workings of the body. Together, these elements create a holistic view that enables coordinated, informed patient care.

Beyond the structured patient information in EHRs, clinical data encompasses rich visual insights captured through medical imaging. These visual narratives reveal the body's inner workings in ways no other data can. In radiology departments across the world, technicians capture X-rays—two-dimensional shadows that have guided medical decisions for over a century. For more complex cases, CT scans create detailed cross-sectional images by combining multiple X-ray measurements taken from different angles, offering clinicians layer-by-layer views of internal structures.

When soft tissue detail is paramount, MRI technology steps in, using powerful magnetic fields and radio waves to generate exquisitely detailed images without radiation exposure. This technology proves invaluable for examining the brain, spinal cord, and joints, revealing subtleties invisible to other imaging methods. Meanwhile, ultrasound imaging offers a dynamic, real-time window into the body using high-frequency sound waves, allowing clinicians to observe structures in motion—from a developing fetus to blood flowing through vessels. For detecting metabolic activity at the cellular level, PET scans track radioactive tracers as they move through the body, highlighting areas of unusual activity that might indicate cancer or neurological disorders.

This rich tapestry of medical imaging data has become particularly valuable in the age of artificial intelligence. Radiologists now partner with sophisticated AI algorithms that can analyze thousands of images with remarkable speed and precision, flagging potential abnormalities for human review and enhancing diagnostic capabilities. The marriage of human expertise with computational power is transforming diagnostic support, allowing earlier detection of conditions from lung nodules to brain tumors.

Complementing these visual insights, laboratory data provides objective, quantifiable evidence of the body's internal chemistry and function. The most common laboratory investigations begin with blood tests—analyzing samples for everything from basic cell counts and electrolyte balances to complex markers of inflammation, infection, or organ dysfunction. These tests serve as crucial windows into a patient's overall health status, identifying imbalances or abnormalities that might not yet manifest as symptoms.

Beyond blood analysis, urine tests offer insights into kidney function, metabolic disorders, and potential infections, often serving as first-line screening tools due to their non-invasive nature. For more specialized investigations, clinicians turn to genetic tests that examine a patient's DNA, identifying inherited conditions, predispositions to certain diseases, or genetic mutations that might guide personalized treatment approaches. The laboratory landscape also includes detailed pathology reports, where specially trained physicians examine tissue samples under microscopes, determining whether cells appear normal or show signs of disease—information critical for cancer diagnosis and treatment planning.

Together, these laboratory findings form a foundational element of evidence-based medicine, providing objective data points that guide diagnosis, treatment selection, and ongoing monitoring of patient health. When aggregated across populations, this same laboratory data becomes invaluable for research, revealing patterns and correlations that drive medical innovation forward.

Next, I've summarized a few more Data categories: Administrative, -

Omics, Patient Generated, Population Health, and ending with Research and Clinical Trials Data.

➢ Administrative Data

Administrative data relates to the operational and financial aspects of healthcare delivery.

- **Billing and Claims Data**: Information related to the financial transactions in healthcare, including:
    - Procedures performed
    - Diagnoses codes (e.g., ICD-10 codes)
    - Costs and payments
    - Insurance claims
- **Scheduling Data**: Information about patient appointments, staff schedules, and resource allocation.
- **Operational Data**: Data related to hospital operations, such as:
    - Bed occupancy rates
    - Equipment utilization
    - Staff workload

➢ -Omics Data

-Omics data refers to large-scale data sets in biological and molecular studies. This is a rapidly growing area of healthcare data, particularly important for personalized medicine.

- **Genomics Data**: Information about an individual's genetic makeup, including:
    - DNA sequences
    - Genetic variations

- o Gene expression data

- **Proteomics Data**: Data about the structure and function of proteins in the body.

- **Metabolomics Data**: Information about metabolites and metabolic processes.

- **Microbiomics Data**: Data about the microorganisms in the human body.

➢ **Patient-Generated Data**

With the rise of wearable devices and mobile health apps, patients are increasingly generating their own health data outside of clinical settings.

- **Wearable Device Data**: Information from devices like fitness trackers and smartwatches, including:

  - o Heart rate

  - o Sleep patterns

  - o Physical activity levels

- **Mobile Health App Data**: Data from various health-related mobile applications, such as:

  - o Food and nutrition logs

  - o Mood tracking

  - o Medication adherence records

- **Patient-Reported Outcomes**: Standardized questionnaires that capture the patient's perspective on their health status, quality of life, or functional status.

➢ **Population Health Data**

This category includes data that provides insights into the health status and determinants of health for populations.

- **Public Health Surveillance Data**: Information collected by public health agencies, including:
    - Disease prevalence and incidence rates
    - Vaccination rates
    - Health behaviors (e.g., smoking rates, obesity rates)

- **Social Determinants of Health Data**: Information about non-medical factors that influence health outcomes, such as:
    - Education levels
    - Income and employment
    - Housing conditions
    - Environmental factors

- **Epidemiological Study Data**: Data from large-scale studies on the patterns, causes, and effects of health and disease conditions in defined populations.

➢ **Research and Clinical Trials Data**

Data generated from medical research and clinical trials, including:

- Study protocols
- Participant data
- Outcome measures
- Adverse event reports

Healthcare's diverse data types power AI's potential to transform patient care and operational efficiency. While integrating clinical, administrative, -omics, and patient-generated data is essential, it presents significant challenges.

AI effectiveness hinges on data quality—consistent, complete information with clear provenance. Healthcare data often suffers from variability, gaps, and format inconsistencies that can undermine AI performance.

Understanding these limitations and potential biases is crucial when developing reliable models.

The future of healthcare AI depends on our ability to connect varied data streams while maintaining privacy and standardization. Ironically, AI itself may offer solutions to the very data quality challenges that currently limit its effectiveness.

Importance of Data Quality in Healthcare

High-quality data is essential for several reasons:

1. **Patient Safety**: Inaccurate or incomplete data can lead to medical errors and compromised patient safety.
2. **Effective Decision Making**: Healthcare providers rely on accurate data to make informed clinical decisions.
3. **Research Integrity**: Medical research and public health initiatives depend on reliable data to draw valid conclusions.
4. **AI Model Performance**: The performance of AI models is directly tied to the quality of the data they are trained on.
5. **Interoperability**: High-quality, standardized data facilitates better information exchange between different healthcare systems.

Common Data Quality Issues in Healthcare

Several issues can compromise the quality of healthcare data:

1. **Incompleteness**: Missing or partial data entries.
2. **Inaccuracy**: Incorrect data entries, often due to human error.
3. **Inconsistency**: Conflicting information within or across records.
4. **Duplication**: Multiple entries for the same patient or event.
5. **Timeliness**: Data that is not up-to-date or reflective of the current state.
6. **Bias**: Systematic errors that skew the data in particular directions.

Addressing Data Quality Issues

Improving and maintaining data quality involves several strategies:

1. **Data Validation**: Implementing checks to ensure data meets predefined quality criteria.
2. **Data Cleaning**: Identifying and correcting (or removing) corrupt or inaccurate records.
3. **Regular Audits**: Conducting systematic reviews of data quality.
4. **Training**: Educating staff on the importance of data quality and proper data entry techniques.
5. **Automated Data Capture**: Utilizing technology to reduce manual data entry errors.

Healthcare data forms the foundation upon which modern medicine builds its insights, decisions, and innovations. As we've explored throughout this chapter, this data landscape is remarkably diverse—from the structured clinical information in electronic health records to the molecular-level detail of -omics data, from administrative records documenting healthcare operations to patient-generated information captured outside traditional clinical settings. Each data type contributes unique perspectives to the complex mosaic of healthcare information.

Yet the transformative potential of this data hinges on its quality, accessibility, and integration. Poor data quality can compromise patient safety, while inconsistent standards limit interoperability between systems. Privacy concerns must be balanced with the need to share information for better care coordination and research advancement. The challenges we face—fragmented systems, variable data quality, and evolving privacy regulations—are significant but not insurmountable.

The future of healthcare lies at this intersection of data science and medicine. By understanding the fundamental nature of healthcare data— its sources, structures, and limitations—we position ourselves to harness its full potential. As artificial intelligence and machine learning continue to evolve, their capabilities will increasingly depend on our ability to provide high-quality, diverse, and representative healthcare data. The organizations that invest in data quality, standardization, and governance today will be best positioned to deliver innovative, personalized care tomorrow.

The journey toward data-driven healthcare is ultimately about people—patients whose lives can be improved, clinicians whose decisions can be enhanced, and researchers whose discoveries can be accelerated. By building robust data foundations, we create the essential infrastructure for a healthcare system that is more precise, proactive, and patient-centered. The fundamentals of healthcare data explored in this chapter serve not as technical abstractions, but as critical building blocks for a healthier future.

Chapter 4:

Data Standardization and Big Data

Data Standardization Efforts in Healthcare

Standardization is crucial for ensuring data consistency and facilitating interoperability. Several standardization efforts are prominent in healthcare:

1. **ICD (International Classification of Diseases):**

   - Purpose: Standardizing the coding of diagnoses and procedures.
   - Current version: ICD-10, with ICD-11 being gradually adopted.
   - AI Relevance: Crucial for training models on diagnostic and procedural data.

2. **SNOMED CT (Systematized Nomenclature of Medicine -- Clinical Terms):**

   - Purpose: Comprehensive clinical terminology for electronic health records.
   - Characteristics: Hierarchical structure, suitable for detailed clinical documentation.
   - AI Relevance: Enables sophisticated querying and analysis of clinical data.

3. **LOINC (Logical Observation Identifiers Names and Codes):**

   - Purpose: Standardizing laboratory and clinical observations.
   - Characteristics: Universally applicable coding system for lab results.
   - AI Relevance: Essential for models involving lab data analysis.

4. **RxNorm**:

     o   Purpose: Standardizing medication names and codes.
     o   Characteristics: Provides normalized names for clinical drugs.
     o   AI Relevance: Critical for medication-related AI applications.

5. **HL7 (Health Level Seven) Standards**:

     o   Purpose: Standards for exchanging clinical and administrative data between software applications.
     o   Key Standard: HL7 FHIR (Fast Healthcare Interoperability Resources)
     o   AI Relevance: Facilitates data exchange and integration, crucial for comprehensive AI models.

6. **DICOM (Digital Imaging and Communications in Medicine)**:

     o   Purpose: Standard for handling, storing, printing, and transmitting medical imaging information.
     o   Characteristics: Includes file format definition and network communications protocol.
     o   AI Relevance: Essential for AI applications in medical imaging.

Challenges in Healthcare Data Standardization

Despite the substantial progress in healthcare data standardization, several persistent challenges continue to hamper full implementation across the industry. Legacy systems—some dating back decades—present perhaps the most immediate barrier, as these aging technological foundations often cannot accommodate newer data standards without significant modifications. Many healthcare facilities, particularly smaller practices and rural hospitals, continue to rely on these outdated systems due to financial constraints.

This highlights another significant obstacle: the substantial implementation costs associated with adopting new standards. Healthcare organizations face not only the direct expenses of new software and hardware but also the considerable time investment required for system transitions, staff training, and workflow adjustments. These financial and temporal demands create a fragmented landscape of adoption, where large academic medical centers might embrace cutting-edge standards while smaller community providers lag years behind.

The inherent complexity of healthcare data further complicates standardization efforts. Medical information spans countless specialized domains, each with unique documentation requirements and terminologies. From the nuanced language of psychiatric assessments to the precise measurements of laboratory values, capturing this diversity within standardized frameworks remains exceedingly difficult. Standard developers continuously navigate the delicate balance between comprehensive detail and practical usability—standards that are too simplistic fail to capture essential clinical information, while overly complex ones create implementation barriers and reduce adoption rates.

This balancing act exemplifies the central challenge in healthcare data standardization: creating systems sophisticated enough to support modern medicine's complexity while remaining accessible enough for widespread implementation across diverse healthcare settings.

Data Quality and Standardization for AI in Healthcare

For AI applications, data quality and standardization are particularly crucial:

1. **Training Data Quality**: AI models are only as good as the data they're trained on. High-quality, standardized data is essential for developing reliable AI models.

2. **Feature Engineering**: Standardized data facilitates more effective feature engineering for AI models.

3. **Model Generalizability**: Models trained on standardized data are more likely to generalize well across different healthcare settings.

4. **Interpretability**: Standardized data can enhance the interpretability of AI model outputs.

5. **Continuous Learning**: Quality, standardized data enables more effective continuous learning and updating of AI models.

Future Directions

As healthcare becomes increasingly digitized, we can expect automation to streamline data quality management and standardization processes. AI itself will likely become a solution to data challenges, helping to clean, standardize, and harmonize information across systems. Internationally, efforts toward global healthcare data standards will intensify to facilitate cross-border collaboration and research, while new frameworks will better incorporate patient-generated health data.

Privacy innovations will emerge in parallel, including enhanced governance frameworks, privacy-preserving AI techniques, and potentially blockchain applications for secure data management. We'll likely see greater international harmonization of security standards and a shift toward patient-controlled data models that give individuals more say in how their health information is used in AI applications.

The foundation of effective healthcare AI remains high-quality, standardized data. As these technologies advance, maintaining robust data quality through collaboration between healthcare providers, IT specialists, data scientists, and standards organizations will be essential for developing ethical, reliable AI-driven healthcare solutions.

Protecting Healthcare Data Privacy and Security

Ensuring healthcare data privacy and security is both a legal requirement and ethical obligation. As AI and data analytics advance, robust safeguards are essential to maintain public trust, protect patient safety, and fully realize these technologies' potential without compromising individual rights. This topic will be discussed in greater detail in a later chapter of this book.

Interoperability in Healthcare

Interoperability—healthcare's digital connectivity backbone—enables systems to communicate and share information meaningfully across organizational boundaries. This capability exists along a progression of sophistication. At its most basic foundational level, systems simply transfer data packets without necessarily understanding content. Moving up to structural interoperability, the data maintains its format and meaning during exchange, while semantic interoperability represents true comprehension where systems can interpret and act upon the information they receive. The highest form, organizational interoperability, transcends technical considerations to encompass the complex social, policy, and procedural frameworks that facilitate seamless information sharing between different healthcare entities.

This multi-layered connectivity isn't merely a technical convenience—it forms the critical infrastructure for coordinated care delivery and is particularly essential for AI systems that require diverse, integrated data sources to function effectively. As healthcare grows increasingly data-driven, establishing robust interoperability becomes not just beneficial but necessary for realizing the full potential of artificial intelligence in improving patient outcomes.

Persistent Challenges:
- **Legacy Systems & Data Silos:** Outdated tech limits data sharing.
- **Lack of Standards:** Inconsistent data formats hinder exchange.
- **Privacy, Security, & Compliance:** Protecting data while navigating regulations.
- **Vendor Lock-in & Complex Workflows:** Proprietary systems and varying processes add barriers.

Standards and Emerging Solutions:
- **HL7 FHIR, DICOM, IHE:** Promote standardized, structured data exchange.

- **API-Driven Interoperability:** Facilitates real-time access and data sharing.
- **Blockchain & Direct Protocol:** Explore secure, decentralized exchange.
- **C-CDA:** Standardizes clinical summary documents.

Government and Industry Initiatives:
- **21st Century Cures Act & Interoperability Rules (USA):** Combat information blocking, mandate APIs.
- **European Health Data Space (EU):** Improve cross-border data exchange.
- **Global Digital Health Partnership:** International collaboration for digital health.

AI's Role in Advancing Interoperability:
- **NLP & Automated Mapping:** Extract and align unstructured data.
- **Predictive Interoperability:** Anticipates needed data for specific cases.
- **Anomaly Detection & Intelligent Interfaces:** Ensure accuracy and usability.

Implementation Barriers:
- **Cost & Resistance to Change:** High expenses and organizational inertia.
- **Data Governance & Semantic Alignment:** Ensuring data meaning is preserved.
- **Scalability:** Addressing growing healthcare data volumes.
  Looking Ahead: Future Interoperability Trends
- **AI-Enhanced Interoperability:** Smarter, automated data exchange.
- **Patient-Centered Systems:** Empower patients to control and share their data.
- **Global Standards:** Harmonization of healthcare data protocols.

- **Real-Time Exchange:** Supporting immediate clinical decisions.
- **IoMT Integration:** Seamless use of data from connected medical devices.

Achieving true interoperability in healthcare is a complex challenge, but it is also a critical goal for improving patient care, enabling more effective use of AI, and advancing medical research. As technology continues to evolve and standards mature, we can expect to see significant progress in this area, leading to more connected, efficient, and patient-centered healthcare systems.

Big Data in Healthcare

The concept of "Big Data" has become increasingly relevant in healthcare, as the volume, variety, and velocity of health-related data have grown exponentially. Big Data in healthcare refers to the vast quantities of data created by the digitization of everything from patient records to payer records, and from wearable sensors to medical imaging. This section explores the characteristics of healthcare big data, its challenges, potential impacts, and the platforms and tools used to manage and analyze it.

Characteristics of Big Data in Healthcare

Healthcare big data is often characterized by the "5 Vs":

1. **Volume**: The sheer amount of data generated in healthcare is enormous. This includes EHR data, medical imaging, genomic data, and data from wearable devices.

2. **Velocity**: Data is being generated at an unprecedented speed. Real-time data from monitoring devices and rapid updates to patient records contribute to this high velocity.

3. **Variety**: Healthcare data comes in many forms - structured (e.g., lab results), unstructured (e.g., clinical notes), semi-structured (e.g., medical imaging data with tags), and complex (e.g., genomic data).

4. **Veracity**: Ensuring the accuracy and trustworthiness of data is crucial in healthcare where decisions can have life-or-death consequences.

5. **Value**: The potential insights that can be derived from healthcare big data are immense, ranging from personalized treatment plans to population health management.

Sources of Healthcare Big Data

1. Electronic Health Records (EHRs)
2. Medical Imaging Data
3. Genomic Data
4. Claims and Billing Data
5. Clinical Trial Data
6. Patient-Generated Health Data (PGHD)
7. Internet of Medical Things (IoMT) Data
8. Public Health Data
9. Social Media and Web Data

Managing healthcare's massive data ecosystem presents interconnected challenges that healthcare organizations must navigate simultaneously. The fundamental issue of data integration requires reconciling information from disparate sources—legacy systems, modern EHRs, laboratory platforms, and patient devices—each with unique formats and structures. This integration challenge directly impacts data quality, as inconsistencies, gaps, and errors inevitably emerge when merging these diverse sources.

Meanwhile, the sensitive nature of health information demands robust privacy protections and security measures that must somehow balance with the need for data accessibility and utility. Effective governance frameworks become essential, establishing clear policies for data collection, storage, access, and usage while maintaining regulatory compliance. As healthcare data volumes grow exponentially, scalability becomes critical, and systems must efficiently handle not just today's data but tomorrow's increased demands.

The analytical challenges prove equally daunting. Healthcare data's high dimensionality and complexity require sophisticated methods that can extract meaningful patterns while ensuring the resulting insights remain interpretable to clinicians making real-world decisions. Increasingly, these analyses must happen in real-time, enabling immediate interventions when patients' conditions change, creating additional technical hurdles for processing infrastructure. Together, these challenges represent the significant but necessary barriers healthcare organizations must overcome to realize big data's transformative potential.

Potential Impacts of Big Data on Healthcare Delivery and Research

1. **Personalized Medicine**:
   - Analyzing large datasets to tailor treatments to individual patients based on their genetic makeup, lifestyle, and environmental factors.
2. **Predictive Analytics**:
   - Using historical data to predict future health events, such as disease outbreaks or patient deterioration.
3. **Population Health Management**:
   - Analyzing data across populations to identify health trends and implement targeted interventions.
4. **Clinical Decision Support**:
   - Providing healthcare providers with data-driven insights to support diagnosis and treatment decisions.
5. **Drug Discovery and Development**:
   - Accelerating the drug discovery process through analysis of large genomic and clinical datasets.
6. **Operational Efficiency**:
   - Optimizing hospital operations, resource allocation, and supply chain management through data analysis.
7. **Fraud Detection**:
   - Using advanced analytics to identify fraudulent claims and billings.

8. **Real-time Monitoring**:
   - o Enabling continuous monitoring of patient health through analysis of data from wearable devices and IoMT.

Looking ahead, healthcare's big data landscape will likely evolve through several transformative technologies. Advanced AI and machine learning will extract increasingly nuanced insights from complex health datasets, while edge computing will shift processing closer to data sources—enabling real-time analytics directly on medical devices at the point of care. Blockchain technology promises more secure, transparent data management without centralized vulnerabilities, and though still emerging, quantum computing may eventually analyze healthcare's most complex datasets at unprecedented speeds. Perhaps most significantly, future analytics will extend beyond traditional clinical information to incorporate social determinants of health, recognizing that factors like housing, education, and environment profoundly impact wellbeing.

This technological evolution is reshaping healthcare from reactive treatment to proactive prevention through personalized, predictive care models. However, meaningful progress requires addressing fundamental challenges in data quality, privacy protection, algorithmic bias, and ethical implementation. As these barriers diminish, AI will increasingly augment clinical decision-making, enhance patient experiences, and optimize healthcare delivery systems—ultimately transforming data from a byproduct of care into its vital foundation.

Chapter 5:

Data Analytics in Healthcare

Healthcare is undergoing a digital revolution, with data analytics emerging as a transformative force that promises to reshape patient care, operational efficiency, and medical research. At its core, healthcare data analytics involves the systematic application of statistical, contextual, and predictive modeling techniques to extract actionable insights from the vast and growing repository of health information.

The potential of data analytics in healthcare extends across the entire ecosystem. Clinicians can enhance their decision-making through evidence-based insights derived from thousands of similar cases. Healthcare administrators can optimize resource allocation by predicting patient volumes and identifying operational bottlenecks. Researchers can accelerate drug discovery and development by uncovering patterns in complex biological data. Patients themselves benefit from more personalized treatment approaches tailored to their unique characteristics.

What makes this moment particularly significant is the unprecedented convergence of data availability and analytical capability. Healthcare organizations now generate and store enormous volumes of diverse data—from structured electronic health records and medical imaging to unstructured clinical notes and patient-reported outcomes. Simultaneously, advances in computing power and analytical methods have created the tools needed to transform this data into meaningful knowledge.

This chapter explores the evolving landscape of healthcare data analytics, beginning with the foundational types of analytics: descriptive, diagnostic, predictive, and prescriptive. We then examine the statistical methods and machine learning techniques that power these analyses, illustrating their applications with real-world examples. The chapter also addresses the crucial aspects of data visualization and reporting, which bridge the gap between complex analyses and practical implementation.

While the promise of data analytics in healthcare is immense, significant challenges remain. Issues of data quality, privacy concerns, interoperability limitations, and organizational resistance can impede effective implementation. We discuss these obstacles and potential approaches to overcome them.

Finally, we look toward the horizon of healthcare analytics, exploring emerging trends like artificial intelligence, real-time analytics, and privacy-preserving techniques that may further revolutionize how we use data to improve health outcomes and healthcare delivery.

Throughout this exploration, we maintain focus on the ultimate purpose of healthcare data analytics: behind every data point is a patient, a provider, or a health system striving to provide better care. The true measure of success for analytics in healthcare is not technological sophistication but meaningful improvement in human health and wellbeing.

Types of Data Analytics in Healthcare: A Revised Approach

Healthcare organizations employ a progressive spectrum of analytical approaches, each building upon the foundation of the previous one. This analytical maturity model enables increasingly sophisticated insights and decision-making capabilities.

Healthcare analytics employs statistical methods that range from straightforward to sophisticated. At the basic level, descriptive statistics summarize data—averages, ranges, and distributions of values like patient wait times or hospital stays. Moving up in complexity, inferential statistics help us draw conclusions beyond our immediate data, such as determining whether a treatment effect is genuine or merely due to chance. At the most advanced level, techniques like Bayesian networks model complex causal relationships between multiple factors, helping clinicians understand how various symptoms and risk factors interact to influence patient outcomes. This progression from description to inference to causal modeling reflects the increasing power of statistical approaches to extract meaningful insights from healthcare data.

Descriptive Analytics: Understanding the Past

Descriptive analytics transforms raw healthcare data into meaningful insights by answering the fundamental question: "What happened?" Through basic statistical methods, healthcare organizations gain clarity about their operations and patient populations.

A modern hospital utilizes descriptive analytics to create dashboards displaying patient throughput, average lengths of stay, and seasonal illness patterns. While seemingly simple, these insights provide the essential foundation for more advanced analysis. For example, tracking emergency department volumes over time might reveal unexpected patterns in utilization that prompt further investigation.

Diagnostic Analytics: Uncovering Root Causes

Building on descriptive insights, diagnostic analytics delves deeper by answering: "Why did it happen?" When troubling trends emerge—such as unexpected readmission spikes or post-surgical complications; healthcare teams employ more sophisticated techniques to uncover underlying causes.

Consider a hospital that discovers elevated readmission rates among patients from specific neighborhoods. Diagnostic analytics might reveal connections to social determinants of health, such as transportation barriers or food insecurity. This deeper understanding enables healthcare providers to address root causes rather than merely treating symptoms, creating targeted intervention programs that address specific community needs.

Predictive Analytics: Anticipating Future Outcomes

Predictive analytics represents a significant evolution in healthcare decision-making, shifting focus from past events to future possibilities by answering: "What is likely to happen?" This forward-looking approach employs advanced statistical modeling and machine learning to forecast outcomes based on historical patterns.

In clinical settings, predictive analytics identifies patients at elevated risk before symptoms fully manifest. For instance, an AI model might flag subtle indicators of pre-diabetes in patients' lab results and demographic data, enabling early intervention through lifestyle modification programs. Similarly, hospital operations benefit from predicting admission patterns, allowing proactive staffing adjustments that ensure appropriate coverage while minimizing unnecessary costs.

Even equipment maintenance becomes more efficient through predictive approaches. By analyzing performance patterns of critical medical devices, maintenance teams can anticipate failures before they occur, preventing dangerous downtime during crucial procedures and extending the lifespan of expensive equipment.

Prescriptive Analytics: Determining Optimal Actions

The most advanced form of healthcare analytics, prescriptive analytics, moves beyond prediction to recommendation by answering: "What should we do about it?" This approach combines predictive insights with action-oriented guidance to create decision roadmaps.

During resource-constrained situations, such as the COVID-19 pandemic, prescriptive systems have proven invaluable. One medical center deployed analytics to optimize limited ventilator resources by continuously analyzing patient acuity levels and projected admission rates across their hospital network, recommending redistribution strategies that maximized survival rates.

On an individual level, prescriptive analytics personalizes treatment plans by analyzing thousands of similar cases and recommending intervention strategies tailored to each patient's unique characteristics. For patients with complex conditions like congestive heart failure, this might mean customized medication regimens and monitoring schedules designed specifically for their situation.

The Analytics Maturity Journey

Healthcare organizations typically progress through these analytical capabilities in stages, gradually building more sophisticated systems as they master each level. The journey from descriptive to prescriptive analytics represents not just technological advancement but an evolution in organizational thinking—from reactive to proactive, from standardized to personalized, and from intuition-based to evidence-driven decision-making.

While each analytical type serves distinct purposes, they function most effectively as an integrated system, with insights flowing between levels to create a comprehensive understanding of healthcare challenges and opportunities. As organizations advance in this journey, they gain increasingly powerful tools to improve clinical outcomes, enhance operational efficiency, and ultimately transform healthcare delivery.

The Analytics Ecosystem: Integration, Challenges, and Evolution

The Interconnected Analytics Landscape

While we've examined each type of analytics separately, in practice, these approaches function as an integrated ecosystem rather than isolated tools. This interconnection creates a virtuous cycle of insight generation:

Descriptive analytics establishes the factual foundation by revealing what happened, providing the necessary context for deeper investigation. When diagnostic analytics uncovers meaningful correlations and causal relationships, these insights naturally feed into predictive models, improving their accuracy and relevance. As predictive capabilities mature, they enable prescriptive systems to recommend optimal interventions based on likely outcomes. Finally, the results of these interventions loop back into descriptive analytics, creating a continuous learning system.

This integrated approach transforms healthcare decision-making from reactive to proactive, from fragmented to holistic, and from intuition-based to evidence-driven. For example, a comprehensive analytics system might first identify an elevated surgical complication rate (descriptive), determine that specific sterilization practices correlate with complications (diagnostic), predict which future patients face highest risk (predictive), and recommend targeted protocol modifications (prescriptive), all while continuously monitoring outcomes to refine its models.

Navigating Implementation Challenges

The journey toward advanced analytics capabilities presents significant challenges that grow more complex at each stage of maturity:

Data Quality and Integration becomes increasingly critical as analytics complexity grows. While descriptive analytics might function adequately with incomplete data, predictive and prescriptive approaches demand comprehensive, high-quality information from multiple sources. Healthcare organizations must invest in robust data governance frameworks, standardization initiatives, and integration technologies to build the necessary foundation.

Technical Complexity increases substantially with each analytical evolution. Moving from basic statistical methods to sophisticated machine learning algorithms requires specialized expertise that many healthcare organizations lack internally. This talent gap often necessitates partnerships with academic institutions or technology vendors while building internal capabilities through targeted education and recruitment.

Organizational Change Management represents perhaps the most formidable challenge. Advanced analytics often disrupts established workflows and decision-making hierarchies, potentially creating resistance among clinicians and administrators accustomed to experience-based approaches. Successful implementation requires thoughtful change management strategies that engage stakeholders early, demonstrate clear value, and integrate analytics into existing workflows rather than replacing them.

Ethical Considerations become more pronounced as analytics increasingly influence clinical and operational decisions. Issues of algorithmic bias, patient privacy, informed consent, and professional autonomy demand careful attention. Organizations must establish ethical frameworks and governance structures to ensure that analytics augment rather than undermine human judgment and that algorithmic recommendations don't perpetuate existing healthcare disparities.

Emerging Directions in Healthcare Analytics

As healthcare organizations overcome these challenges, several transformative trends are emerging that will shape the next generation of healthcare analytics:

Continuous Real-Time Analytics is replacing periodic batch processing as healthcare increasingly operates in real-time. Advanced systems now analyze streaming data from bedside monitors, wearable devices, and IoT sensors, enabling immediate intervention when concerning patterns emerge. This shift from retrospective to real-time analysis fundamentally changes the tempo and responsiveness of healthcare delivery.

Adaptive Learning Systems represent a significant evolution beyond static analytical models. These systems continuously refine their algorithms based on new data and outcomes, becoming more accurate and personalized over time. For chronic condition management, adaptive systems might adjust treatment recommendations based on an individual patient's unique response patterns, creating truly personalized care plans.

Explainable AI addresses the critical "black box" problem in advanced analytics. As healthcare increasingly relies on complex algorithms for decision support, the ability to understand and explain these recommendations becomes essential for clinical adoption and ethical practice. Next-generation systems will provide clear rationales for their suggestions, enabling clinicians to evaluate and incorporate algorithmic insights into their decision-making process.

The evolution of healthcare analytics isn't merely technological—it represents a fundamental transformation in how healthcare organizations understand their operations, make decisions, and deliver care.

Organizations that successfully navigate this transformation will gain powerful tools to improve clinical outcomes, enhance operational efficiency, and ultimately deliver more personalized and effective healthcare.

Key Methods in Healthcare Analytics: From Statistics to Machine Learning

Healthcare analytics employs a spectrum of mathematical approaches that range from traditional statistical methods to advanced machine learning techniques. Rather than viewing these as separate domains, modern healthcare organizations increasingly integrate them into a unified analytical toolkit. This section explores the essential methods that power healthcare analytics, highlighting their applications and interrelationships.

Foundational Statistical Approaches

Statistical methods provide the mathematical backbone for healthcare analytics, enabling organizations to test hypotheses, identify relationships, and quantify uncertainty. These approaches have evolved from simple descriptive statistics to sophisticated modeling techniques.

Regression analysis remains one of the most versatile tools in healthcare analytics. Linear regression helps identify relationships between variables like medication dosage and patient outcomes, while logistic regression enables predictions for binary outcomes such as hospital readmission risk. Cox regression models time-dependent events, proving invaluable for analyzing survival rates and treatment efficacy. At Central Memorial Hospital, regression analysis identified that post-surgical complication risk increased significantly with specific preoperative factors, enabling targeted interventions that reduced complications by 30%.

Time series analysis captures healthcare's inherently temporal nature, revealing patterns in data collected over time. Public health departments employ seasonal decomposition techniques to predict disease outbreaks, while hospitals use ARIMA models to forecast patient admissions. These forecasts enable proactive resource allocation—ensuring adequate staffing during predicted surge periods while avoiding costly overstaffing during quieter times.

Healthcare researchers increasingly leverage **Bayesian methods**, which provide a framework for continuously updating probability estimates as new evidence emerges. Unlike traditional statistics, Bayesian approaches incorporate prior knowledge and update belief distributions with each new observation—mirroring the iterative nature of clinical decision-making. Diagnostic support systems for rare diseases now use Bayesian networks to update disease probability estimates as new symptoms or test results become available.

Machine Learning: Extending Statistical Capabilities

Machine learning extends traditional statistics through algorithms that improve automatically with experience, enabling analysis of more complex patterns and relationships in healthcare data.

Supervised learning algorithms train on labeled data to predict outcomes or classify new observations. Classification algorithms like random forests and support vector machines help identify patients at risk for specific conditions, enabling early intervention. For example, a supervised learning model developed at Northeastern Medical Center analyzes patterns in vital signs, lab values, and demographic data to predict sepsis onset hours before obvious clinical signs appear, improving survival rates by identifying candidates for early intervention.

Unsupervised learning discovers hidden patterns without predefined labels, revealing insights that might otherwise remain undetected. Clustering techniques have proven particularly valuable in identifying patient subgroups with similar characteristics, enabling more personalized treatment approaches. Research hospitals use clustering on genomic data to identify previously unknown disease subtypes, explaining why patients with apparently identical diagnoses respond differently to the same treatments.

Deep learning, based on neural networks with multiple processing layers, has revolutionized medical image analysis. Convolutional neural networks now match or exceed radiologist performance in detecting abnormalities in X-rays, mammograms, and retinal images. Beyond imaging, recurrent neural networks analyze temporal patterns in electronic health records to predict disease progression and treatment response with increasing accuracy.

Integrating Statistical and Machine Learning Approaches

The distinction between traditional statistics and machine learning increasingly blurs in practice, with modern healthcare analytics systems integrating both approaches. This integration combines the interpretability and theoretical foundation of statistics with the pattern recognition capabilities of machine learning.

Ensemble methods exemplify this integration by combining multiple models to improve overall performance. A comprehensive cardiac risk prediction system might incorporate logistic regression for its interpretability, random forests for handling complex interactions, and neural networks for capturing subtle patterns—each contributing complementary insights to the final prediction.

Causal inference methods address healthcare's need to move beyond correlation to understanding cause and effect. Techniques like propensity score matching and instrumental variable analysis help researchers draw causal conclusions from observational data when randomized controlled trials aren't feasible. These methods enable more confident statements about intervention effects, supporting evidence-based clinical and policy decisions.

Federated learning approaches preserve privacy while enabling model training across multiple institutions, solving one of healthcare's most persistent analytics challenges. By sharing model updates rather than raw patient data, healthcare systems can collaborate on developing powerful predictive models while maintaining regulatory compliance and patient confidentiality.

Implementation Considerations

Selecting appropriate analytical methods requires careful consideration of several factors:

Data characteristics fundamentally shape methodological choices. Small datasets may benefit from statistical approaches that perform well with limited data, while massive, complex datasets might necessitate scalable machine learning techniques. Data quality issues like missing values require appropriate handling strategies, from imputation techniques to algorithms specifically designed for incomplete data.

Interpretability requirements vary across healthcare applications. While a deep learning model might provide superior accuracy for certain diagnostic tasks, clinical adoption may require more interpretable approaches like decision trees or logistic regression that provide clear explanations for their predictions. This transparency becomes particularly crucial for high-stakes clinical decisions.

Computational resources constrain method selection, especially for real-time applications. While complex deep learning models might offer theoretical advantages, deployment environments with limited processing power may necessitate more computationally efficient approaches.

Domain expertise integration remains essential for successful analytics implementation. Statistical and machine learning methods work best when combined with clinical knowledge. Model development should involve multidisciplinary collaboration between data scientists and healthcare professionals to ensure that analytical approaches address clinically relevant questions and incorporate domain-specific constraints.

As healthcare analytics continues to evolve, the boundaries between statistical methods and machine learning will further dissolve, creating increasingly sophisticated approaches that leverage the strengths of both traditions. Organizations that effectively integrate these methods into their analytical workflows gain powerful tools for extracting meaningful insights from healthcare's complex and expanding data landscape.

Visualization and Reporting: Translating Insights into Action

Data visualization and reporting represent the crucial bridge between complex analytics and practical implementation in healthcare. Even the most sophisticated statistical models and machine learning algorithms provide little value if their insights remain trapped in technical complexity, inaccessible to clinicians, administrators, and patients. Effective visualization and reporting transform abstract data into actionable knowledge that drives better decisions.

The Power of Visual Communication in Healthcare

Healthcare data is inherently complex—multidimensional, time-dependent, and often filled with nuance. Visual representations leverage the human brain's remarkable ability to process visual information, enabling faster comprehension and more intuitive understanding than tables of numbers or text descriptions alone.

Effective visualization serves multiple critical functions in healthcare analytics:

Insight discovery occurs when patterns emerge visually that might remain hidden in raw data. When epidemiologists at the State Health Department visualized COVID-19 cases geospatially, unexpected clusters revealed transmission patterns that weren't evident in tabular reports, enabling more targeted intervention strategies.

Decision support becomes more effective when complex risk calculations appear as intuitive visual indicators. Emergency departments now employ color-coded dashboards showing patient acuity and wait times, enabling clinicians to quickly prioritize cases without mentally processing multiple data points.

Communication across disciplines improves when visualization creates a common language. When genomics researchers needed to explain complex mutation patterns to clinicians, network visualizations depicting gene interactions proved far more effective than statistical tables alone.

Narrative building becomes possible when visualizations tell a cohesive story about health trends. Public health campaigns frequently use visual data storytelling to demonstrate how behavioral changes affect health outcomes, making abstract statistics personally relevant.

Healthcare Visualization Approaches

Healthcare organizations employ diverse visualization techniques depending on the data characteristics and analytical goals:

Temporal visualizations capture healthcare's inherently time-based nature. Line charts tracking patient vital signs over time enable clinicians to detect subtle deterioration patterns before critical thresholds are crossed. Calendar heatmaps reveal cyclical patterns in hospital admissions, helping administrators anticipate staffing needs for specific days and seasons.

Categorical comparisons highlight differences between groups or interventions. While traditional bar charts compare treatment outcomes across patient cohorts, more sophisticated approaches like forest plots simultaneously display effect sizes and confidence intervals, providing statistical context for observed differences.

Hierarchical relationships appear frequently in healthcare data. Tree maps effectively visualize hierarchical concepts like healthcare expenditures, with nested rectangles showing proportional spending across departments, procedures, and supplies, helping administrators identify unexpected cost centers.

Network visualizations reveal complex interconnections. Social network diagrams tracking patient and provider interactions have helped infection control teams understand and interrupt hospital-acquired infection transmission patterns. Similar approaches visualize comorbidity relationships, showing how certain conditions frequently cluster together.

Geospatial representations connect health data to location. Public health departments use choropleth maps (where regions are shaded proportionally to measured variables) to identify geographic disparities in health outcomes and access to care, guiding resource allocation and intervention efforts.

From Static Reports to Interactive Dashboards

Healthcare reporting has evolved from static, periodic documents to dynamic, interactive systems that enable exploration and personalization:

Clinical dashboards provide at-a-glance views of patient status and care quality metrics. Modern systems allow clinicians to drill down from summary statistics to individual cases, combining high-level perspective with detailed patient information. The most effective dashboards incorporate visual alerts that draw attention to critical values requiring immediate intervention.

Administrative dashboards enable operational oversight by visualizing key performance indicators. Hospital executives monitor metrics like bed utilization, average length of stay, and clinical outcomes through integrated dashboards that highlight trends and anomalies requiring attention. These systems often incorporate predictive elements, showing not just current status but projected trajectories.

Population health dashboards support care management across patient populations. Healthcare systems track quality measures, care gaps, and risk stratification across enrolled populations, enabling proactive outreach to high-risk patients and systematic quality improvement initiatives.

Patient-facing visualizations increasingly empower individuals in their healthcare journey. Patient portals now include visual representations of lab results over time, medication adherence tracking, and personalized risk profiles, making complex health information more accessible and actionable for non-clinical users.

Design Principles for Healthcare Visualization

Creating effective healthcare visualizations requires attention to both aesthetic and functional design principles:

Clarity and simplicity should take precedence over visual complexity. Healthcare visualizations often suffer from information overload that obscures key insights. Effective designs emphasize the most important patterns while allowing users to access additional detail as needed.

Appropriate visual encoding matches data characteristics to visual representations. While line charts effectively show continuous trends over time, attempting to display categorical data this way creates misleading impressions of continuity between distinct categories.

Consistent color schemes improve interpretability and reduce cognitive load. Well-designed healthcare dashboards employ systematic color coding—using consistent colors for the same measures across different visualizations and reserving alert colors like red for truly critical indicators.

Contextual reference points enhance interpretation. Laboratory value visualizations often include reference ranges, helping clinicians immediately distinguish normal from abnormal values. Similarly, performance dashboards frequently incorporate benchmarks or goals, providing context for current metrics.

Accessibility considerations ensure visualizations serve all users. Color choices should accommodate color vision deficiencies, and interactive elements should support keyboard navigation and screen readers for users with disabilities.

Implementation Challenges and Solutions

Despite their potential value, implementing effective visualization and reporting systems presents several challenges:

Data integration issues often complicate visualization efforts when information resides in disparate systems. Modern healthcare organizations increasingly implement data lakes or warehouses that consolidate information from multiple sources, enabling integrated visualizations that cross traditional system boundaries.

Balancing standardization with customization requires careful design. While standardized visualizations ensure consistency, different users have unique information needs. Leading healthcare systems address this tension through role-based dashboards that provide standardized core elements while allowing individual customization.

Technical limitations in legacy healthcare systems can impede advanced visualization. While dedicated visualization platforms offer superior capabilities, integration with existing electronic health records remains essential for clinical adoption. Successful implementations often employ middleware solutions that extract data from legacy systems for visualization while maintaining operational integration.

Visualization literacy varies widely among healthcare stakeholders. Even well-designed visualizations provide limited value if users cannot interpret them correctly. Progressive healthcare organizations now include visualization training in their analytics implementation, helping clinicians and administrators develop the skills to extract meaningful insights from visual data.

As healthcare continues its data-driven transformation, visualization and reporting will remain essential components of the analytics ecosystem; the final critical step that transforms data into insight and insight into action. Organizations that master these capabilities enable decision-makers at all levels to leverage the full potential of healthcare analytics, ultimately improving care delivery, operational efficiency, and patient outcomes.

Real-world Applications: Analytics Driving Healthcare Transformation

The true value of healthcare analytics emerges when theoretical capabilities translate into tangible improvements in patient care, operational efficiency, and population health. This section explores how healthcare organizations are applying analytics to address their most pressing challenges, illustrated through real-world examples that demonstrate both the potential and practical considerations of analytics implementation.

Enhancing Clinical Decision-Making

Analytics increasingly supports clinicians at the point of care, augmenting human expertise with data-driven insights.

Sepsis prediction exemplifies how analytics saves lives through early intervention. The University of Pennsylvania Health System implemented a machine learning model that continuously monitors electronic health record data to identify patients developing sepsis—a life-threatening condition where hours matter. The system analyzes vital signs, laboratory values, and medication data to calculate a real-time risk score, alerting clinicians when patients show subtle deterioration patterns before obvious clinical signs appear. This early warning system has reduced sepsis mortality by 18% while decreasing unnecessary antibiotic use through improved specificity.

Precision medicine initiatives leverage analytics to match treatments to patients based on their unique characteristics. At Mayo Clinic, oncologists use analytics platforms that integrate genomic sequencing, previous treatment responses, and continuously updated research evidence to recommend personalized cancer treatments. These systems identify potentially effective therapies for patients with rare or treatment-resistant cancers by finding molecular similarities to cases that responded to specific interventions, even across different cancer types. This approach has enabled treatment matches for previously untreatable cases, leading to unexpected remissions in some patients.

Diagnostic decision support helps clinicians navigate complex differential diagnoses. Intermountain Healthcare deployed an analytics system that analyzes combinations of symptoms, test results, and patient characteristics to suggest diagnoses that might otherwise be overlooked, particularly for rare conditions. Rather than replacing clinical judgment, the system works collaboratively with physicians, reducing diagnostic delays and unnecessary testing through more targeted workups.

Transforming Healthcare Operations

Healthcare organizations increasingly apply analytics to optimize their operational processes, improving efficiency while maintaining or enhancing care quality.

Capacity management has evolved from reactive responses to predictive planning. Cleveland Clinic implemented an analytics platform that forecasts patient census by unit, accounting for seasonal patterns, scheduled surgeries, and community disease outbreaks. The system predicts staffing needs up to two weeks in advance with over 85% accuracy, enabling more stable scheduling for clinical staff while ensuring appropriate coverage. During a recent influenza surge, the system anticipated capacity constraints three days before they occurred, allowing proactive redistribution of patients and resources across the hospital network.

Operating room optimization demonstrates how analytics improves resource utilization in high-cost environments. Massachusetts General Hospital applied machine learning techniques to identify inefficiencies in surgical scheduling and turnover processes. The resulting recommendations led to a 30-minute reduction in average turnover time and a 15% increase in surgical volume without adding operating rooms or staff—creating both financial benefits and improved access for patients awaiting surgery.

Supply chain analytics has become increasingly sophisticated as healthcare organizations address both cost pressures and supply vulnerabilities. Banner Health implemented predictive ordering systems that analyze usage patterns across their facilities, adjusting inventory levels based on predicted case volumes and seasonal demand variations. During pandemic-related supply disruptions, this system enabled proactive sourcing of alternative products before critical shortages occurred, while also identifying $4.2 million in annual savings through standardization and waste reduction.

Advancing Population Health

As healthcare models increasingly focus on maintaining health rather than simply treating illness, analytics enables more effective population health management.

Risk stratification helps healthcare organizations identify patients who would benefit most from proactive interventions. Kaiser Permanente's analytics platform integrates clinical, claims, socioeconomic, and consumer data to predict which patients face highest risk for avoidable emergency department visits and hospitalizations. Care managers use these insights to target outreach efforts and develop personalized care plans addressing both medical and social determinants of health, resulting in a 28% reduction in preventable hospitalizations among high-risk patients.

Intervention effectiveness analysis helps organizations determine which programs deliver the greatest value. When Geisinger Health System implemented multiple chronic disease management initiatives simultaneously, analytics enabled precise evaluation of each program's impact. By comparing outcomes across similar patient groups receiving different interventions, they identified which components produced meaningful improvements and which could be modified or discontinued, optimizing their resource allocation for maximum population health impact.

Community health planning increasingly relies on analytics to identify geographic areas with unmet needs. The Camden Coalition of Healthcare Providers uses geospatial analytics to map "hot spots" of high healthcare utilization and poor outcomes, revealing neighborhood-level patterns that guide targeted community interventions. This approach has enabled more effective deployment of community health workers and social services, addressing root causes of health disparities rather than repeatedly treating their consequences.

Accelerating Medical Research

Analytics transforms medical research through faster hypothesis generation, more efficient clinical trials, and real-world evidence evaluation.

Pattern discovery in large datasets reveals relationships that might otherwise remain hidden. Researchers at Vanderbilt University Medical Center used machine learning techniques to analyze de-identified electronic health records from over two million patients, discovering unexpected associations between common medications and reduced Alzheimer's disease risk. These computational findings generated novel hypotheses now being evaluated in traditional clinical studies—demonstrating how analytics can accelerate the early stages of medical discovery.

Adaptive trial designs use real-time analytics to optimize research protocols. The I-SPY 2 breast cancer trial employed Bayesian adaptive algorithms to continuously analyze treatment responses, allowing investigators to adjust patient randomization toward more promising treatments while maintaining statistical validity. This approach identified effective therapies with fewer participants and in less time than traditional trial designs, accelerating the path from discovery to clinical implementation.

Real-world evidence generation increasingly complements controlled trials through analytics applied to routine clinical data. FDA-approved programs now use sophisticated analytics to identify treatment effects across diverse patient populations in regular care settings. These approaches provide insights into medication effectiveness and safety in populations often excluded from clinical trials, such as elderly patients with multiple comorbidities, filling critical knowledge gaps in the evidence base.

Implementation Lessons

Organizations successfully implementing analytics share several common approaches:

Starting with clearly defined problems rather than technology-driven solutions ensures analytics efforts address genuine organizational priorities. Successful implementations typically begin with specific questions where data-driven insights can directly inform actionable decisions.

Building multidisciplinary teams integrates technical expertise with clinical and operational knowledge. Organizations find that data scientists working in isolation rarely produce implementable solutions; effective teams include clinicians, administrators, and data experts collaborating throughout the analytics lifecycle.

Creating feedback loops ensures analytics tools improve over time. High-performing organizations implement systematic processes to evaluate analytics performance, incorporate user feedback, and continuously refine their models and visualizations based on real-world experience.

As healthcare analytics continues to mature, we can expect increasingly sophisticated applications that further transform how healthcare is delivered, managed, and experienced. The examples described here represent not endpoints but early demonstrations of what becomes possible when healthcare organizations effectively harness their data through analytics.

The Path Forward: Navigating the Future of Healthcare Analytics

As we conclude our exploration of healthcare data analytics, it's worth reflecting on both the remarkable progress already achieved and the journey that lies ahead. Healthcare analytics has evolved from basic descriptive reporting to sophisticated predictive and prescriptive systems that influence decisions throughout the healthcare ecosystem. Yet we stand at an inflection point, with emerging technologies, evolving methodologies, and persistent challenges shaping the future landscape.

Convergent Forces Driving Analytics Evolution

Several powerful forces are converging to accelerate analytics advancement in healthcare:

Computational innovation continues to expand what's technically possible. Quantum computing approaches, though still emerging, show promise for modeling complex biological systems at unprecedented scale. Edge computing brings analytical capabilities closer to the point of care, enabling real-time processing of high-volume data streams from medical devices and sensors. These technical advances will enable analytics applications that today remain computationally infeasible.

Methodological advancement extends beyond pure technology to new analytical approaches. Causal inference techniques increasingly move healthcare analytics from correlation to causation, enabling more confident conclusions about intervention effects. Federated learning methods preserve privacy while allowing models to learn from diverse datasets across organizational boundaries. These methodological innovations address healthcare's unique analytical challenges around privacy, causality, and data fragmentation.

Healthcare digitization continues to generate richer, more diverse data. As digital health tools proliferate and interoperability improves, analytics will have access to more comprehensive patient journeys spanning clinical encounters, home monitoring, lifestyle factors, and social determinants. This expanded data ecosystem will enable more holistic approaches to understanding and improving health.

Persistent Challenges Requiring Attention

Despite this promising trajectory, significant challenges remain that will require sustained focus from the healthcare analytics community:

Ethical frameworks for AI must evolve alongside technological capabilities. As analytics increasingly influences high-stakes healthcare decisions, ensuring that these systems operate fairly, transparently, and responsibly becomes crucial. Developing governance structures that prevent algorithmic bias, protect patient autonomy, and maintain appropriate human oversight will be essential for maintaining trust in healthcare analytics.

Workforce development remains a critical need across healthcare. The gap between analytics capabilities and clinical implementation often stems from insufficient data literacy among healthcare professionals and inadequate domain knowledge among data scientists. Building this bilingual talent pool—professionals who understand both healthcare and analytics—represents perhaps the most significant implementation challenge facing the field.

Regulatory clarity continues to evolve unevenly. Healthcare organizations navigate complex and sometimes contradictory regulations around data usage, algorithm validation, and analytics implementation. As regulators work to balance innovation with patient protection, creating clearer pathways for analytics adoption will help accelerate beneficial implementations while ensuring appropriate safeguards.

A Vision for Healthcare Analytics

Looking ahead, we can envision a healthcare system where analytics is fully integrated into the fabric of care delivery, operations, and research—not as a separate technical domain but as an intrinsic capability enhancing all aspects of healthcare:

Clinicians will practice augmented medicine, where their expertise and judgment remain central but are enhanced by analytical insights customized to each patient's unique circumstances. These systems will function as collaborative partners, handling routine pattern recognition while preserving human judgment for complex clinical decisions requiring empathy and ethical reasoning.

Patients will engage with personalized analytics through intuitive interfaces that translate complex health data into actionable insights. These tools will empower individuals to make more informed decisions about their health, understand the implications of different choices, and actively participate in their care planning.

Healthcare organizations will operate as learning health systems, where every patient interaction generates insights that improve future care. Real-time analytics will enable continuous quality improvement, resource optimization, and adaptation to changing patient needs and healthcare environments.

Health policy will increasingly rely on sophisticated modeling and simulation to evaluate potential interventions before implementation. These approaches will enable more evidence-based policymaking and rapid assessment of policy effects across diverse populations and care settings.

The Human Element in Data-Driven Healthcare

As we advance toward this vision of analytics-enhanced healthcare, we must remember that data, algorithms, and visualizations are means to an end, not ends in themselves. The ultimate measure of success for healthcare analytics is not technical sophistication but human impact—improved patient outcomes, enhanced care experiences, greater healthcare equity, and more sustainable healthcare systems.

The most successful analytics implementations maintain this human-centered perspective, designing systems that augment rather than replace human capabilities, that enhance rather than undermine relationships between patients and providers, and that address healthcare's most meaningful challenges rather than its most technically interesting problems.

By maintaining this focus on human needs and impacts while leveraging advancing technological capabilities, healthcare analytics can fulfill its promise as a transformative force in healthcare—creating a future where data-driven insights help healthcare fulfill its fundamental mission of improving human health and wellbeing.

The data analytics approaches we've explored—from descriptive to prescriptive—provide the methodological foundation for healthcare transformation. Now we'll see how these analytical capabilities combine with artificial intelligence to address perhaps the most fundamental clinical activity: diagnosis. By applying advanced analytics to the diagnostic process, AI is not merely automating traditional approaches but enabling entirely new ways to identify disease patterns and determine optimal interventions. This shift from general analytics to specific clinical applications represents a crucial step in translating data science into direct patient benefit.

Chapter 6:

AI in Clinical Diagnosis

Introduction: The Diagnostic Revolution

Medicine has always been defined by its diagnostic challenges—the ability to accurately identify disease has historically depended on the clinician's knowledge, experience, and observational skills. Today, we stand at the threshold of a remarkable transformation as artificial intelligence begins to reshape this fundamental aspect of healthcare.

Diagnosis represents the critical first step in the patient journey, determining treatment paths and ultimately influencing outcomes. The stakes could not be higher: delayed or incorrect diagnoses contribute to approximately 40,000-80,000 preventable deaths annually in U.S. hospitals alone. Against this backdrop, AI offers unprecedented capabilities to process vast datasets, recognize subtle patterns, and augment clinical decision-making in ways previously unimaginable.

What makes this moment particularly significant is the convergence of three powerful forces: the digitization of healthcare data, advances in computational power, and breakthroughs in machine learning algorithms. Electronic health records, digital imaging, genomic data, and even unstructured clinical notes now provide the raw material that AI systems can analyze at scales and speeds beyond human capability.

This chapter explores how AI is transforming clinical diagnosis across multiple domains. We begin by examining AI's role in symptom-based diagnosis and laboratory analysis, where machine learning algorithms are helping clinicians navigate complex presentations and identify patterns in patient data. We then explore the remarkable advances in medical imaging, where AI is not merely assisting radiologists but sometimes exceeding human performance in specific diagnostic tasks.

Natural language processing—AI's ability to understand and analyze human language—represents another frontier, enabling machines to extract meaningful insights from unstructured clinical notes, pathology reports, and medical literature. Finally, we examine how AI is addressing one of medicine's most persistent challenges: the diagnosis of rare diseases, where pattern recognition across vast datasets can identify conditions that might otherwise remain elusive.

Throughout this exploration, we consider not just the technological capabilities but also the nuanced integration of AI into clinical workflows. The goal is not to replace human clinicians but to create synergistic partnerships that leverage the complementary strengths of human and artificial intelligence—the clinician's contextual understanding, empathy, and judgment working alongside AI's pattern recognition, data processing, and tireless consistency.

As we examine these advances, we maintain a balanced perspective—acknowledging both the remarkable potential and the significant challenges in implementing AI for clinical diagnosis. The promise is profound: more accurate, timely, and equitable diagnosis, ultimately leading to better patient outcomes. The path to realizing this promise, however, requires navigating technical, ethical, and practical complexities that we will explore throughout this chapter.

AI-Assisted Diagnosis: Augmenting Clinical Decision-Making

For centuries, diagnosis has represented the quintessential application of human medical expertise—combining knowledge, observation, and reasoning to identify disease. Today, AI is enhancing this process through sophisticated pattern recognition and data analysis capabilities that complement clinical judgment in powerful ways.

Machine Learning for Symptom-Based Diagnosis

Clinical diagnosis often begins with a constellation of symptoms that must be interpreted within the context of a patient's history and risk factors. This complex process is precisely where machine learning shows particular promise.

AI approaches to symptom-based diagnosis leverage supervised learning algorithms trained on vast databases of patient presentations and confirmed diagnoses. These systems analyze patterns that might elude even experienced clinicians, particularly for conditions with atypical presentations or symptoms that could indicate multiple possible diagnoses.

Early applications focused on basic triage have evolved into more sophisticated diagnostic support tools. The Mayo Clinic has developed machine learning algorithms that analyze patient-reported symptoms to help prioritize urgent cases and suggest potential diagnoses for clinician consideration. Similarly, systems like Ada Health and Babylon combine natural language processing with diagnostic algorithms to analyze symptom descriptions and generate potential diagnoses with associated probabilities.

The impact of these systems extends beyond merely suggesting diagnoses. At Boston Children's Hospital, an AI system called HealthMap monitors patterns in emergency department presentations, detecting early signals of disease outbreaks before they would be apparent through traditional surveillance methods. During a recent influenza season, the system identified an unusual pattern of respiratory symptoms three days before official reporting mechanisms registered the outbreak, enabling earlier public health interventions.

Perhaps most promising is AI's potential to identify rare disease conditions that individual clinicians might encounter only a few times in their careers, if at all. By analyzing symptoms across millions of patient records, these systems can recognize patterns associated with uncommon conditions, potentially reducing the "diagnostic odyssey" that many rare disease patients endure. One clinician using such a system noted, "It suggested a metabolic disorder I hadn't considered, prompting additional testing that confirmed the diagnosis and changed our treatment approach completely."

Laboratory Data Analysis and Interpretation

Laboratory testing provides essential diagnostic data, but interpreting results—particularly across multiple tests and over time—presents significant challenges. AI is transforming this aspect of diagnosis through advanced pattern recognition and predictive analytics.

Modern machine learning algorithms can analyze complex patterns across laboratory values, identifying subtle relationships that might indicate emerging health issues before they become clinically apparent. At Vanderbilt University Medical Center, an AI system continuously monitors patient laboratory data to predict acute kidney injury up to 48 hours before clinical recognition would typically occur. This early warning system allows preventive interventions that can mitigate or prevent kidney damage, demonstrating how AI can shift diagnosis from reactive to proactive.

Beyond individual test interpretation, AI excels at integrating laboratory data with other clinical information. Systems in development at Stanford Medicine analyze patterns across laboratory results, vital signs, medication data, and demographics to predict clinical deterioration in hospitalized patients. By identifying at-risk patients earlier, these systems enable timely interventions that can prevent critical events.

Perhaps the most revolutionary is AI's ability to discover novel biomarkers—combinations of laboratory values that together indicate increased risk for specific conditions. Traditional statistical approaches might miss these complex relationships, but machine learning algorithms can identify patterns across hundreds of variables. Researchers using such an approach recently discovered a novel laboratory signature predictive of sepsis, a life-threatening condition where early recognition significantly improves survival rates.

However, implementing these systems in clinical practice requires careful attention to workflow integration. As one laboratory director observed, "The AI doesn't replace our expertise—it helps us prioritize abnormal results and see patterns developing over time. But it needs to fit seamlessly into our workflow to be useful." Successful integration involves thoughtful design of alerts, visualization of AI insights, and clear communication of uncertainty in predictions.

Predictive Analytics for Early Detection

Perhaps the most transformative application of AI in diagnosis is the ability to detect disease at earlier, more treatable stages through predictive analytics. By analyzing patterns across diverse data sources, AI can identify subtle signals that precede clinical symptoms, potentially transforming our approach to diagnosis from reactive to proactive.

At the Duke Clinical Research Institute, researchers developed a machine learning model that analyzes patient records to identify individuals at high risk for heart failure before they develop symptoms. The algorithm integrates multiple risk factors—including subtle laboratory changes, medication patterns, and even administrative codes—that together signal increased risk. Validated in a population of over 50,000 patients, the system identified at-risk individuals with significantly higher accuracy than traditional risk scores, enabling preventive interventions that reduced heart failure hospitalizations by 25%.

Similar approaches show promise in oncology, where early detection directly impacts survival rates. A deep learning system developed at Google Health demonstrated the ability to detect malignant breast lesions in mammograms with greater sensitivity than experienced radiologists, potentially identifying cancers at earlier stages. Equally important, the system reduced false positives by 5.7%, potentially sparing thousands of women unnecessary biopsies and the associated psychological distress.

The impact of these predictive approaches extends beyond hospital settings to community and primary care environments. Population health management platforms increasingly incorporate AI-driven risk prediction to identify patients who would benefit from preventive screening or intervention. For example, a system deployed across a large primary care network identified previously unrecognized patients at high risk for undiagnosed type 2 diabetes, enabling targeted screening that led to earlier diagnosis and treatment.

However, the implementation of predictive analytics raises important considerations about false positives, patient anxiety, and healthcare resource utilization. As one primary care physician noted, "These systems help us identify patients who need additional attention, but we need to be thoughtful about how we communicate risk predictions to avoid unnecessary fear." The most effective implementations combine AI predictions with thoughtful clinical protocols for follow-up and patient communication.

Medical Imaging and AI: Seeing Beyond Human Vision

Medical imaging represents one of the most promising and advanced applications of AI in diagnosis. The highly visual nature of radiology, pathology, and other imaging-based specialties creates an ideal environment for machine learning algorithms that excel at image analysis and pattern recognition.

Transforming Radiological Diagnosis

Radiology has emerged as the leading edge of AI implementation in clinical practice, with algorithms now capable of analyzing various imaging modalities including X-rays, CT scans, MRI, and ultrasound. These systems excel at tasks that challenge human perception, such as detecting subtle abnormalities, precisely measuring structures, and tracking changes over time.

Chest radiography provides a compelling example of AI's impact. Deep learning algorithms can now detect pulmonary nodules, pneumonia, tuberculosis, and other abnormalities with sensitivity comparable to or exceeding that of experienced radiologists. A multi-center study involving over 100,000 chest X-rays demonstrated that an AI system detected pulmonary nodules with 96% sensitivity, compared to 85% for radiologists reading the same images. Perhaps more significantly, the system maintained consistent performance across diverse patient populations and image qualities, addressing the variability that often affects human performance.

Beyond simple detection, AI systems increasingly provide quantitative analysis and disease characterization. In neuroimaging, algorithms can precisely measure brain structures affected by neurodegenerative diseases, tracking subtle volume changes over time with greater precision than visual assessment. This capability enables earlier detection of conditions like Alzheimer's disease, where structural changes precede clinical symptoms by years or even decades.

The workflow impact of these technologies is equally significant. AI-based triage systems now analyze images immediately after acquisition, flagging critical findings for prioritized review. At Northwell Health, implementation of such a system for intracranial hemorrhage detection reduced the average time to radiologist interpretation for critical cases from 58 minutes to 13 minutes—a difference that can directly impact patient outcomes in time-sensitive conditions.

However, the integration of AI into radiological practice faces substantial challenges. Radiologists express concerns about the "black box" nature of many algorithms, where the reasoning behind AI findings remains opaque. As one radiologist noted, "I need to understand why the AI flagged something to integrate that information with my own assessment." This has driven development of more explainable AI approaches that highlight the image features influencing the algorithm's conclusions.

Digital Pathology and AI Analysis

While radiology has led AI implementation in medical imaging, pathology is rapidly embracing similar approaches through the digitization of tissue slides and development of advanced image analysis algorithms. This digital transformation is enabling more accurate, efficient, and quantitative analysis of pathological specimens.

Oncologic pathology represents a primary focus for these innovations. AI algorithms can now assist in detecting cancer cells, grading tumors, and identifying molecular features from histopathological images. A landmark study at Harvard Medical School demonstrated that a deep learning system could distinguish between two lung cancer types with 97% accuracy, matching the performance of experienced pathologists while requiring a fraction of the time.

Beyond basic classification, AI is enhancing the precision of pathological assessment through quantitative analysis. Traditional manual approaches to quantifying features like mitotic count or tumor infiltrating lymphocytes are time-consuming and subject to significant inter-observer variability. AI systems perform these measurements with greater consistency and speed, potentially standardizing pathological assessment across institutions and improving the reliability of prognostic indicators.

The integration of AI with emerging molecular techniques represents perhaps the most promising frontier in pathological diagnosis. Algorithms can now predict certain molecular characteristics directly from H&E-stained slides, potentially eliminating the need for additional specialized testing. Researchers at the University of California, Los Angeles demonstrated an algorithm that could predict microsatellite instability status in colorectal cancer from routine histopathology slides with 95% accuracy, potentially guiding immunotherapy decisions without requiring additional molecular testing.

However, pathologists emphasize that AI augments rather than replaces their expertise. As one pathologist observed, "The AI excels at quantification and pattern recognition, but pathological diagnosis requires integration with clinical context that still depends on human judgment." The most effective implementations position AI as a collaborator that handles routine tasks and flags areas of interest, allowing pathologists to focus their expertise on complex cases and integration with clinical information.

Emerging Applications in Dermatology and Ophthalmology

Beyond radiology and pathology, AI is transforming diagnostic imaging in specialties where visual assessment plays a central role, particularly dermatology and ophthalmology.

In dermatology, deep learning algorithms can now analyze images of skin lesions to distinguish between benign and malignant conditions. A groundbreaking study published in Nature demonstrated that a convolutional neural network could classify skin cancers with accuracy comparable to dermatologists. Similar systems are now being deployed through smartphone applications, potentially expanding access to dermatological expertise in underserved regions. While these consumer applications raise regulatory and quality concerns, they represent an important step toward democratizing specialized diagnostic capabilities.

Ophthalmology has embraced AI for screening and diagnostic applications, particularly for conditions like diabetic retinopathy where early detection can prevent vision loss. The FDA-approved IDx-DR system can autonomously detect diabetic retinopathy from retinal images without clinician interpretation, potentially expanding screening capabilities in primary care settings. Similar approaches are showing promise for age-related macular degeneration, glaucoma, and other conditions where subtle retinal changes indicate disease.

These applications share a common theme: extending specialized diagnostic capabilities beyond traditional settings. As one ophthalmologist noted, "There simply aren't enough specialists to screen every patient who needs it. AI can help identify the patients who truly need our expertise." This represents a recurring pattern in clinical AI—not replacing specialists but extending their reach through systems that can perform initial assessment and triage.

The next section will explore how AI is transforming another critical aspect of diagnosis through natural language processing in clinical documentation and medical literature analysis.

Natural Language Processing: Unlocking Clinical Documentation and Medical Literature

The wealth of information in healthcare exists not only in structured data and images but also in the rich, unstructured text of clinical notes, medical literature, and patient communications. Natural language processing (NLP)—AI's ability to understand, analyze, and generate human language—represents a critical capability for extracting diagnostic insights from these textual sources.

Mining Clinical Documentation for Diagnostic Insights

Clinical documentation contains invaluable diagnostic information often trapped in unstructured formats. Progress notes, consultation reports, discharge summaries, and pathology reports all contain nuanced observations captured in natural language rather than structured data fields.

Advanced NLP algorithms now extract and categorize clinically relevant concepts from free text, identifying symptoms, conditions, medications, and procedural information that might otherwise remain inaccessible for systematic analysis. At Mass General Brigham, implementation of an NLP system to analyze clinical notes improved the identification of patients with heart failure by 34% compared to structured data alone, enabling more comprehensive disease management and revealing previously undetected cases.

Beyond simple extraction, contextual understanding represents a significant advancement in clinical NLP. Modern algorithms distinguish between confirmed diagnoses and those merely suspected or ruled out—a critical distinction that earlier systems struggled to make. They can also capture temporal relationships, determining when symptoms began, whether conditions have improved or worsened, and if treatments were previously attempted.

The diagnostic impact extends to monitoring subtle changes in patient status over time. At the University of California San Francisco Medical Center, an NLP system analyzes daily progress notes to track neurological status in intensive care patients, detecting subtle deterioration signals that might not trigger changes in structured vital signs or laboratory values. One neurointensivist noted, "The system identified concerning language patterns in progress notes twelve hours before clinical deterioration became obvious, giving us a critical early warning." A neurointensivist a specialist physician who provides critical care for patients with acute neurological and neurosurgical conditions.

However, implementation challenges remain significant. Clinical language varies dramatically across specialties, institutions, and individual clinicians. Abbreviations, shorthand, and idiomatic expressions pose particular difficulties, often having different meanings in different contexts. As one developer observed, "SOB can mean 'shortness of breath' or 'brother' depending on whether it appears in a pulmonology note or social history." Successful systems must adapt to these linguistic variations while maintaining accuracy.

Diagnostic Decision Support Through Literature Analysis

The exponential growth of medical literature presents an insurmountable challenge for individual clinicians—over 3,000 new articles are published daily in indexed medical journals alone. NLP enables AI systems to continuously analyze this literature, extracting and synthesizing knowledge to support diagnostic decision-making.

Systems like IBM Watson for Genomics and Oncology combine NLP analysis of scientific literature with patient-specific data to suggest diagnostic possibilities and treatment options. These platforms can analyze thousands of articles, clinical trials, and treatment guidelines in seconds, identifying relevant information that might take a clinician weeks to discover through traditional literature review.

The impact is particularly significant for rare or complex conditions where relevant research might be scattered across diverse journals and specialties. A pediatric neurologist using such a system shared: "When presented with an unusual constellation of symptoms, the system identified three recent case reports describing a rare genetic syndrome that matched our patient perfectly. Without this, we might have missed the diagnosis entirely."

Beyond keeping clinicians updated, these systems help bridge specialty knowledge gaps. Primary care physicians face the impossible task of staying current across all medical fields, but NLP-powered systems can provide specialty-level knowledge through continuous literature analysis. One physician noted, "It's like having dozens of specialists reviewing each case alongside me, each bringing their specialized knowledge to bear."

The implementation of these systems requires careful attention to workflow integration and user experience. Clinicians express frustration with systems that overwhelm them with information or fail to prioritize findings appropriately. The most successful implementations deliver insights at relevant decision points, providing evidence summaries and confidence levels rather than simply presenting long lists of potentially relevant publications.

Diagnostic Signal Detection in Patient-Generated Text

A relatively unexplored frontier in diagnostic NLP involves analyzing text generated directly by patients, including messages to providers, responses to questionnaires, and even social media content (with appropriate consent).

Emerging research demonstrates that NLP can detect subtle linguistic signals associated with conditions like depression, cognitive impairment, and early dementia. A study at the University of Pennsylvania analyzed message portal communications between patients and providers, identifying linguistic patterns predictive of depression with 80% accuracy before clinical diagnosis. Similar approaches have shown promise for early detection of cognitive changes associated with neurodegenerative diseases, where subtle language alterations often precede obvious clinical symptoms.

Patient-reported symptoms captured through digital platforms present another valuable data source. NLP algorithms can analyze these descriptions to identify patterns suggesting specific diagnoses or disease subtypes. This approach proves particularly valuable for conditions with subjective symptoms like chronic pain, fatigue, or cognitive changes, where patient descriptions may contain diagnostic clues not captured in structured assessments.

However, these applications raise important ethical considerations regarding privacy, consent, and the appropriate boundaries of diagnostic monitoring. As one bioethicist noted, "Patients may not realize their language is being analyzed for diagnostic purposes, raising questions about transparency and informed consent." Successful implementation requires clear communication with patients about how their data will be used and the option to opt out of such analyses.

Enhancing Documentation Through Ambient Clinical Intelligence

While much NLP development focuses on analyzing existing documentation, emerging "ambient clinical intelligence" systems aim to transform how documentation is created in the first place. These systems use voice recognition and NLP to listen to natural patient-clinician conversations, automatically generating structured documentation while identifying potential diagnostic considerations.

Early implementations like Nuance's Dragon Ambient eXperience (DAX) and Suki Assistant demonstrate the potential of this approach. By automatically documenting patient encounters, these systems not only reduce administrative burden but also potentially improve diagnostic accuracy by allowing clinicians to focus completely on the patient rather than documentation. As one primary care physician using such a system observed, "I can maintain eye contact and truly listen to the patient's story, which has helped me catch subtle diagnostic clues I might have missed while typing notes."

Beyond simple transcription, advanced systems can identify potentially missed questions or inconsistencies in the clinical interview, suggesting additional areas for exploration. This "diagnostic coaching" function helps ensure thorough evaluation, particularly for less experienced clinicians or those working outside their primary specialty.

The next evolution of these systems involves real-time diagnostic suggestion during patient encounters. Prototype systems currently in development listen to the clinical conversation and discreetly suggest potential diagnoses or follow-up questions based on the symptoms and history being discussed. A physician testing such a system shared, "During a complex case, it suggested asking about a medication side effect I hadn't considered, which turned out to be the actual cause of the patient's symptoms."

While promising, these applications face significant implementation challenges, including concerns about privacy, accuracy, and the potential impact on the patient-clinician relationship. Successful deployment requires careful attention to these issues, with transparent communication and clear professional guidelines for appropriate use.

The integration of NLP capabilities with other diagnostic AI approaches represents perhaps the most exciting frontier in this domain. By combining insights from clinical documentation, medical literature, imaging reports, and structured data, AI systems can provide increasingly comprehensive diagnostic support that extends beyond the capabilities of any single modality.

AI for Rare Disease Diagnosis: Finding the Needle in the Haystack

Rare diseases represent one of medicine's most persistent diagnostic challenges. Though individually uncommon, rare diseases collectively affect an estimated 300 million people worldwide. Patients with rare conditions often endure a "diagnostic odyssey," visiting an average of seven specialists over 4.8 years before receiving an accurate diagnosis. This delay not only prolongs suffering but often prevents timely interventions that could alter disease progression.

Artificial intelligence offers unique capabilities to address this challenge through its ability to recognize patterns across vast datasets, connect seemingly unrelated symptoms, and consider thousands of rare conditions simultaneously—tasks that exceed human cognitive capacity.

Pattern Recognition Across Diverse Data Sources

The power of AI in rare disease diagnosis lies in its ability to analyze patterns across multiple data modalities simultaneously; genomic information, laboratory results, imaging studies, and clinical observations.

The Undiagnosed Diseases Network (UDN) exemplifies this approach, combining AI analysis of phenotypic and genomic data to diagnose previously undiagnosable conditions. Their machine learning system compares a patient's presentation against databases containing millions of symptom-disease and gene-disease relationships. This approach has achieved diagnostic success in approximately 35% of cases that had eluded conventional methods, including the identification of several previously unknown genetic disorders.

Beyond identifying known rare diseases, AI enables the discovery of new disease subtypes through unsupervised learning techniques. By analyzing patterns in patient data without predetermined categories, these algorithms reveal natural groupings that may represent distinct disease mechanisms requiring different therapeutic approaches. Researchers at Stanford Medicine used this approach to identify three previously unrecognized subtypes of idiopathic pulmonary fibrosis, each with different progression patterns and treatment responses.

The ability to integrate real-time data streams represents another significant advancement. AI systems can continuously update their analysis as new information becomes available—laboratory results, specialist consultations, or response to therapeutic trials—progressively refining diagnostic hypotheses. This dynamic approach mirrors the clinical reasoning process while considering exponentially more possibilities than a human clinician could evaluate.

Facial Analysis and Rare Genetic Disorders

Some of the most tangible successes in AI-assisted rare disease diagnosis have come from facial recognition technology applied to genetic disorders. Many genetic conditions manifest with subtle but distinctive facial features that may be imperceptible to all but the most experienced specialists.

The Face2Gene application exemplifies this approach, using deep learning algorithms to analyze facial photographs and identify features associated with over 300 genetic syndromes. The system compares a patient's facial characteristics against a database of thousands of confirmed cases, suggesting potential diagnoses for clinician consideration. In a landmark study, this system demonstrated an ability to place the correct diagnosis within its top ten suggestions in 91% of cases across a diverse set of genetic conditions.

The accessibility of this technology proves particularly valuable in settings without specialized genetics expertise. Primary care physicians and general pediatricians can now access sophisticated diagnostic support previously available only at major academic centers. As one rural pediatrician noted, "With this technology, I identified two rare genetic conditions in six months that might otherwise have gone undiagnosed for years."

Importantly, these systems continue to improve through a virtuous cycle of implementation and learning. Each confirmed diagnosis enriches the training dataset, enabling more accurate future predictions—particularly valuable for ultra-rare conditions with limited documented cases. The technology has already contributed to the phenotypic delineation of several newly identified genetic disorders by recognizing consistent facial patterns among patients with similar genetic variants.

However, implementation challenges remain significant, including ensuring algorithmic fairness across diverse populations. Initial versions of facial analysis algorithms performed less effectively for patients from underrepresented ethnic backgrounds due to training data limitations. Developers have worked to address these disparities by diversifying their training datasets, but ongoing vigilance is required to ensure equitable performance across all patient populations.

Natural Language Processing and the Diagnostic Odyssey

The diagnostic journey for rare disease patients generates extensive clinical documentation—consultation notes, test results, attempted treatments, and patient-reported experiences. Natural language processing offers powerful tools to analyze this textual information, identifying patterns that suggest specific rare diagnoses.

AI systems can now analyze clinical notes to extract and normalize symptoms, creating comprehensive phenotypic profiles that might span dozens of clinical encounters and multiple healthcare systems. These normalized profiles are then compared against rare disease knowledge bases to identify potential matches. The German-based Ada Health system demonstrated the ability to suggest the correct diagnosis among its top three possibilities in 73% of rare disease cases, often identifying conditions that had eluded multiple specialists.

Perhaps most valuable is NLP's ability to identify temporal patterns in symptom development—distinguishing between stable, progressive, or relapsing-remitting presentations. This temporal dimension proves particularly important for rare diseases with evolving clinical pictures, where the sequence and progression of symptoms often provide critical diagnostic clues.

Beyond analyzing provider documentation, NLP can extract valuable insights from patient-authored content. Patients with rare diseases often become experts in their own conditions, documenting subtle symptoms and experiences in forums, social media, and direct communications with providers. Analysis of this patient-generated content has led to several documented cases where AI systems identified correct diagnoses missed by conventional approaches. As one rare disease specialist observed, "Sometimes the diagnostic clues are hidden in the patient's own words, if we have the tools to listen properly."

The Human-AI Partnership in Rare Disease Diagnosis

While AI demonstrates remarkable capabilities in rare disease diagnosis, the most effective approaches combine algorithmic analysis with human expertise. This partnership leverages the complementary strengths of both: AI's ability to process vast datasets and consider thousands of rare possibilities, alongside the clinician's contextual understanding, intuition, and direct patient interaction.

The Rare Disease Centers of Excellence network exemplifies this collaborative approach. These centers combine AI diagnostic tools with multidisciplinary expert teams, significantly improving diagnostic rates for complex cases. When encountering diagnostic uncertainty, clinicians input structured and unstructured patient data into AI systems, which generate diagnostic hypotheses ranked by probability. Clinicians then evaluate these suggestions in the context of their expertise and direct patient assessment, determining which warrants further investigation.

This human-AI partnership extends beyond initial diagnosis to ongoing refinement of diagnostic categories. Clinicians provide critical feedback on AI performance, identifying both successful diagnoses and errors, which continuously improves system accuracy. This feedback loop proves particularly valuable for extremely rare conditions where limited cases make traditional algorithm training challenging.

The impact of this partnership extends to the diagnostic experience itself. While AI can suggest potential diagnoses, human clinicians remain essential for communicating with patients, contextualizing findings, and guiding them through the emotional journey of rare disease diagnosis. As one patient advocate noted, "The technology may identify the condition, but we still need compassionate providers to help us understand what it means for our lives."

Conclusion: The Future of AI in Clinical Diagnosis

The integration of artificial intelligence into clinical diagnosis represents a profound evolution in healthcare—not a replacement of human clinicians but an enhancement of their capabilities through powerful new tools for pattern recognition, data analysis, and knowledge synthesis.

As we've explored throughout this chapter, AI is transforming diagnostic practice across multiple domains: enhancing symptom-based reasoning, revealing patterns in laboratory data, identifying subtle features in medical images, extracting insights from clinical documentation, and recognizing rare diseases that might otherwise remain undiagnosed. In each area, the most effective implementations create synergistic partnerships between human and artificial intelligence, combining the complementary strengths of each.

Looking ahead, several emerging trends will likely shape the continued evolution of AI in clinical diagnosis. The integration of multimodal data— combining insights from clinical notes, images, genomics, laboratory values, and sensor data—promises increasingly comprehensive diagnostic capabilities. Federated learning approaches will enable AI systems to learn from diverse datasets across institutions while preserving privacy and security. Advances in explainable AI will make algorithmic reasoning more transparent to clinicians, addressing the "black box" problem that has limited adoption of some current systems.

Perhaps most significantly, AI diagnosis will increasingly shift from reactive to proactive approaches—identifying disease at earlier, more treatable stages or even predicting risk before clinical presentation. This evolution has profound implications for preventive medicine, potentially transforming our fundamental approach to disease detection and management.

However, significant challenges remain on this journey. Ensuring algorithmic fairness across diverse patient populations requires ongoing vigilance and commitment. Integration with clinical workflows must be thoughtfully designed to enhance rather than disrupt patient care. Privacy considerations, data quality issues, and regulatory frameworks all require careful navigation as these technologies continue to evolve.

The true measure of success for AI in clinical diagnosis will not be technological sophistication but improved patient outcomes—more accurate and timely diagnoses, reduced disparities in diagnostic capabilities, and ultimately better health for individuals and populations. Achieving this promise requires not just technological innovation but thoughtful implementation that places these powerful tools in service of the fundamental values of medicine: beneficence, non-maleficence, justice, and respect for persons.

As we transition to the next chapter, which explores AI applications in treatment planning and clinical interventions, we carry forward a key insight: the future of healthcare lies not in artificial intelligence alone, but in the intelligent integration of artificial and human capabilities, each augmenting the other to achieve what neither could accomplish alone.

Chapter 7:

AI in Treatment and Implementation

Beyond Diagnosis to Intervention

While diagnosis represents the critical first step in the patient journey, treatment decisions and clinical interventions ultimately determine patient outcomes. Artificial intelligence is now extending its transformative potential beyond diagnostic applications to reshape how treatments are planned, delivered, and evaluated across healthcare.

This evolution marks a profound shift in AI's role—from primarily analytical to increasingly interventional. AI systems are not only helping clinicians understand what is happening but are beginning to guide decisions about what should be done. This transition brings both remarkable opportunities and significant responsibilities as algorithms begin to influence treatment decisions that directly impact patient lives.

What makes this moment particularly consequential is the integration of AI across multiple dimensions of treatment: informing clinical decisions through evidence synthesis, enhancing surgical precision through robotics, personalizing therapies based on individual patient characteristics, and optimizing complex treatment protocols through predictive modeling. These capabilities are converging to create a more precise, personalized, and proactive approach to healthcare delivery.

However, the implementation of AI in treatment contexts raises unique challenges beyond those encountered in diagnostic applications. Treatment decisions involve value judgments, risk assessments, and consideration of patient preferences in ways that are more complex than diagnostic determinations. The stakes of algorithmic recommendations increase significantly when they guide interventions rather than merely support understanding.

This chapter explores how AI is transforming treatment planning and implementation across multiple domains of healthcare. We begin by examining how AI is enhancing clinical decision support systems, making them more personalized, evidence-based, and context-aware. We then explore the integration of AI with surgical robotics, creating new capabilities for precision, minimally invasive interventions, and extending surgical expertise beyond traditional limitations.

The promise of personalized medicine—treatments tailored to individual patient characteristics—represents another frontier where AI is proving transformative. We examine how AI enables more precise matching of therapies to patients based on genetic, molecular, and clinical features, potentially revolutionizing fields from oncology to chronic disease management.

Throughout this exploration, we maintain focus on the ethical dimensions of AI in treatment contexts, particularly questions of autonomy, responsibility, and the appropriate balance between algorithmic guidance and human judgment. We also address the practical challenges healthcare organizations face when implementing these systems, from workflow integration to training requirements.

As we consider the future trajectory of AI in clinical treatment, we recognize that success will be measured not by technological sophistication but by tangible improvements in patient outcomes, clinical efficiency, and healthcare accessibility. The true promise lies in creating synergistic partnerships between human clinicians and artificial intelligence—combining the compassion, judgment, and ethical reasoning of healthcare professionals with the data processing power, pattern recognition capabilities, and tireless consistency of AI systems.

AI in Treatment Planning and Decision Support

For centuries, treatment decisions have represented the quintessential application of clinical judgment—weighing evidence, evaluating risks and benefits, and considering patient-specific factors to determine the optimal therapeutic approach. Today, AI is enhancing this process through advanced analytics that synthesize evidence, personalize recommendations, and predict outcomes with unprecedented precision.

Evidence-Based Decision Support

The exponential growth of medical knowledge has made it increasingly challenging for clinicians to stay current with emerging evidence across their scope of practice. AI-powered clinical decision support systems (CDSS) help bridge this knowledge gap by continuously analyzing the latest research and applying it to individual patient scenarios.

Modern CDSS have evolved far beyond simple rule-based systems to incorporate sophisticated machine learning algorithms that can weigh multiple factors simultaneously. At Intermountain Healthcare, an AI-powered CDSS for antibiotic selection analyzes patient data, local resistance patterns, and current guidelines to recommend optimal antimicrobial regimens. This system has demonstrated a 70% increase in guideline-concordant prescribing and a significant reduction in antibiotic-resistant infections.

The true power of these systems emerges from their ability to personalize evidence application based on patient-specific factors. Traditional guidelines often exclude patients with complex comorbidities or unusual presentations—precisely the cases where clinicians need the most support. AI systems can consider these complexities, applying relevant evidence from similar cases even when perfect guideline matches don't exist.

This capability proves particularly valuable for conditions with evolving treatment landscapes. In oncology, platforms like IBM Watson for Oncology analyze thousands of scientific articles, clinical trials, and treatment outcomes to generate evidence-based treatment recommendations tailored to individual patient characteristics. A study at Manipal Comprehensive Cancer Center demonstrated 93% concordance between the system's recommendations and those of a multidisciplinary tumor board for breast cancer cases.

However, implementation experience reveals both promises and challenges. Clinicians express concern about the "black box" nature of some systems, where the reasoning behind recommendations remains opaque. As one oncologist noted, "I need to understand why the system is recommending this approach to determine if it makes sense for my specific patient." This has driven the development of more explainable AI approaches that provide supporting evidence and confidence levels alongside recommendations.

Predictive Modeling for Treatment Outcomes

Perhaps the most transformative aspect of AI in treatment planning is the ability to predict individual patient responses to various interventions, moving beyond population-based statistics to truly personalized prognostication.

Advanced predictive models now integrate diverse data types—clinical characteristics, biomarkers, imaging features, and even lifestyle factors—to forecast how individual patients might respond to specific treatments. For complex conditions like inflammatory bowel disease, these models help clinicians choose between multiple treatment options by predicting which is most likely to induce remission for a specific patient.

The impact extends beyond treatment selection to optimization of treatment protocols. Machine learning algorithms can identify the optimal dosing, timing, and combination of therapies for individual patients. In cancer care, such approaches have demonstrated the ability to reduce treatment toxicity while maintaining efficacy by personalizing chemotherapy dosing based on patient-specific factors.

Treatment sequencing represents another area where predictive modeling shows particular promise. For conditions requiring multiple lines of therapy, AI can analyze large datasets to determine optimal treatment sequences based on patient characteristics. This approach has shown value in multiple sclerosis management, where the order of disease-modifying therapies significantly impacts long-term outcomes.

Beyond predicting treatment efficacy, AI models increasingly forecast potential complications, enabling proactive prevention. The University of Pennsylvania developed a deep learning algorithm that identifies patients at high risk for adverse events during chemotherapy, allowing for preventive interventions that reduced hospitalizations by 35% in the highest-risk group.

The communication of these predictions to patients represents an important implementation consideration. As one clinician observed, "These systems don't just provide probabilities—they influence hope, anxiety, and decision-making in profound ways." The most successful implementations combine algorithmic predictions with thoughtful approaches to risk communication, helping patients understand both the capabilities and limitations of these forecasts.

Continuous Learning Systems for Treatment Optimization

Traditional clinical decision support relies on periodic updates to incorporate new evidence. Modern AI systems increasingly employ continuous learning approaches that evolve in real-time based on observed outcomes, creating a virtuous cycle of improvement.

These systems monitor treatment responses across patient populations, identifying patterns that might indicate certain approaches work better for specific patient subgroups. At Memorial Sloan Kettering Cancer Center, an AI platform continuously analyzes outcomes data to refine treatment recommendations for rare cancer subtypes, where limited evidence makes traditional guideline development challenging.

The value of this approach becomes particularly evident during rapid therapeutic evolution, such as during the COVID-19 pandemic. AI systems analyzing treatment outcomes across multiple hospitals identified effective approaches more quickly than traditional research methods could, helping clinicians adapt treatment protocols as understanding of the disease evolved.

However, these continuous learning systems raise important considerations about data quality, validation, and the balance between rapid adaptation and scientific rigor. As one healthcare quality director noted, "We need to ensure that the system is learning from representative data and that changes to recommendations are clinically validated before implementation." Organizations implementing such systems have developed governance frameworks to balance innovation with appropriate oversight.

AI-Enabled Shared Decision Making

Treatment decisions ultimately belong not to algorithms or even clinicians alone, but to patients in consultation with their healthcare providers. Advanced AI systems are increasingly designed to support this shared decision-making process rather than simply providing recommendations.

These platforms help visualize complex risk-benefit tradeoffs in ways patients can more easily understand, converting statistical information into personalized, accessible formats. For surgical decisions, AI-generated predictive visualizations can illustrate the likely functional outcomes of different approaches based on an individual patient's characteristics, helping patients align treatment choices with their personal priorities and values.

Mayo Clinic has pioneered such approaches for complex cardiac procedures, using AI to generate personalized outcome predictions that facilitate more informed consent discussions. Clinicians report that these tools not only improve patient understanding but also help elicit important values and preferences that might otherwise remain unexpressed.

The future evolution of these systems will likely involve increasingly sophisticated modeling of patient preferences alongside clinical factors. Early research demonstrates that AI can help predict which aspects of treatment outcomes matter most to individual patients based on their values, demographics, and prior decisions, potentially enabling more personalized guidance.

As we transition to exploring robotics and AI in surgery, we carry forward a crucial insight: the most powerful applications of AI in treatment planning don't replace clinical judgment but augment it—providing clinicians and patients with enhanced information, personalized predictions, and evidence synthesis that enables more informed, individualized decisions about the interventions that will best achieve desired outcomes.

AI in Personalized Medicine

Medicine has long aspired to move beyond one-size-fits-all approaches toward treatments tailored to individual patients. Today, AI is accelerating this transformation by analyzing complex patterns across biological, clinical, and environmental factors to enable truly personalized therapeutic strategies. This shift represents one of healthcare's most profound evolutions—from population-based to precision medicine.

Genomic Medicine and AI Analytics

The genomic revolution has generated unprecedented data about the molecular basis of disease, but translating this information into clinical action requires computational approaches that far exceed human analytical capabilities. AI has emerged as the essential bridge between raw genomic data and actionable clinical insights.

Machine learning algorithms can now analyze a person's genetic information (their genetic profile) to predict three key factors: their risk of developing certain diseases, how they might respond to medications, and which treatment approaches might work best for them. What makes these systems powerful is their ability to look at thousands of small variations in genes simultaneously, rather than focusing on just one gene at a time. This comprehensive approach helps us understand complex conditions that are influenced by many genes working together (what scientists call 'polygenic conditions'), offering a much more complete picture than earlier genetic analyses could provide.

At Geisinger Health System, implementation of such approaches has enabled preemptive pharmacogenomic testing, with AI algorithms identifying patients likely to experience adverse drug reactions based on their genetic profiles. This program reduced adverse medication events by 35% among high-risk patients by enabling genetically informed prescribing decisions before adverse reactions occurred.

Beyond analyzing germline genetics, AI is transforming cancer care through sophisticated tumor genomic interpretation. Traditional approaches to cancer have relied on anatomical classification (lung cancer, breast cancer), but AI-powered analysis of tumor genetic profiles enables molecular classification that better predicts treatment response. Foundation Medicine's genomic analysis platform uses machine learning to interpret complex tumor genomic profiles, identifying actionable mutations and matching patients to targeted therapies or appropriate clinical trials. A study at Memorial Sloan Kettering demonstrated that this approach identified effective targeted therapy options for 42% of patients who had exhausted standard treatment approaches.

The integration of genomic with clinical and environmental data represents the next frontier in this domain. AI systems increasingly incorporate family history, environmental exposures, lifestyle factors, and social determinants alongside genomic information to create comprehensive risk models that far outperform traditional approaches. As one precision medicine specialist noted, "Genes predict possibilities, but environment and behavior determine which possibilities become realities. AI helps us integrate all these dimensions."

AI-Enabled Treatment Selection and Optimization

Beyond risk prediction, AI is transforming how treatments are selected and optimized for individual patients based on their unique characteristics.

In oncology, treatment selection increasingly relies on comprehensive molecular profiling interpreted through sophisticated algorithms. These systems analyze a tumor's genetic, proteomic, and transcriptomic features to identify vulnerabilities that can be targeted with specific therapies. At the Knight Cancer Institute, researchers developed a machine learning system that integrates multiple "-omic" data types to predict which patients will respond to immunotherapy, a breakthrough that could spare non-responders from unnecessary treatment while ensuring responders receive potentially life-saving therapy.

The impact extends well beyond cancer care. In infectious disease management, AI algorithms now predict antimicrobial resistance patterns at the individual patient level, enabling more targeted antibiotic selection. A system implemented at Johns Hopkins Hospital analyzes patient-specific factors, local resistance patterns, and pathogen characteristics to recommend optimal antibiotic regimens, reducing treatment failures by 47% for complex infections.

Mental health treatment has traditionally relied heavily on trial-and-error approaches, but AI is enabling more personalized interventions in this domain as well. Researchers at Stanford developed algorithms that analyze brain imaging, genetic markers, and clinical history to predict antidepressant response, potentially sparing patients the months of sequential medication trials that characterize current practice. As one psychiatrist observed, "This could transform our field from empirical guesswork to precision neuroscience."

The optimization of treatment protocols represents another promising application. In chronic disease management, AI systems now analyze continuous glucose monitoring data to create personalized insulin dosing recommendations for diabetes patients. These algorithms learn from individual response patterns, adapting recommendations to account for factors like exercise, stress, and dietary variations that affect insulin requirements. Similar approaches are emerging for anticoagulation management, seizure prevention, and chronic pain control—conditions where treatment needs vary significantly between individuals and even within the same individual over time.

Digital Biomarkers and Continuous Monitoring

The concept of personalized medicine is evolving beyond discrete treatment decisions to continuous adaptation based on real-time patient data. AI enables this approach by translating complex data streams from wearable devices, smartphones, and home sensors into clinically meaningful insights.

These systems identify "digital biomarkers," patterns in data from everyday devices that correlate with important health states or outcomes. Researchers at UC San Francisco developed algorithms that can detect atrial fibrillation from smartwatch data with 97% accuracy, enabling early intervention for stroke prevention. Similar approaches have shown promise for detecting early signs of Parkinson's disease from smartphone typing patterns, identifying respiratory exacerbations in COPD patients through voice analysis, and predicting mood fluctuations in bipolar disorder from social media language and smartphone usage patterns.

The integration of these continuous monitoring capabilities with treatment adaptation represents a fundamental shift in healthcare delivery. Traditional medicine operates on an episodic model where treatments are adjusted during periodic clinic visits, but AI-enabled systems increasingly support continuous optimization. Diabetes management exemplifies this evolution—closed-loop insulin delivery systems now use AI algorithms to continuously adjust insulin dosing based on real-time glucose readings, essentially creating an artificial pancreas that adapts to changing patient needs.

This continuous personalization approach is expanding to other conditions. In heart failure management, AI systems monitor multiple parameters including weight, blood pressure, activity levels, and even voice characteristics to detect early signs of decompensation and recommend preemptive interventions. A randomized trial of such a system demonstrated a 38% reduction in heart failure hospitalizations through this proactive, personalized approach.

Implementation Challenges and Health Equity Considerations

While AI holds tremendous promise for personalizing medicine, implementation challenges remain significant. Perhaps most concerning is the potential for algorithmic approaches to exacerbate existing healthcare disparities if not carefully designed and deployed.

Many AI systems are trained on datasets that underrepresent certain populations, potentially leading to less accurate or effective recommendations for these groups. A widely publicized study found that a genetic risk score for cardiovascular disease performed significantly worse for patients of African descent than for those of European ancestry, reflecting the predominance of European-derived data in the training dataset. As one researcher noted, "Personalized medicine isn't truly personalized if it works better for some groups than others."

Addressing these disparities requires deliberate efforts to diversify training datasets, validate algorithms across different populations, and continuously monitor performance across demographic groups. The NIH's All of Us Research Program represents one such initiative, aiming to build a diverse genomic and health database that better represents the full spectrum of human diversity.

Cost and access considerations also affect implementation. Advanced genomic testing and AI-powered treatment selection can be prohibitively expensive, potentially limiting these approaches to well-resourced healthcare settings and exacerbating inequities. Innovative payment models and technology democratization efforts are essential to ensure that personalized medicine benefits all patients, not just the privileged few.

Despite these challenges, the trajectory of AI in personalized medicine continues to accelerate. As healthcare shifts from treating disease to maintaining health, AI-enabled personalization will increasingly focus on prevention rather than intervention—identifying individual risk factors and delivering precisely targeted preventive strategies before disease manifests. This evolution promises not just more effective healthcare but fundamentally different healthcare—moving from standardized, reactive, and disease-focused to personalized, proactive, and health-oriented approaches that could transform patient outcomes across the healthcare spectrum.

Ethical Considerations in Clinical AI

As artificial intelligence increasingly influences treatment decisions and clinical interventions, it raises profound ethical questions that extend beyond technical considerations to the very foundations of healthcare. These ethical dimensions must be thoughtfully addressed to ensure that AI enhances rather than undermines the core values of medicine.

Patient Autonomy and Informed Consent

The integration of AI into clinical decision-making raises important questions about patient autonomy: the right of individuals to make informed decisions about their own care. How much should patients know about the role of AI in their treatment decisions? What level of explanation is sufficient for meaningful consent? These questions become increasingly complex as AI systems grow more sophisticated.

Traditional informed consent focuses on providing patients with information about the nature, risks, and benefits of proposed interventions. When AI influences these recommendations, patients may need additional information about the role of algorithmic processes. A survey of patients at Mayo Clinic revealed that 75% wanted to know when AI contributed to their diagnosis or treatment plan, with many expressing desire for information about the system's accuracy and the data upon which it was trained.

Healthcare organizations have responded with varying approaches to AI disclosure and consent. Cleveland Clinic implemented a tiered consent process, where patients receive basic information about AI usage with options for more detailed explanations if desired. Their experience suggests that most patients appreciate transparency about AI use but vary considerably in their desire for technical details.

The level of explanation required for meaningful consent remains an area of active debate. As one bioethicist noted, "Complete technical transparency about AI systems is neither possible nor helpful for most patients. What matters is functional transparency—enough information to understand the implications for their care." This functional transparency might include information about the system's overall accuracy, potential limitations or biases, and the role of human oversight in the process.

The concept of "algorithmic authority" adds another dimension to autonomy considerations. Some patients may defer to AI recommendations due to perceived technological authority, potentially diminishing true autonomy in decision-making. Conversely, others might categorically reject AI-influenced recommendations due to distrust or misunderstanding. Healthcare professionals play a crucial role in contextualizing AI insights within the broader clinical picture and ensuring patients maintain meaningful agency in their care decisions.

Responsibility and Liability

As AI systems increasingly influence clinical decisions, questions of responsibility and accountability become increasingly complex. When an adverse outcome occurs following an AI-influenced intervention, how should responsibility be allocated among technology developers, healthcare organizations, individual clinicians, and the AI system itself?

Legal frameworks for medical liability traditionally focus on human actors and clear causal relationships. The introduction of AI creates new challenges in establishing causation and determining standards of care. Does following an AI recommendation constitute reasonable care, or should clinicians be expected to independently verify algorithmic suggestions? If clinicians override AI recommendations that later prove correct, does this constitute negligence?

Healthcare organizations have developed various approaches to navigate these questions. Partners HealthCare established a governance framework that clearly delineates responsibility for AI-influenced decisions, specifying that clinicians retain ultimate responsibility while recognizing the organization's duty to ensure AI system quality and appropriate implementation. Their policy requires documentation of reasoning when overriding high-confidence AI recommendations, creating an accountability trail while preserving clinical judgment.

Professional liability insurers have begun developing frameworks for coverage in AI-enabled practice environments. These policies increasingly require healthcare organizations to implement robust validation, monitoring, and training programs around AI implementation. As one healthcare attorney observed, "The standard of care is evolving to include not just how clinicians use AI, but how organizations validate, implement, and monitor these systems."

The concept of "meaningful human oversight" has emerged as a guiding principle in this domain. This approach recognizes that while AI may influence decisions, humans must maintain sufficient knowledge and authority to evaluate algorithmic recommendations critically. Implementing meaningful oversight requires careful attention to workflow design, clinician training, and system transparency to ensure humans remain engaged rather than deferring uncritically to algorithmic outputs.

Transparency and Explainability

The "black box" nature of many advanced AI systems poses significant ethical challenges in healthcare contexts. When algorithms influence life-altering treatment decisions, should clinicians and patients be able to understand how these recommendations are generated? What level of explainability is necessary for appropriate trust and use?

Different clinical contexts may require different levels of explanation. For low-risk applications like appointment scheduling optimization, detailed explanations of algorithmic reasoning may be unnecessary. However, for high-stakes decisions like cancer treatment selection or transplant allocation, more comprehensive explainability becomes ethically essential.

Healthcare organizations have implemented various approaches to address the explainability challenge. Duke University Health System developed a tiered transparency framework for clinical AI applications, with required explainability levels proportional to the potential impact on patient outcomes. Their highest transparency tier requires systems to provide case-specific explanations of key factors influencing recommendations, confidence levels, and limitations.

The concept of "appropriate trust" has emerged as a useful framework for considering explainability requirements. As one medical informaticist noted, "The goal isn't blind trust in AI or reflexive skepticism, but appropriate trust—understanding enough about the system's reasoning to know when to rely on it and when to question it." Achieving appropriate trust requires explainability tailored to the needs of different stakeholders—technical explanations for system developers, clinical reasoning explanations for healthcare providers, and outcome-focused explanations for patients.

Efforts to develop more inherently explainable AI models represent another approach to this challenge. While deep learning models often operate as black boxes, alternative approaches like attention mechanisms, case-based reasoning models, and hybrid systems incorporating explicit rule-based components can provide greater transparency while maintaining performance. Mayo Clinic's AI platform for cardiac imaging prioritized explainable architecture over raw performance, enabling cardiologists to understand the anatomical features influencing the system's assessments.

Fairness and Health Equity

Perhaps the most profound ethical concern surrounding clinical AI involves fairness and the potential for these systems to exacerbate existing health disparities. AI algorithms trained on historical healthcare data may inadvertently learn and perpetuate biases embedded in that data, potentially leading to different quality of care for different population groups.

A landmark study published in Science revealed that a widely used algorithm for identifying patients needing enhanced care management exhibited significant racial bias, systematically underestimating the needs of Black patients compared to White patients with similar health status. The algorithm wasn't explicitly considering race but used healthcare costs as a proxy for health needs—and due to historical disparities in healthcare access and utilization, Black patients generated lower costs than White patients with equivalent conditions.

This case illustrates how bias can emerge even without explicit discriminatory intent, highlighting the need for proactive approaches to ensuring algorithmic fairness. Leading healthcare organizations have developed comprehensive frameworks for assessing and mitigating bias in clinical AI. The Algorithmic Bias Prevention Framework implemented at Mount Sinai Health System includes diverse training data requirements, pre-implementation testing across demographic groups, continuous post-implementation monitoring for outcome disparities, and regular bias audits by independent reviewers.

The concept of "algorithmic affirmative action" has emerged as one approach to addressing historical inequities. Rather than simply aiming for algorithms that are blind to protected characteristics, these approaches explicitly consider factors like race, ethnicity, and socioeconomic status to counterbalance historical disadvantages. However, such approaches raise complex legal and ethical questions about appropriate methods for remedying historical injustices.

Beyond the algorithms themselves, implementation contexts significantly influence equity impacts. As one health equity researcher observed, "Even a perfectly unbiased algorithm can increase disparities if deployed in ways that make it differentially accessible across populations." Ensuring equitable implementation requires attention to factors like cost, technological requirements, language accessibility, and integration with diverse care settings.

The Role of Ethics in AI Governance

As healthcare organizations increasingly recognize these ethical dimensions of clinical AI, many have established dedicated AI ethics committees and comprehensive governance frameworks. These structures typically include diverse stakeholders: clinicians, patients, ethicists, legal experts, and technical specialists, all to provide balanced perspectives on complex issues.

The Mayo Clinic's AI Ethics Framework exemplifies this approach, establishing a dedicated committee responsible for reviewing proposed AI applications before implementation and monitoring deployed systems for ethical concerns. Their framework specifies principles including transparency, justice, non-maleficence, responsibility, and privacy, with specific standards for each principle based on the application's potential impact and risk level.

Professional societies have also developed ethical guidelines for AI in healthcare. The American Medical Association's policy on augmented intelligence emphasizes that AI should enhance human capabilities rather than replace them, should be designed to accommodate the needs of all stakeholders, and should be deployed in ways that advance health equity. Similarly, the American College of Radiology's ethics framework for AI specifies requirements for transparency, algorithm validation, and ongoing monitoring for unintended consequences.

Regulatory approaches to clinical AI ethics continue to evolve. The FDA's proposed regulatory framework for AI/ML-based Software as a Medical Device includes not only technical performance requirements but also considerations of algorithmic bias, transparency, and real-world performance monitoring. The European Union's proposed AI Act takes a risk-based approach, imposing stricter requirements for "high-risk" applications including many healthcare uses.

As we look toward the future of AI in clinical practice, these ethical frameworks will require continuous evolution to address emerging challenges. The rapid advancement of AI capabilities necessitates ongoing dialogue among technology developers, healthcare providers, patients, ethicists, and policymakers to ensure that these powerful tools enhance rather than undermine the fundamental values of healthcare—beneficence, non-maleficence, autonomy, and justice.

This ethical foundation becomes particularly important as we consider the practical challenges of implementing AI in clinical settings—the focus of our next section. Successful implementation requires not just technical excellence but careful attention to the human, organizational, and systemic dimensions that ultimately determine whether AI truly improves patient care.

Challenges in Implementing AI in Clinical Settings

The journey from promising AI prototype to effective clinical implementation involves navigating a complex landscape of technical, organizational, human, and systemic challenges. Even the most sophisticated algorithms provide little value until successfully integrated into healthcare delivery systems and clinical workflows.

Integration with Clinical Workflows and Information Systems

Perhaps the most fundamental implementation challenge involves integrating AI systems into existing clinical workflows without disrupting patient care or overburdening healthcare professionals. AI tools that add steps to clinical processes or require separate login systems often face significant adoption barriers regardless of their technical capabilities.

Successful implementations carefully map existing workflow patterns before designing AI integration points. At Brigham and Women's Hospital, an AI system for identifying patients at risk for clinical deterioration was initially deployed as a standalone dashboard but saw minimal usage. After redesigning the system to deliver targeted alerts within the existing EHR workflow, utilization increased eightfold and was associated with a 20% reduction in unexpected ICU transfers.

Beyond workflow considerations, interoperability with existing information systems represents another significant challenge. Healthcare organizations typically operate complex ecosystems of clinical and administrative systems, many using proprietary data formats or legacy technologies. AI systems must interface seamlessly with these existing infrastructures to access necessary data and deliver insights at appropriate decision points.

The Cleveland Clinic addressed this challenge by implementing an enterprise data platform that standardizes information from diverse sources before making it available to AI applications. This approach creates a consistent data foundation while insulating individual AI applications from the complexity of underlying systems. As their Chief Information Officer noted, "We can't rebuild our entire technical infrastructure for each AI use case, so we created an abstraction layer that makes AI integration more plug-and-play."

The temporal dimension of clinical workflows adds another layer of complexity. Unlike many industries where AI can operate on flexible timelines, healthcare often requires real-time insights aligned with specific clinical activities. Algorithms must deliver recommendations within compressed timeframes—during a brief patient encounter or before a scheduled procedure—to influence care decisions effectively.

Data Quality, Standardization, and Governance

AI systems are fundamentally dependent on data quality, a particular challenge in healthcare where information is often fragmented, inconsistently structured, and variable in completeness. Implementation efforts frequently reveal data quality issues that weren't apparent during system development.

Organizations with successful AI implementations typically begin with comprehensive data quality assessments across the specific data elements required for their intended applications. Partners HealthCare developed a "data readiness index" that evaluates completeness, consistency, and accuracy of key data elements before AI implementation. This approach helps identify and remediate data issues proactively rather than discovering them through algorithm failures.

Beyond quality issues, lack of data standardization poses significant challenges. Healthcare data elements are often recorded differently across—and even within—organizations. Something as fundamental as blood pressure might be documented in multiple formats, measurement units, or recording frequencies. Without standardization, algorithms trained in one context may perform poorly when deployed in another.

Mayo Clinic addressed this challenge by implementing enterprise-wide data standardization initiatives before scaling AI applications. Their approach included not just technical standardization but also organizational policies and training to ensure consistent data capture practices. As their Chief Data Officer explained, "AI implementation isn't just about deploying algorithms—it's about creating the data ecosystem those algorithms need to function reliably."

Governance structures for data access and algorithm validation represent another implementation consideration. Healthcare organizations must balance making data accessible for AI development and validation while maintaining appropriate privacy protections and security controls. Leading organizations have established dedicated AI governance committees that include privacy officers, security specialists, and compliance experts alongside clinical and technical leaders.

Change Management and Healthcare Professional Adoption

Even technically perfect AI systems deliver little value without acceptance and appropriate use by healthcare professionals. Resistance to AI implementation often stems from concerns about job displacement, liability, workflow disruption, or skepticism about algorithmic recommendations.

Successful implementations address these concerns through comprehensive change management strategies that emphasize AI as an augmentation rather than replacement of clinical expertise. University of Pennsylvania Health System developed a "clinical AI partnership model" that involves clinicians throughout the implementation process—from use case selection through design, validation, and deployment. This approach not only produces more clinically relevant solutions but also builds trust and ownership among the professionals who will ultimately use the technology.

Education and training represent another crucial aspect of change management. Healthcare professionals need understanding not just of user interfaces but also of AI capabilities, limitations, and appropriate use cases. Mount Sinai Health System implemented a tiered AI literacy curriculum with basic awareness training for all clinicians and more comprehensive education for those working directly with AI applications. Their program addresses both technical aspects and ethical considerations, helping clinicians develop appropriate trust in algorithmic recommendations.

Generational differences often influence AI adoption, with some studies indicating that clinicians trained in the pre-digital era may be more hesitant to incorporate AI into their practice. Organizations have addressed this challenge through peer mentorship programs where digitally native clinicians support colleagues in developing comfort with AI-enabled approaches. As one chief medical information officer observed, "The technology adoption curve in healthcare is often less about age and more about perceived value and usability. When clinicians see tangible benefits and intuitive interfaces, resistance diminishes regardless of generation."

Regulatory Compliance and Legal Considerations

Healthcare operates within a complex regulatory environment that presents unique challenges for AI implementation. Regulatory frameworks for AI-based medical technologies continue to evolve, creating uncertainty about approval pathways, validation requirements, and compliance standards.

The FDA has established various pathways for AI-based medical technologies, including 510(k) clearance, de novo classification, and premarket approval, depending on the level of risk and novelty. However, the iterative, learning nature of many AI systems creates regulatory challenges when algorithms evolve after initial approval. The FDA's proposed regulatory framework for AI/ML-based Software as a Medical Device addresses this through a "predetermined change control plan" approach, but implementation details continue to develop.

Beyond regulatory approval, AI implementation must comply with various healthcare regulations including HIPAA privacy rules, information blocking provisions of the 21st Century Cures Act, and anti-kickback statutes that may apply to vendor relationships. Organizations with successful implementations typically establish multidisciplinary compliance teams that address these requirements throughout the AI lifecycle, from data acquisition through deployment and monitoring.

Liability considerations add another layer of complexity. When adverse events occur in cases involving AI recommendations, determining responsibility among technology vendors, healthcare organizations, and individual clinicians remains legally ambiguous. Leading organizations are developing explicit policies regarding clinician responsibility when using AI systems, documentation requirements for algorithm-influenced decisions, and processes for reviewing cases where clinicians override algorithmic recommendations.

Scaling and Sustaining AI Implementation

Many healthcare organizations have successfully implemented individual AI applications but struggle to scale these successes across multiple use cases or sustain their impact over time. The transition from promising pilots to enterprise-wide implementation represents a significant challenge requiring systematic approaches and organizational commitment.

Organizations that successfully scale AI implementations typically establish dedicated infrastructure for AI development, validation, and deployment. Intermountain Healthcare created an "AI Center of Excellence" that provides standardized processes, technical infrastructure, and expertise to support AI initiatives across the organization. This approach reduces duplication of effort, ensures consistent governance practices, and facilitates knowledge sharing across projects.

Financial sustainability represents another scaling challenge. Many AI implementations begin with grant funding or innovation budgets but struggle to transition to sustainable business models. Organizations with enduring implementations develop clear value frameworks that quantify benefits—whether through improved outcomes, reduced costs, or enhanced capacity—and establish appropriate funding mechanisms for ongoing operation and enhancement.

Integration with quality improvement and clinical transformation initiatives enhances sustainability. Rather than positioning AI as a standalone technology initiative, successful organizations embed it within broader clinical transformation efforts. As one healthcare executive noted, "AI isn't a solution by itself; it's an enabler of better clinical processes and decisions. When we integrate it with our broader quality and transformation agenda, it becomes sustainable."

The human infrastructure for AI sustainability deserves equal attention to technical considerations. As healthcare AI evolves from specialized projects to mainstream capabilities, organizations must develop appropriate staffing models, career pathways, and ongoing education programs. Leading systems are creating hybrid roles that bridge clinical, technical, and operational domains; professionals who understand both the algorithms and the clinical contexts in which they operate.

These implementation challenges are not merely obstacles to overcome but essential considerations that shape how AI technologies translate from promising concepts into meaningful clinical impact. As we look toward future trends in this domain, understanding these practical realities helps distinguish between theoretical possibilities and innovations likely to transform actual clinical practice.

Future Trends in AI for Clinical Practice

As we look toward the horizon of healthcare AI, several emerging trends promise to reshape how these technologies augment clinical practice. These developments extend beyond incremental improvements to represent potential paradigm shifts in how AI interfaces with healthcare professionals, patients, and healthcare systems.

From Black Boxes to Glass Boxes: The Evolution of Explainable AI

The "black box" nature of many current AI systems represents a significant limitation for clinical applications where understanding algorithmic reasoning is crucial for appropriate trust and use. The next generation of clinical AI systems will increasingly incorporate "explainable AI" (XAI) approaches that provide transparent insights into their decision-making processes.

These techniques range from attention mechanisms that highlight the most influential features in a prediction to counterfactual explanations that illustrate how different inputs would change the system's output. Rather than merely providing confidence scores, advanced XAI systems will articulate their reasoning in clinically meaningful terms that align with healthcare professionals' conceptual frameworks.

Duke University researchers are developing neural network architectures that mirror clinical reasoning pathways, allowing their systems to explain diagnostic and treatment recommendations using familiar medical concepts rather than abstract statistical relationships. Their early implementations in cardiology demonstrate the ability to trace algorithmic recommendations to specific ECG patterns and clinical risk factors in ways that cardiologists find intuitive and trustworthy.

Beyond technical approaches, interface design plays a crucial role in explainability. Future systems will present algorithmic insights through visual and interactive displays that allow clinicians to explore the basis for recommendations rather than simply receiving them as pronouncements. These interfaces will support collaborative human-AI decision-making by enabling clinicians to test "what if" scenarios and understand the reasoning behind AI suggestions.

The evolution toward explainable AI represents not just a technical advancement but a fundamental shift in the relationship between clinicians and algorithms—moving from opaque outputs that require leap-of-faith acceptance to transparent reasoning that clinicians can evaluate alongside their own clinical judgment.

Multimodal AI: Integrating Diverse Data Types

Current healthcare AI systems typically operate within data silos, analyzing single modalities like images, text, or structured data independently. The next evolution involves multimodal systems that simultaneously analyze diverse data types to generate more comprehensive insights.

These systems will integrate information from electronic health records, medical images, genomic data, continuous monitoring devices, and even ambient clinical intelligence to create holistic patient representations. Rather than requiring clinicians to mentally synthesize insights from multiple systems, these integrated platforms will present unified recommendations that consider all relevant information simultaneously.

Researchers at Stanford Medicine are developing multimodal systems that combine radiological images, pathology slides, genomic sequencing, and clinical notes to generate comprehensive cancer assessments. Their early results demonstrate that this integrated approach outperforms single-modality analysis for both diagnostic accuracy and treatment response prediction, particularly for complex or atypical presentations.

Beyond clinical data, future systems will increasingly incorporate contextual information about social determinants of health, environmental factors, and community-level data. This broader view enables more holistic understanding of health influences and more effective interventions that address root causes rather than just symptoms.

The impact of multimodal integration extends beyond diagnosis and treatment selection to longitudinal health management. These systems will track patterns across diverse data streams over time, identifying subtle correlations between different health parameters that might escape human observation. This capability proves particularly valuable for complex chronic conditions like autoimmune disorders or neurological diseases where multiple body systems interact in complex ways.

Federated Learning and Privacy-Preserving AI

The tension between data access needs for AI development and privacy protection requirements has constrained healthcare AI advancement. Federated learning and other privacy-preserving approaches promise to resolve this tension by enabling algorithm training across distributed datasets without centralizing sensitive patient information.

In federated learning approaches, algorithms are sent to where data resides rather than transferring data to centralized repositories. The models learn locally at each participating institution, and only model parameters—not patient data—are shared centrally. This approach maintains data privacy while allowing algorithms to learn from diverse patient populations across organizations.

The FDA-sponsored Project Dandelion demonstrates this approach through a federated learning network connecting 10 healthcare systems across different geographic regions. Their breast cancer detection algorithm achieved performance comparable to centrally trained models while maintaining complete data locality, establishing a template for privacy-preserving AI development that complies with strict healthcare privacy requirements.

Beyond federated learning, other privacy-enhancing technologies are emerging to support healthcare AI development. Differential privacy techniques add carefully calibrated noise to datasets to prevent identification of individual patients while maintaining overall statistical properties. Homomorphic encryption allows computation on encrypted data without decryption, potentially enabling algorithm training without exposing sensitive information even to analysts.

These approaches will accelerate healthcare AI development by expanding access to diverse training data while maintaining stringent privacy protections. They also address data sovereignty concerns in international contexts where cross-border data transfer faces legal restrictions, potentially enabling global collaboration on AI development while respecting local privacy regulations.

Autonomous and Semi-Autonomous AI Systems

Current clinical AI systems predominantly provide recommendations for human consideration, but certain applications are evolving toward greater autonomy for suitable clinical tasks. These range from semi-autonomous systems that operate under human supervision to fully autonomous applications for specific constrained functions.

The FDA has already approved several autonomous AI systems, including IDx-DR for diabetic retinopathy screening and Caption Health's ultrasound guidance software. These systems operate independently for specific tasks while maintaining clear boundaries around their autonomous functions. This trend will likely accelerate for well-defined tasks with clear decision boundaries and limited risk profiles.

Semi-autonomous systems represent another promising direction, particularly for time-sensitive situations where immediate action provides clear benefit. AI-enabled continuous monitoring systems are evolving from passive alerting to active intervention for certain parameters. For example, closed-loop insulin delivery systems now automatically adjust insulin doses based on continuous glucose readings, essentially functioning as an artificial pancreas with minimal human intervention.

The concept of "adjustable autonomy" will likely guide future development, with systems that dynamically shift between recommendation and autonomous operation based on situation characteristics and confidence levels. In high-confidence, low-risk scenarios, systems might act autonomously while reverting to recommendation mode when encountering unusual situations or low-confidence predictions.

Healthcare organizations implementing such systems are developing comprehensive governance frameworks that clearly delineate autonomous functions, oversight requirements, and human involvement thresholds. Mayo Clinic's Autonomous System Review Board evaluates proposed autonomous applications using a risk-based framework that considers factors including clinical impact, reversibility, transparency, and fail-safe mechanisms.

AI-Enabled Precision Health and Prevention

Perhaps the most transformative potential of clinical AI lies in shifting healthcare focus from treatment to prevention through increasingly sophisticated prediction and personalization capabilities. Future systems will integrate diverse data sources to identify individual health risks and deliver precisely targeted preventive interventions before disease manifests.

These systems will analyze patterns across traditional clinical data, genomic information, wearable device readings, environmental exposures, and social determinants to generate comprehensive health risk profiles at both individual and population levels. Rather than waiting for disease symptoms, healthcare systems will increasingly deploy proactive interventions based on these predictive insights.

Kaiser Permanente's predictive health initiative exemplifies this approach through AI systems that identify members at elevated risk for conditions including heart disease, diabetes, and certain cancers. Their platform doesn't just flag risk but generates personalized prevention plans tailored to individual characteristics, preferences, and social circumstances. Early results demonstrate significant improvements in health outcomes through these precision prevention approaches.

The granularity of these predictions will continue to increase, moving beyond general disease risk to specific molecular pathways and mechanisms. Researchers at Geisinger are developing systems that predict not just whether someone might develop diabetes, but which specific pathophysiological processes are most likely involved, enabling precisely targeted preventive interventions that address individual disease pathways rather than using one-size-fits-all approaches.

This evolution toward precision prevention represents a fundamental paradigm shift in healthcare delivery—from reactive treatment of established disease to proactive maintenance of health through continuous monitoring, precise risk prediction, and personalized preventive interventions. While significant implementation challenges remain, this direction promises both better health outcomes and more sustainable healthcare economics by reducing the burden of chronic disease.

The Collaborative Future of AI in Healthcare

As artificial intelligence continues its integration into clinical practice, we stand at an inflection point that will define the future relationship between technology and healthcare delivery. The trajectory of this evolution depends not just on technological capabilities but on how thoughtfully we navigate the human, ethical, and systemic dimensions of implementation.

The most promising future for clinical AI lies not in autonomous systems that replace human judgment but in collaborative partnerships that combine the complementary strengths of artificial and human intelligence. AI excels at processing vast datasets, recognizing subtle patterns, and maintaining vigilance without fatigue. Human clinicians contribute contextual understanding, ethical judgment, empathy, and the ability to navigate ambiguity in ways algorithms cannot replicate.

This collaborative model requires designing systems explicitly for human-AI partnership rather than focusing solely on algorithmic performance.

Interfaces must support joint cognitive work, explanations must align with clinical thinking patterns, and workflows must integrate algorithmic and human insights seamlessly. As one clinician researcher observed, "The goal isn't creating the smartest possible AI, but creating the most effective possible team of human and artificial intelligence."

The ethical foundation for this partnership requires continued attention to the values and principles that guide healthcare. AI systems must be designed and implemented in ways that enhance rather than undermine patient autonomy, that promote rather than diminish health equity, and that augment rather than replace the human connection at the heart of healing relationships. These considerations cannot be afterthoughts but must be integrated into development and implementation from the earliest stages.

Implementation challenges will continue to shape the evolution of clinical AI, with successful adoption depending as much on organizational, cultural, and workforce factors as on technological capability. Organizations that approach AI as a sociotechnical intervention rather than merely a technical one—addressing the human, process, and system dimensions alongside the algorithms themselves—will achieve the greatest clinical impact.

Looking ahead, we can envision a healthcare ecosystem where AI serves as a ubiquitous yet often invisible force multiplier for human capabilities—continuously monitoring for subtle signs of deterioration, synthesizing relevant evidence for clinical decisions, personalizing interventions based on individual characteristics, and extending clinical expertise beyond traditional boundaries of time and place. This vision represents not a replacement of human healthcare but its augmentation and extension to deliver more precise, proactive, and personalized care.

The path toward this future requires continued collaboration across disciplines and stakeholders—clinicians, data scientists, patients, ethicists, administrators, and policymakers—each bringing essential perspectives to this complex landscape. By maintaining focus on the fundamental purpose of healthcare technology—improving human health and wellbeing—we can harness the tremendous potential of artificial intelligence while ensuring it remains in service to the humans at the center of healthcare.

As we conclude our exploration of AI in treatment and implementation, we recognize that these technologies represent powerful tools rather than solutions in themselves. Their true value emerges not from their technical sophistication but from how effectively they enhance the capacity of healthcare professionals and systems to fulfill their fundamental mission: providing compassionate, effective care to those in need.

While the treatment applications we've discussed demonstrate AI's power to enhance clinical decision-making, they represent just the beginning of a broader transformation. As we'll explore in the next chapter, AI's true potential lies in moving beyond standardized treatment protocols toward truly personalized care—approaches tailored to each patient's unique biological, psychological, and social characteristics. This evolution from enhancing traditional treatment models to enabling precision medicine represents one of healthcare's most promising frontiers, where data and AI combine to recognize and respond to human individuality in ways previously impossible.

Chapter 8:

AI for Personalized Patient Care

Healthcare stands at the threshold of a new era where artificial intelligence promises to transform the patient experience from standardized protocols to truly personalized care. This shift represents the culmination of medicine's long evolution toward precision—from population-based approaches to individualized treatment strategies that recognize each patient's unique biological, environmental, and lifestyle factors.

At its core, AI-powered personalized care aims to deliver the right intervention, to the right patient, at the right time. Unlike traditional approaches that often follow rigid treatment pathways based on broad population averages, AI enables healthcare providers to analyze vast amounts of individual patient data—genomic information, medical history, real-time vitals, environmental factors, and lifestyle patterns—to develop truly customized care plans.

This chapter explores how AI is reshaping the patient journey across three critical domains: personalized medicine, predictive analytics, and continuous monitoring. We examine how these technologies work in concert to create a more proactive, precise, and patient-centered healthcare experience. From preventing disease before symptoms appear to tailoring treatments for optimal efficacy, AI is enabling a fundamental reimagining of what personalized care can achieve.

While the technical capabilities of AI in healthcare are remarkable, our focus remains on the ultimate goal: improving outcomes that matter to patients. The technologies we discuss are not ends in themselves but powerful tools in service of enhancing patient wellness, extending healthy lifespans, reducing suffering, and improving quality of life. As we explore these applications, we'll emphasize both their transformative potential and the practical challenges that must be addressed to realize their full benefits.

AI in Personalized Medicine and Treatment Plans

The concept of "one-size-fits-all" medicine is rapidly becoming obsolete as AI unlocks unprecedented capabilities to tailor treatments to individual patients. Personalized medicine represents a fundamental shift from reactive to proactive healthcare, where interventions are customized based on a patient's unique characteristics rather than population averages.

Genomics and Precision Therapeutics

AI's ability to analyze complex genomic data has revolutionized how we approach treatment selection and dosing. By identifying relationships between genetic variants and treatment responses, AI helps clinicians select therapies with the highest likelihood of success for each patient.

Consider the transformation in oncology, where AI systems now routinely analyze tumor genomic profiles to identify targeted therapies. IBM Watson for Genomics exemplifies this approach, analyzing genetic test results against the latest medical literature to identify potential treatments that human experts might overlook. In a University of North Carolina study, the system identified actionable genetic mutations in 32% of cancer patients that had been missed in conventional analysis.

Beyond oncology, pharmacogenomic applications of AI are helping predict how patients will metabolize medications based on their genetic profiles. These algorithms can identify which patients might experience adverse reactions or require non-standard dosing, potentially preventing harmful side effects before they occur.

Multimodal Data Integration for Treatment Optimization

The true power of AI in personalized medicine lies in its ability to integrate diverse data types—genomic, clinical, imaging, lifestyle, and environmental—to create comprehensive patient profiles. This holistic view enables treatment plans that address multiple factors simultaneously.

"The challenge in personalized medicine isn't just having more data—it's making sense of it," explains Dr. Elena Martínez, Director of Precision Medicine at Stanford University Medical Center. "AI can identify patterns across data types that humans simply cannot perceive."

Modern AI systems can dynamically adjust treatment regimens based on real-time patient responses and changing conditions. For example, in diabetes management, AI algorithms analyze continuous glucose monitoring data alongside activity, diet, and medication information to recommend precise insulin dosing adjustments throughout the day, significantly improving glycemic control compared to standard approaches.

Challenges and Ethical Considerations

While powerful, AI-driven personalized medicine raises important challenges. Ensuring data privacy becomes increasingly complex as we collect more intimate patient information. Additionally, addressing algorithmic bias is critical—if training data lacks diversity, AI systems may deliver less effective recommendations for underrepresented populations.

Perhaps most importantly, we must navigate the balance between AI recommendations and human clinical judgment. Rather than replacing physician expertise, effective AI systems enhance it by processing information at scales beyond human capability while allowing clinicians to incorporate contextual factors and patient preferences into final decisions.

Predictive Analytics for Patient Outcomes

While personalized medicine focuses on optimizing treatments for individual patients, predictive analytics harnesses AI to anticipate health events before they occur. This proactive approach represents a fundamental shift from reactive care—waiting for symptoms to appear— to preventive interventions triggered by early risk signals.

Early Warning Systems: From Hospitals to Homes

Predictive models have transformed care in hospital settings, where algorithms analyze real-time patient data to detect subtle signs of deterioration hours or days before clinical symptoms appear. The impact of these systems is particularly evident in conditions where early intervention dramatically improves outcomes.

Sepsis, a life-threatening response to infection that can rapidly lead to organ failure and death, illustrates the power of predictive analytics. Early warning systems like the Epic Sepsis Model analyze patterns across vital signs, laboratory values, and medication data to identify at-risk patients up to 24 hours before clinical manifestation. A study at the University of Pennsylvania Health System found this approach identified 33% of sepsis cases before clinical recognition, significantly reducing mortality rates.

Beyond hospital walls, predictive analytics is extending into everyday life through consumer wearables and remote monitoring devices. AI algorithms can now analyze data from smartwatches and other sensors to detect subtle abnormalities in heart rhythm, sleep patterns, or activity levels that may signal developing health problems. The Apple Heart Study demonstrated this potential by identifying atrial fibrillation in users based on smartwatch data, enabling early intervention for a condition that often remains undetected until a stroke occurs.

Risk Stratification for Targeted Interventions

Not all patients face equal risks, and healthcare resources achieve maximum impact when directed toward those most likely to benefit. AI excels at stratifying patient populations based on risk profiles, enabling more efficient allocation of preventive resources.

For chronic disease management, machine learning models can analyze electronic health records, genetic data, and lifestyle factors to identify which patients are at highest risk of complications. For example, in diabetes care, AI systems can predict which patients are most likely to develop kidney disease, retinopathy, or neuropathy, allowing for intensified preventive measures specifically for these individuals.

Hospital readmissions—often preventable with appropriate post-discharge support—provide another compelling application of risk stratification. Deep learning models developed by Google Health have demonstrated significantly higher accuracy than traditional methods in predicting 30-day unplanned readmissions using only data available at discharge. These models help hospitals target enhanced follow-up care and resources to patients who need them most, improving outcomes while optimizing resource utilization.

From Population to Precision Prediction

Traditional predictive models relied on relatively few variables and population-level statistics. Modern AI approaches are moving toward increasingly personalized predictions based on comprehensive individual data profiles.

"The future of predictive analytics isn't just about identifying high-risk groups—it's about understanding the specific risk trajectory for each individual patient," explains Dr. James Chen, Director of Clinical AI Research at Mayo Clinic. "This allows us to move from general preventive measures to precision interventions tailored to each person's unique risk factors."

This evolution toward precision prediction is particularly evident in cardiovascular disease prevention. Rather than relying solely on traditional risk factors like blood pressure and cholesterol, AI models now incorporate hundreds of variables—including subtle ECG patterns, cardiac imaging features, genomic markers, and even social determinants of health—to generate highly individualized risk profiles. These models not only predict overall cardiovascular risk but can identify which specific pathways (inflammation, lipid metabolism, hypertension) drive risk for each patient, enabling precisely targeted preventive strategies.

The integration of predictive analytics with personalized medicine creates a powerful synergy—predictive models identify who needs intervention and when, while personalized medicine principles determine exactly which intervention will be most effective for each individual. Together, they form the foundation of a truly proactive healthcare system focused on maintaining wellness rather than merely treating illness.

AI-Driven Patient Monitoring and Early Intervention

While predictive analytics helps identify who might develop health problems, continuous monitoring systems powered by AI enable real-time detection of subtle changes in patient condition—creating opportunities for intervention at the earliest possible moment. This represents the next logical step in our progression from reactive to proactive care.

The Continuous Monitoring Revolution

Healthcare monitoring has traditionally been episodic—vitals checked during intermittent hospital rounds or at occasional office visits. This approach inevitably misses critical changes that occur between measurements. AI-enabled continuous monitoring fundamentally transforms this paradigm by providing uninterrupted visibility into patient status.

Wearable devices and IoT sensors now capture a wealth of physiological data—heart rate, respiratory patterns, activity levels, sleep quality, and more—which AI algorithms analyze continuously to establish personalized baselines and detect meaningful deviations. This shift from periodic snapshots to continuous assessment enables detection of subtle changes that would be invisible in traditional monitoring approaches.

"What makes AI monitoring transformative isn't just the constant data collection—it's the ability to establish what's normal for each individual patient and identify meaningful deviations from that personal baseline," explains Dr. Sarah Johnson, Medical Director of Remote Patient Monitoring at Cleveland Clinic. "This personalization dramatically reduces false alarms while catching true deterioration earlier."

The impact of continuous monitoring is particularly evident in chronic condition management. For heart failure patients, for example, AI systems can analyze weight fluctuations, heart rate patterns, and activity levels to detect fluid retention days before patients would notice symptoms, enabling medication adjustments that prevent hospitalizations. A study by the University of California San Francisco found that this approach reduced heart failure hospitalizations by 38% compared to standard care.

From Detection to Intervention: Closing the Loop

The true power of AI-driven monitoring emerges when detection systems connect seamlessly with intervention protocols. These "closed-loop" systems not only identify problems but trigger appropriate responses—whether automated adjustments, clinician alerts, or patient notifications.

Diabetes management exemplifies this approach. Advanced continuous glucose monitoring systems now pair with AI algorithms that predict glucose trends hours in advance. These systems can automatically adjust insulin delivery through connected pumps or provide timely nutritional recommendations to prevent hypoglycemic or hyperglycemic episodes before they occur. The automation of this detection-intervention cycle allows patients to spend significantly more time in optimal glucose ranges with less cognitive burden.

Mental health represents another frontier for closed-loop monitoring and intervention. AI systems can now analyze patterns in digital behavior, voice characteristics, sleep data, and physical activity to detect subtle signs of depression or anxiety. When concerning patterns emerge, these systems can initiate appropriate interventions—from suggesting stress management exercises to facilitating connection with mental health professionals—before severe episodes develop.

Balancing Vigilance with Well-being

While the potential benefits of continuous monitoring are substantial, implementing these systems requires careful attention to several challenges. Privacy concerns are paramount when collecting intimate health data outside clinical settings. Additionally, the psychological impact of constant monitoring requires consideration—patients may experience anxiety from heightened awareness of their health metrics.

"The goal isn't to create a state of hypervigilance where patients constantly worry about their health data," notes Dr. Michael Chen, Director of Digital Health Ethics at Johns Hopkins University. "It's to provide reassurance through invisible safety nets that only become visible when truly needed."

Finding this balance requires thoughtful design of monitoring systems that provide protection without promoting anxiety. The most successful implementations establish clear thresholds for alerts, provide context for measurements, and give patients control over how and when they engage with their health data.

Enhancing Patient Engagement and Adherence through AI

Even the most precisely personalized treatments and sophisticated monitoring systems ultimately depend on patient participation. Treatment plans only improve outcomes when patients follow them, yet non-adherence rates often exceed 50% for chronic conditions. AI offers innovative approaches to bridge this critical gap between medical recommendations and patient action.

From Information to Understanding: Personalized Education

Traditional patient education relies on standardized materials that rarely account for individual learning styles, health literacy levels, or specific concerns. AI transforms this approach by tailoring educational content to each patient's unique needs and preferences.

Natural language processing and machine learning algorithms now analyze patient questions and responses to assess comprehension levels and information needs. Based on this analysis, AI systems can adjust the complexity of explanations, provide additional context for unfamiliar concepts, and emphasize aspects of education most relevant to the individual's condition and concerns.

Wellframe, an AI-powered patient education platform, demonstrates the impact of this approach. By continuously adapting content based on patient engagement and comprehension, the system achieved significant improvements in health literacy and self-management skills compared to standard educational approaches, particularly among populations traditionally underserved by healthcare systems.

Visual learning tools powered by AI further enhance understanding by creating personalized explanatory animations and interactive models.

These systems can show patients how their specific condition affects their body, how proposed treatments work, and how lifestyle changes influence their health trajectory—making abstract medical concepts concrete and personally relevant.

Motivation Through Personalization

Beyond understanding, effective engagement requires motivation—patients must believe that treatment plans are worth following and that their actions make a meaningful difference. AI enhances motivation by connecting treatments to personally meaningful outcomes and providing evidence of progress.

Machine learning algorithms analyze individual patient data to identify which factors most strongly influence adherence for each person. For some, social connection drives behavior change; for others, quantifiable progress metrics or alignment with personal values proves more motivating. By identifying these individual motivational patterns, AI systems can customize adherence strategies accordingly.

For medication adherence specifically, AI applications like AiCure have demonstrated remarkable results. Using smartphone cameras with facial recognition to confirm proper medication taking, these systems increased adherence rates by over 25% in clinical trials. The technology works by combining verification with personalized reminders and behavioral reinforcement techniques tailored to each patient's adherence patterns.

Human Connection in the Digital Age

While AI technologies enable new forms of engagement, the most successful implementations recognize that technology works best as a complement to human connection rather than a replacement for it.

"The future of patient engagement isn't AI or human—it's AI and human," emphasizes Dr. Lisa Patel, Chief of Patient Experience at Massachusetts General Hospital. "AI handles the continuous monitoring and personalization at scale, while human providers offer the empathy, judgment, and connection that technology cannot."

This integrated approach is exemplified by hybrid care models where AI systems continuously monitor patient status and adherence patterns, but escalate to human providers when emotional support, complex decision-making, or relationship-building is needed. These models leverage each component's strengths—AI's tireless monitoring and pattern recognition combined with humans' emotional intelligence and contextual judgment.

The Journey Toward Truly Patient-Centered Care

Throughout this chapter, we've traced the evolution of personalized care enabled by artificial intelligence—from tailoring treatments based on individual biology to predicting health risks before symptoms appear, continuously monitoring patient status for early intervention, and enhancing engagement through personalized approaches.

These innovations represent interconnected facets of a broader transformation in healthcare delivery. Together, they enable a care model that is:

- **Proactive** rather than reactive, identifying and addressing risks before they manifest as disease

- **Precise** rather than standardized, tailoring interventions to each patient's unique characteristics

- **Continuous** rather than episodic, maintaining connection with patients throughout their health journey

- **Collaborative** rather than prescriptive, engaging patients as active participants in their care

While significant technical and implementation challenges remain, the trajectory is clear: AI is enabling a fundamental shift toward care that truly centers around the needs, characteristics, and preferences of each individual patient.

Looking Ahead: From Individual to System

As we've seen, AI offers powerful tools to personalize and enhance care for individual patients. However, healthcare doesn't exist in isolation—it operates within complex systems involving multiple providers, populations, and policy considerations.

In the next chapter, we'll explore how AI extends beyond individual care to transform healthcare systems more broadly. We'll examine applications in population health management, error reduction, clinical decision support, and care coordination. We'll also address the critical ethical considerations and implementation challenges that must be navigated as AI becomes increasingly embedded in healthcare delivery.

The journey from AI-enhanced individual care to AI-transformed healthcare systems represents the next frontier in leveraging these technologies to improve health outcomes for all patients, regardless of their circumstances or where they receive care.

Chapter 9:
AI for Healthcare Systems and Ethical Considerations

From Individual Care to System Transformation

In the previous chapter, we explored how AI is revolutionizing personalized patient care through tailored treatments, predictive analytics, continuous monitoring, and enhanced engagement. While these applications significantly improve outcomes for individual patients, healthcare ultimately functions as an interconnected ecosystem of providers, populations, and processes. The true potential of AI emerges when we extend its capabilities beyond individual encounters to transform entire healthcare systems.

Healthcare systems face unprecedented challenges—rising costs, provider burnout, persistent disparities, and increasing complexity of care. Traditional approaches to system improvement, often focused on incremental changes to existing processes, have proven insufficient to address these fundamental issues. AI offers a different paradigm—one that can identify patterns across vast populations, streamline complex workflows, reduce system-level inefficiencies, and promote more equitable care delivery.

This chapter examines AI applications that operate at the system level rather than the individual level. We explore how AI transforms population health management by identifying vulnerable groups and optimizing resource allocation. We investigate its role in reducing systematic medical errors through enhanced safety protocols and decision support. We analyze how AI improves coordination among providers and across care settings. Finally, we address the critical ethical considerations and implementation challenges that arise when deploying AI across healthcare systems.

Throughout this exploration, we maintain focus on the ultimate goal: creating healthcare systems that deliver better outcomes for all patients while operating more efficiently and equitably. The promise of AI at the system level is not merely to do the same things faster, but to fundamentally reimagine how healthcare is organized, delivered, and experienced.

AI in Population Health Management

While personalized medicine focuses on optimizing care for individuals, population health management takes a broader view—identifying patterns across communities, addressing social determinants of health, and allocating resources to maximize collective well-being. AI dramatically enhances these capabilities by uncovering complex relationships within population data and enabling more precise interventions at scale.

Identifying Vulnerable Populations Through Advanced Analytics

Traditional population health approaches often rely on limited datasets and simple risk factors to identify vulnerable groups. AI transforms this process by integrating diverse data sources—clinical records, social determinants, environmental factors, and community-level information—to create multidimensional risk profiles that capture the complex reality of health disparities.

"The power of AI in population health isn't just identifying who's at risk, but understanding why they're at risk," explains Dr. Robert Johnson, Director of Health Equity Research at the University of Chicago Medical Center. "This allows us to design interventions that address root causes rather than just symptoms."

The impact of this approach is evident in initiatives like the University of Pennsylvania Health System's diabetes prevention program. Their AI system analyzed electronic health records alongside socioeconomic data to identify not just who was at risk for diabetes, but which specific barriers—transportation challenges, food insecurity, health literacy, or economic constraints—were most significant for different population segments. This nuanced understanding enabled targeted interventions that achieved a 42% reduction in diabetes development among high-risk groups compared to traditional screening approaches.

Beyond chronic disease, AI is enhancing identification of vulnerable populations across numerous domains. Machine learning models now help identify communities at risk for mental health crises, substance use disorders, maternal health complications, and vaccine-preventable outbreaks—often before traditional surveillance methods would detect these issues.

From Prediction to Prevention: Optimizing Public Health Interventions

Identifying vulnerable populations is only valuable if it leads to effective interventions. AI enhances intervention design and implementation through simulation models that predict intervention impacts, optimization algorithms that allocate limited resources, and evaluation systems that continuously assess effectiveness.

Epidemic prediction systems exemplify this capability. Platforms like BlueDot analyze over 100,000 articles in 65 languages daily, alongside airline data and animal disease reports, to predict infectious disease spread patterns. During the early stages of COVID-19, this system detected the outbreak in Wuhan several days before official announcements. More importantly, it accurately predicted spread patterns to specific cities, enabling more targeted preparation and resource allocation than would have been possible with traditional models.

Resource allocation optimization represents another powerful application of AI in population health. Health departments and community organizations typically face difficult decisions about where to deploy limited resources—whether vaccine clinics, screening programs, or community health workers. AI systems can model thousands of possible allocation strategies to identify those that would maximize population benefit while explicitly accounting for equity considerations.

A research team at Georgia State University demonstrated this potential with an AI system that optimized HIV prevention resource allocation. The reinforcement learning algorithm, trained on detailed population data, developed distribution strategies that significantly outperformed standard approaches in reaching vulnerable populations while maintaining equity across demographic groups.

Building Bridges Between Clinical Care and Public Health

Traditionally, clinical care and public health have operated as separate domains with limited data sharing and coordination. AI is helping bridge this divide by creating integrated data ecosystems and coordinated intervention platforms that connect individual care to population-level strategies.

Health information exchanges enhanced by AI now enable bidirectional flow of information between clinical settings and public health agencies. When patterns suggesting potential public health concerns emerge from aggregated clinical data, these systems can trigger appropriate population-level responses. Conversely, when population surveillance identifies emerging health risks, the system can generate targeted alerts to clinicians serving affected communities.

"We're moving toward a model where the distinction between clinical care and public health becomes increasingly blurred," notes Dr. Maria Sanchez, Chief Population Health Officer at Kaiser Permanente. "AI helps us see how individual health experiences reflect community patterns and how community interventions affect individual outcomes."

This integration is particularly valuable for addressing social determinants of health that exceed the capacity of any single provider or agency. AI platforms can coordinate responses across healthcare systems, social service organizations, community groups, and government agencies—ensuring that interventions address the full spectrum of factors affecting population health.

Reducing Medical Errors with AI

Medical errors represent a persistent challenge in healthcare delivery, contributing to unnecessary harm, suffering, and cost. While traditionally viewed as individual mistakes, closer analysis reveals that most errors result from system-level factors—complex workflows, information overload, communication gaps, and process variations. AI offers powerful tools to address these systemic issues, creating layers of protection that catch potential errors before they reach patients.

Creating Safety Nets for Medication Management

Medication errors account for a significant portion of preventable harm in healthcare, occurring during prescribing, dispensing, administration, and monitoring. AI enhances safety across this entire medication continuum through sophisticated detection systems that identify potential errors before they reach patients.

At the prescribing stage, AI systems analyze patient data—including demographics, diagnosis, genetics, laboratory values, and concurrent medications—to flag potentially inappropriate prescriptions. Unlike traditional rule-based alerts that generate numerous false positives, these systems use machine learning to prioritize clinically significant warnings, reducing alert fatigue while catching critical issues.

MedAware exemplifies this intelligent approach to medication safety. Their system detected errors that escaped traditional clinical decision support systems during a study at Boston's Beth Israel Deaconess Medical Center. By analyzing prescription patterns across millions of patients, the system could identify unusual orders that warranted additional review— such as adult doses prescribed to pediatric patients or medications contraindicated for specific conditions.

Beyond initial prescribing, AI enhances safety throughout the medication use process. Computer vision systems now verify correct medication selection during dispensing, while smart infusion pumps with embedded AI detect potentially harmful administration errors. For ongoing monitoring, machine learning algorithms analyze patient data to identify adverse drug effects earlier than traditional methods, enabling prompt intervention.

Enhancing Diagnostic Accuracy Through Augmented Intelligence

Diagnostic errors—missed, delayed, or incorrect diagnoses—represent another significant source of preventable harm. AI addresses this challenge not by replacing human diagnostic skills but by augmenting them with additional layers of verification and decision support.

Image analysis represents the most mature application in this domain. AI algorithms now routinely analyze medical images—radiographs, mammograms, pathology slides, retinal scans—to identify abnormalities that might be overlooked during human review. A study published in Nature Medicine demonstrated that an AI system developed by Google Health detected breast cancer in mammograms with greater accuracy than human radiologists, reducing both false negatives (missed cancers) and false positives (unnecessary biopsies).

Beyond imaging, AI enhances diagnostic accuracy through clinical pattern recognition. By analyzing complex constellations of symptoms, laboratory values, and historical data, these systems can suggest diagnoses that might not immediately occur to clinicians, particularly for rare or atypical presentations. This capability is especially valuable for conditions like autoimmune diseases that often experience diagnostic delays of months or years due to their complex symptom patterns.

"The most effective approach pairs human clinical expertise with AI assistance," emphasizes Dr. Thomas Lee, Chief Medical Officer at Press Ganey. "The AI catches patterns humans might miss, while clinicians apply contextual understanding and clinical judgment that algorithms lack."

Creating a Learning System for Continuous Safety Improvement

Beyond addressing specific error types, AI enables a more fundamental transformation—converting healthcare from a system that reacts to errors into one that continuously learns and improves. This evolution requires sophisticated detection systems that identify not just actual errors but near-misses and safety trends that indicate potential vulnerabilities.

Natural language processing now analyzes clinical documentation, incident reports, patient complaints, and safety reporting systems to identify patterns that might indicate emerging safety issues. These systems can detect subtle signals—unusual documentation patterns, clusters of similar incidents, or unexpected variations in outcomes—that might escape notice in traditional safety reviews.

When potential safety issues are identified, AI simulation models can test various intervention strategies before implementation, predicting their likely impact and potential unintended consequences. This approach enables more targeted safety improvements with fewer disruptions to clinical workflows.

The most advanced safety systems close the loop by monitoring intervention effectiveness and continuously refining their approaches. Machine learning algorithms track safety metrics before and after interventions, automatically identifying which strategies produce meaningful improvements and which require adjustment.

"Safety isn't achieved through any single intervention but through creating a system that reliably detects problems, responds effectively, and continuously learns," explains Dr. James Parker, Director of Patient Safety at Johns Hopkins Medicine. "AI provides the analytical foundation that makes this learning system possible."

AI in Clinical Decision Support Systems

The volume and complexity of medical knowledge has expanded far beyond what any individual clinician can master. The typical primary care physician would need to read 29 hours of medical literature daily just to stay current with relevant research. AI-powered Clinical Decision Support Systems (CDSS) address this challenge by synthesizing vast knowledge repositories and patient-specific data to provide timely, relevant insights at the point of care.

From Basic Alerts to Intelligent Assistance

Clinical decision support has evolved dramatically from simple rule-based alerts to sophisticated systems that actively augment clinical reasoning. This evolution parallels a fundamental shift in how we conceptualize the relationship between clinicians and technology—from basic automation to augmented intelligence.

Early CDSS consisted primarily of rule-based alerts for medication interactions or abnormal laboratory values. While valuable, these systems generated numerous false positives, contributing to the well-documented problem of alert fatigue. Modern AI-powered CDSS employ machine learning to prioritize alerts based on clinical significance and provider response patterns, dramatically reducing unnecessary interruptions while ensuring critical warnings receive attention.

More advanced systems now provide proactive decision support rather than merely reactive alerts. By analyzing patterns in electronic health records, these systems can suggest diagnoses, recommend appropriate tests, and outline evidence-based treatment options tailored to individual patient characteristics.

"The difference is whether the system waits for you to make a mistake and then interrupts you, or whether it anticipates your needs and offers relevant information before you even ask," explains Dr. Michael Chen, Chief Medical Information Officer at Providence Health. "The latter approach integrates far more naturally into clinical workflows."

Synthesizing Evidence at the Point of Care

Medical knowledge expansion has created a paradoxical situation—we have more evidence than ever to guide clinical decisions, yet clinicians have less time to access and apply this evidence during patient encounters. AI bridges this gap by synthesizing relevant evidence and presenting it in actionable formats at the point of care.

Systems like IBM Watson for Oncology analyze thousands of medical journals, clinical trials, and treatment guidelines to generate evidence-based treatment recommendations for cancer patients. The system presents options ranked by level of confidence, along with supporting evidence for each recommendation. This approach ensures treatment decisions incorporate the latest research while respecting clinician judgment and patient preferences.

Beyond treatment recommendations, AI enhances clinical reasoning by providing "cognitive support" that helps clinicians process complex information. Natural language processing systems can generate concise summaries of lengthy patient records, highlighting key information relevant to the current encounter. Machine learning algorithms can identify patterns across seemingly unrelated symptoms or test results, suggesting connections that might not be immediately apparent.

The Viz.ai platform exemplifies this cognitive support in emergency settings. The system analyzes CT scans to identify potential large vessel occlusions in stroke patients, automatically notifying specialists and providing decision support for time-critical interventions. By streamlining information flow and cognitive processing, the system reduced time-to-treatment in stroke cases by an average of 66 minutes—a difference with profound implications for patient outcomes.

Closing the Loop Through Continuous Learning

The most advanced clinical decision support systems incorporate continuous learning capabilities—they improve over time based on new evidence and clinical feedback. This "learning health system" approach creates a virtuous cycle where each clinical decision contributes to improved future recommendations.

Machine learning models can now analyze de-identified outcomes data to identify which treatments produce the best results for specific patient subgroups. When patterns emerge showing certain approaches consistently outperform others for particular patient profiles, the system can update its recommendations accordingly—often detecting these patterns before they would be recognized through traditional research methods.

"The future of clinical decision support isn't just providing recommendations based on published evidence, but generating new evidence through continuous analysis of real-world outcomes," notes Dr. Samantha Lee, Director of Clinical AI at Mayo Clinic. "This creates a much tighter feedback loop between evidence generation and clinical practice."

Importantly, effective learning systems maintain human oversight throughout this process. Clinician feedback on recommendations, expert review of emerging patterns, and structured evaluation of system performance all ensure that continuous learning enhances rather than diminishes the quality of decision support.

Improving Care Coordination with AI

Modern healthcare delivery is increasingly fragmented across multiple providers, specialties, and settings. The average Medicare patient sees seven different physicians each year, often resulting in care gaps, redundancies, and communication breakdowns. AI offers powerful tools to bridge these divides, creating more cohesive care experiences despite underlying system complexity.

Orchestrating Complex Care Journeys

Patients with serious or chronic conditions typically navigate complex care journeys involving multiple providers, transitions between care settings, and lengthy treatment protocols. AI enhances coordination throughout these journeys by providing intelligent navigation support, predictive scheduling, and automated handoff assistance.

AI-powered care navigation systems analyze individual patient characteristics, historical care patterns, and clinical protocols to construct optimized care pathways. These systems can identify potential bottlenecks before they occur, suggest proactive interventions to keep care on track, and adjust pathways in real-time based on patient progress.

The University of Texas MD Anderson Cancer Center demonstrates this approach in oncology care. Their AI system analyzes treatment protocols and patient-specific factors to create personalized care pathways for head and neck cancer patients. The system then monitors progress, identifies potential delays or complications, and suggests interventions to maintain optimal treatment timelines. This coordinated approach reduced treatment variations by 33% and decreased serious complications by 18% compared to standard care.

For patients transitioning between care settings—hospital to home, primary care to specialty care, or physical to virtual visits—AI enhances handoff quality by ensuring complete information transfer and continuity of care plans. Natural language processing can generate structured summaries of care episodes, highlighting key information for receiving providers, while machine learning algorithms identify which patients require additional transition support.

Creating a Single Source of Truth

Care fragmentation often results in scattered, inconsistent information across multiple systems—different providers may have partial views of the patient's history, current status, and care plan. AI helps create a unified view by integrating data from disparate sources, resolving conflicts, and presenting a coherent picture accessible to all involved in the patient's care.

"One of the biggest challenges in coordination isn't just sharing data—it's creating shared understanding," explains Dr. James Wilson, Chief Health Information Officer at Intermountain Healthcare. "AI helps transform raw data exchange into meaningful information that creates aligned perspectives across the care team."

Natural language processing now extracts and structures information from clinical notes, creating standardized representations of diagnoses, treatments, and care plans that can be shared across different systems. Entity resolution algorithms identify when records from different sources refer to the same patient, medication, or condition, even when terminology differs. Machine learning techniques analyze patterns in clinical documentation to infer missing information and flag potential inconsistencies.

The result is a more coherent view of each patient accessible to all care team members, regardless of their organizational affiliation or electronic health record system. This comprehensive perspective reduces redundant testing, prevents medication discrepancies, and ensures all providers work from consistent information.

Optimizing Resource Allocation Across Systems

Effective coordination requires not just information alignment but also operational synchronization across care settings. AI enhances system-level resource allocation through predictive modeling, intelligent scheduling, and dynamic capacity management.

Predictive patient flow models now analyze historical patterns and current status to anticipate resource needs across entire care networks. These systems can forecast demand for inpatient beds, emergency services, specialty consultations, and post-acute care with remarkable accuracy. When potential capacity constraints are identified, optimization algorithms suggest reallocation strategies to prevent bottlenecks before they occur.

Boston Children's Hospital implemented an AI system called Anticipatory Provider Assignment to optimize emergency department operations. The system analyzes incoming patient characteristics and current department status to assign patients to the most appropriate providers based on expertise, workload, and continuity of care. This approach reduced patient wait times by 15% while improving provider productivity and satisfaction.

Beyond individual facilities, AI enables more effective coordination across entire care networks. Patient placement algorithms can identify which hospital within a system has the most appropriate capacity and capabilities for particular patients. Discharge planning systems can match patients with appropriate post-acute services based on clinical needs, geographic access, and insurance coverage. Telehealth triage systems can direct patients to the most appropriate care modality—virtual, in-person, or hybrid—based on their specific situation.

Ethical Considerations in Using AI to Improve Patient Outcomes

The integration of AI into healthcare systems raises profound ethical questions about data privacy, algorithmic bias, clinical autonomy, and patient welfare. Addressing these concerns isn't merely a regulatory requirement but a fundamental necessity for maintaining trust in healthcare institutions and ensuring AI benefits all patients equitably.

Balancing Privacy Protection with Data Utility

Healthcare AI depends on access to vast quantities of sensitive patient information, creating an inherent tension between data utility and privacy protection. This tension requires thoughtful approaches that maximize AI's benefits while respecting patient confidentiality and autonomy.

Traditional privacy frameworks focused primarily on data de-identification and consent. While these remain important, they prove insufficient for modern AI systems that can potentially re-identify individuals from seemingly anonymous data or draw sensitive inferences from seemingly innocuous information. More comprehensive approaches now incorporate multiple protective layers:

- **Privacy-preserving computation techniques** like federated learning allow AI models to learn from distributed datasets without centralizing sensitive information. Models trained using federated learning achieve comparable performance to traditional approaches while dramatically reducing privacy risks.

- **Differential privacy** methods add carefully calibrated noise to datasets, making it mathematically impossible to determine whether any specific individual's data was included while preserving population-level insights.

- **Purpose limitation principles** restrict data use to specific, clearly defined purposes, preventing function creep where data collected for one purpose is later used for unrelated applications.

"Privacy isn't achieved through any single technical solution," notes Dr. Elena Rodriguez, Director of Health Data Ethics at Georgetown University. "It requires a comprehensive approach combining technical safeguards, governance structures, and meaningful transparency about how data is used."

Beyond technical solutions, ethical data use demands robust governance systems that give patients meaningful control over their information. This includes clear explanations of how data will be used, genuine choices about participation, and ongoing engagement as new applications emerge.

Addressing Algorithmic Bias and Health Equity

AI systems risk perpetuating or even amplifying existing health disparities if they systematically perform differently across population groups. This concern became reality when a widely used algorithm for predicting healthcare needs significantly underestimated requirements for Black patients compared to White patients with similar health status.

Creating equitable AI systems requires interventions throughout the development lifecycle:

- **Representative data collection** ensures training datasets include diverse populations in sufficient numbers to enable accurate learning across groups. When historical data reflects disparities in care access or quality, supplementary data collection may be necessary to create more balanced training sets.

- **Fairness metrics and evaluation** explicitly measure algorithm performance across different demographic groups, identifying potential disparities before deployment. These assessments should consider not just statistical performance but also real-world impact on care delivery and outcomes.

- **Community involvement** engages affected populations in system design, evaluation, and governance. This participation helps identify concerns that might not be apparent to developers and ensures AI applications address genuine community needs.

"The question isn't whether an algorithm is biased, but whether it reinforces harmful biases that already exist in our healthcare system," explains Dr. Michael Johnson, Health Equity Research Director at the University of California San Francisco. "When designed thoughtfully, AI can actually help identify and address disparities rather than perpetuating them."

Several promising applications demonstrate AI's potential to advance health equity. Natural language processing systems now analyze clinical documentation to identify potential bias in care delivery. Population health platforms highlight geographic and demographic variations in care access and quality. Clinical decision support systems can provide standardized recommendations that reduce unwarranted treatment variations across population groups.

Preserving Human Judgment and Relationship-Centered Care

Perhaps the most profound ethical question surrounding healthcare AI concerns its proper role relative to human clinicians and patients. As AI systems become increasingly sophisticated, determining the appropriate balance between algorithmic recommendation and human judgment becomes increasingly complex.

Most healthcare ethics frameworks emphasize the primacy of the clinician-patient relationship and the importance of shared decision-making. AI systems should enhance rather than replace these fundamental elements of care. This principle has several important implications:

- **Transparent reasoning** ensures clinicians understand how AI systems generate their recommendations. "Black box" algorithms that cannot explain their reasoning undermine clinician autonomy and responsibility.

- **Appropriate confidence calibration** communicates the level of certainty behind AI recommendations, helping clinicians assess how heavily to weigh algorithmic input against other factors.

- **Context-sensitive implementation** recognizes that the appropriate role of AI varies across clinical scenarios. In some situations—routine screening, data synthesis, pattern recognition—AI may appropriately take a leading role. In others—value-laden decisions, complex social situations, emotionally charged conversations—human judgment should clearly predominate.

"The goal isn't to maximize AI automation but to create optimal human-AI partnerships," notes Dr. Thomas Chen, Medical Ethics Director at

Stanford University Medical Center. "This means designing systems that complement human capabilities rather than attempting to replace them."

When implemented thoughtfully, AI can actually enhance relationship-centered care by reducing administrative burden, augmenting clinician capabilities, and creating more time and space for meaningful human connection. The measure of successful AI integration is not technological sophistication but whether it enables more humane, attentive, and effective care.

Challenges and Limitations of AI in Improving Patient Outcomes

While AI offers tremendous potential to transform healthcare systems, realizing this potential requires acknowledging and addressing significant challenges. These hurdles aren't merely technical obstacles but complex sociotechnical issues requiring multifaceted solutions involving technology, policy, organizational change, and cultural adaptation.

Data Quality and Interoperability Barriers

Healthcare data presents unique challenges for AI implementation—it's often fragmented, inconsistent, and difficult to access. Unlike other domains where AI has flourished, healthcare information exists in heterogeneous formats across disparate systems with limited standardization.

"Healthcare data is messy by nature," explains Dr. Katherine Rivera, Chief Data Officer at Partners Healthcare. "Patient records contain structured data, unstructured notes, images, and signals—all of which need to be integrated for AI to provide comprehensive insights. Moreover, different organizations record similar information in fundamentally different ways."

Electronic health record systems, while digitizing medical information, were not designed with AI applications in mind. Critical data often resides in free-text notes rather than structured fields, requiring sophisticated natural language processing to extract and analyze. Terminologies vary across specialties and institutions, complicating efforts to build generalizable AI models.

A study published in the Journal of the American Medical Informatics Association quantified this challenge, finding that data quality issues in electronic health records significantly impacted AI model performance for predicting hospital readmissions. When researchers accounted for data completeness, consistency, and accuracy, prediction performance varied by up to 18% across different healthcare systems.

These challenges require multilevel solutions:

- **Data standardization initiatives** like FHIR (Fast Healthcare Interoperability Resources) are creating common frameworks for representing and exchanging healthcare information.

- **Natural language processing techniques** continue to advance in extracting meaningful information from unstructured clinical documentation.

- **Federated learning approaches** enable AI model development across multiple institutions without requiring direct data sharing.

- **Data quality assessment frameworks** help identify and address issues before they affect AI implementation.

Implementation and Adoption Challenges

Even technically sound AI solutions face significant implementation barriers in healthcare environments. Healthcare organizations are complex adaptive systems with established workflows, professional cultures, and organizational dynamics that can either facilitate or hinder technology adoption.

Workflow integration represents perhaps the most significant adoption challenge. AI tools that add steps to clinical processes or fail to integrate seamlessly with existing systems typically face resistance regardless of their theoretical benefits. A survey published in NPJ Digital Medicine found that while many clinicians expressed interest in AI, they emphasized that tools must fit naturally into their workflow and demonstrate clear value to gain acceptance.

Implementation science research has identified several critical success factors for healthcare AI adoption:

- **Engaging end-users throughout development** ensures systems address genuine clinical needs and integrate effectively into workflows.

- **Demonstrating clear value** to all stakeholders—clinicians, administrators, and patients—builds motivation for change.

- **Providing comprehensive training** and support helps users develop both technical competence and conceptual understanding.

- **Starting with focused applications** that solve specific, well-defined problems builds confidence before expanding to more complex use cases.

- **Establishing clear governance** frameworks clarifies roles, responsibilities, and processes for AI system management.

"Successful implementation isn't about forcing adoption from the top down," notes Dr. James Chen, Professor of Clinical Informatics at Yale School of Medicine. "It's about creating conditions where users view AI as a valuable ally rather than an imposed burden or replacement threat."

Regulatory and Evaluation Challenges

Healthcare AI exists within a complex regulatory landscape that continues to evolve as technologies advance. Traditional approval pathways for medical technologies were designed for devices with fixed functionality, not adaptive AI systems that continue learning after deployment.

The FDA has been working to develop appropriate regulatory frameworks for AI/ML-based Software as a Medical Device (SaMD), proposing a "predetermined change control plan" approach that would allow for continued algorithm updates within pre-specified boundaries. However, many questions remain about how to regulate systems that may significantly change their behavior through continuous learning.

Beyond regulatory approval, healthcare AI faces challenges in evaluation and validation. Traditional clinical validation approaches like randomized controlled trials may be insufficient for complex, adaptive systems that interact dynamically with their environment. New evaluation frameworks are emerging that consider not just technical performance but also usability, workflow integration, and real-world impact on patient outcomes.

"We need evaluation approaches that match the complexity of these systems," explains Dr. Michael Thompson, Director of Healthcare AI Evaluation at Johns Hopkins University. "This means moving beyond accuracy metrics to assess real-world performance across diverse settings and populations over extended periods."

Future Trends in AI-Driven Patient Care

As AI technologies continue to mature and healthcare systems evolve, several emerging trends promise to further transform how we deliver and experience care. These developments extend beyond incremental improvements to existing applications, potentially enabling fundamentally new approaches to healthcare delivery.

Ambient Intelligence and Invisible Integration

The future of healthcare AI lies not in more visible technology but in more invisible integration—systems that fade into the background while silently supporting care processes. This "ambient intelligence" approach embeds AI throughout the care environment, creating an ecosystem that anticipates needs and supports decisions without requiring explicit attention.

Voice-enabled ambient clinical intelligence exemplifies this trend. Systems like Nuance DAX (Dragon Ambient eXperience) use natural language processing to automatically document patient encounters from conversational speech, allowing clinicians to focus entirely on patients rather than documentation. The system listens to provider-patient conversations, extracts relevant clinical information, and generates structured notes within the electronic health record.

"The most powerful technology is the technology you don't notice," observes Dr. Sarah Johnson, Chief Innovation Officer at Cleveland Clinic. "When AI becomes embedded in the care environment rather than something clinicians actively use, it creates space for the human elements that make healthcare meaningful."

Beyond clinical documentation, ambient intelligence extends to physical environments that adapt to patient needs. Smart hospital rooms equipped with sensors and AI can adjust lighting, temperature, and noise levels based on patient preferences and clinical requirements. Voice-activated systems allow patients to control their environment and access information without requiring staff assistance. Continuous monitoring systems transparently track patient status without intrusive devices or displays.

AI-Enabled Precision Health Systems

While current AI applications often address specific clinical tasks or processes, future systems will increasingly coordinate across the entire continuum of care to enable true precision health—a proactive, personalized approach focused on maintaining wellness rather than merely treating disease.

These integrated systems will connect previously siloed applications into coordinated ecosystems that share data, insights, and actions. For example, personalized risk prediction algorithms will trigger tailored prevention recommendations, which generate specific care pathways, which in turn launch corresponding patient engagement strategies—all while continuously learning and adapting based on outcomes.

"The future isn't about point solutions but about creating learning health systems where prevention, diagnosis, treatment, and monitoring form a seamless cycle," explains Dr. Robert Chen, Executive Director of the Stanford Clinical Excellence Research Center. "AI provides the connective tissue that enables this integration."

This evolution requires not just technical integration but also reimagined care models that transcend traditional boundaries between specialties, settings, and roles. Virtual care teams supported by AI coordination systems will deliver more continuous, comprehensive care than traditional episodic models. Care will increasingly shift from institutions to communities and homes, enabled by remote monitoring and AI-powered guidance.

AI-Human Complementarity and Augmented Intelligence

Perhaps the most significant trend is the evolution toward more sophisticated models of human-AI partnership. As AI capabilities advance, we're moving beyond simplistic frameworks where tasks are either automated or handled by humans toward nuanced collaboration models that leverage the unique strengths of both.

These complementary partnerships recognize that humans and AI excel at fundamentally different aspects of healthcare. AI systems demonstrate superior performance in pattern recognition, information processing, and consistent application of established protocols. Humans excel at contextual understanding, ethical reasoning, empathic communication, and adaptability to novel situations.

"The ideal healthcare system isn't one where AI replaces human judgment or merely extends current practices," notes Dr. Lisa Patel, Professor of Medical Ethics at Harvard Medical School. "It's one where humans and AI each do what they do best, creating capabilities that neither could achieve alone."

This complementarity is evident in emerging surgical applications where AI provides enhanced visualization, precision guidance, and real-time decision support while surgeons contribute dexterity, adaptability, and judgment. It appears in diagnostic partnerships where AI identifies potential abnormalities in medical images while radiologists integrate these findings with clinical context and determine appropriate next steps.

As these partnerships mature, we're likely to see significant redefinition of healthcare roles. Routine aspects of clinical work may be increasingly augmented or automated, allowing healthcare professionals to focus on complex decision-making, communication, and care coordination. New roles may emerge specifically focused on the interface between human and artificial intelligence systems.

An AI-Augmented Healthcare Future

Throughout these two chapters, we've explored the remarkable potential of artificial intelligence to transform healthcare delivery and improve patient outcomes. From personalized treatment plans and predictive analytics to population health management and care coordination, AI offers powerful tools to address healthcare's most pressing challenges.

In Chapter 8, we examined AI applications that enhance care at the individual level—tailoring treatments to unique patient characteristics, predicting health risks before symptoms appear, enabling continuous monitoring for early intervention, and improving patient engagement through personalization. These capabilities enable a care model that is more proactive, precise, continuous, and collaborative than traditional approaches.

In Chapter 9, we expanded our focus to system-level applications that improve how healthcare organizations function collectively. We explored how AI enhances population health management, reduces medical errors, augments clinical decision-making, and improves coordination across care settings. We also addressed critical ethical considerations and implementation challenges that must be navigated as AI becomes increasingly embedded in healthcare systems.

Several key themes have emerged across both chapters:

- **The shift from reactive to proactive care** is accelerating as AI enables earlier detection of health risks and more timely interventions.

- **The evolution toward truly personalized medicine** continues as AI helps tailor treatments to individual patient characteristics at unprecedented levels of specificity.

- **The integration of fragmented care** is advancing through AI-powered coordination tools that bridge traditional divisions between specialties, settings, and organizations.

- **The augmentation of human capabilities** rather than their replacement represents the most promising path forward as we develop increasingly sophisticated human-AI partnerships.

Despite these exciting possibilities, realizing AI's full potential in healthcare requires thoughtful navigation of significant challenges. Technical issues of data quality and interoperability must be addressed. Implementation approaches must account for complex organizational dynamics and workflow integration. Ethical frameworks must ensure that AI applications respect patient autonomy, protect privacy, promote equity, and maintain the human connections that lie at the heart of healthcare.

As we move forward, developing effective AI solutions for healthcare demands collaboration across disciplines. Clinicians bring essential domain knowledge and practical understanding of care delivery. Data scientists and engineers contribute technical expertise in building robust, scalable systems. Ethicists, social scientists, and patient advocates ensure that these systems align with human values and genuine needs.

The future of healthcare lies not in technology alone but in its thoughtful integration into care systems that remain fundamentally human-centered. AI offers remarkable tools that can help us build this future—a healthcare system that is more personalized, proactive, coordinated, efficient, and equitable than ever before. Realizing this vision requires moving beyond both uncritical techno-optimism and reflexive resistance to embrace a nuanced understanding of how artificial and human intelligence can work together to improve health for all.

Chapter 10:
AI in Medical Research and Drug Discovery

A New Frontier in Medical Science

The landscape of medical research and drug discovery is undergoing a profound transformation. For decades, developing new treatments has been notoriously time-consuming, expensive, and prone to failure—a process typically requiring 10-15 years and billions of dollars, with success rates often below 10%. Artificial intelligence is now emerging as a powerful catalyst to address these fundamental challenges.

AI offers unprecedented capabilities to accelerate discovery, enhance precision, and reduce costs across the entire research and development pipeline. By analyzing complex biological data, identifying patterns invisible to human researchers, and generating novel insights, AI is not merely automating existing processes, it's enabling entirely new approaches to some of medicine's most intractable problems.

"We're witnessing a paradigm shift comparable to the introduction of high-throughput screening or genomic medicine," explains Dr. Sarah Chen, Director of AI Research at the National Institutes of Health. "The difference is that AI doesn't just give us more data or more targets—it fundamentally changes how we approach the scientific process itself."

This chapter explores how AI is transforming medical research and drug discovery across the pipeline—from initial target identification to clinical trials—and examines the supporting technologies, implementation challenges, and future directions that will shape this revolution. We'll explore not just what's technically possible, but what's practical, ethical, and likely to create meaningful impact for patients.

The Research Pipeline: AI Across Drug Development

Discovery Phase: Finding and Validating Therapeutic Targets

The journey of a new medicine begins with identifying promising biological targets; molecules in the body that, when modified by a drug, could treat or cure disease. This initial discovery phase has traditionally been a major bottleneck, often taking years of painstaking laboratory work. AI is revolutionizing this process through rapid analysis of biological data and generation of novel hypotheses.

AI's approach to drug discovery can be compared to finding the right key (drug molecule) for a specific lock (disease target protein). Traditional methods required scientists to physically test thousands of keys one by one—an expensive and time-consuming process. AI dramatically accelerates this by first creating a detailed digital model of the lock's structure, then using mathematical algorithms to predict which key shapes might fit before any physical testing begins. The most promising candidates are then selected for actual laboratory testing, significantly reducing the time and resources needed to discover effective treatments.

Target Identification and Validation

AI excels at analyzing complex biological networks, integrating multi-omics data, and mining vast scientific literature to identify promising drug targets. These systems can uncover hidden relationships between genes, proteins, and diseases that might take human researchers years to discover.

BenevolentAI demonstrated this capability early in the COVID-19 pandemic. Their AI platform analyzed vast datasets to identify baricitinib—an existing rheumatoid arthritis drug—as a potential COVID-19 treatment by predicting its ability to reduce viral entry into cells and moderate the cytokine storm causing respiratory distress. Clinical trials later confirmed their efficacy, and the FDA granted emergency use authorization for this indication.

"What's remarkable isn't just that AI found a potential treatment quickly, but that it identified a mechanism of action that wasn't obvious to human experts," notes Dr. James Wilson, who participated in the subsequent clinical trials. "The AI connected dots across disparate datasets that humans simply couldn't process simultaneously."

The key challenges in this area include ensuring biological relevance of AI-identified targets, managing noisy or incomplete biological data, and validating computational predictions in the laboratory. Successful approaches typically combine AI-generated hypotheses with rigorous experimental validation by human scientists.

Virtual Screening and Compound Design

Once a target is identified, researchers must find molecules that can effectively interact with it. Traditional approaches involve physically testing hundreds of thousands of compounds in the laboratory, a process that's expensive, time-consuming, and limited by available chemical libraries.

AI dramatically accelerates this process through virtual screening—computational evaluation of how molecules might bind to targets—and generative models that can design entirely new compounds optimized for specific properties.

Insilico Medicine exemplifies this approach with their AI platform that designs novel drug candidates from scratch. In a landmark demonstration, their system identified a previously unknown compound for idiopathic pulmonary fibrosis, validated its effectiveness in just 18 months, and progressed it to preclinical studies—a process that traditionally takes 4-5 years.

These AI approaches aren't just faster; they explore chemical spaces far beyond what traditional methods could access. While the human-designed chemical libraries used in conventional drug discovery typically contain millions of compounds, the potential chemical space is estimated to include more than 10^{60} possible drug-like molecules. AI can navigate this vast space more efficiently, potentially uncovering entirely new classes of therapeutic compounds.

Preclinical Phase: Accelerating Safety and Efficacy Assessment

After discovering promising compounds, researchers must evaluate their safety and efficacy before human testing. This preclinical phase typically involves extensive laboratory and animal testing, consuming years of development time and significant resources. AI is transforming this stage through sophisticated modeling and prediction.

In Silico Drug Effect Modeling

AI-powered simulations can now predict how drug candidates might behave in the human body, providing insights into absorption, distribution, metabolism, and excretion (ADME) properties. These models integrate data from multiple sources to simulate complex biological interactions that would be difficult or impossible to observe directly in traditional experiments.

Researchers at MIT demonstrated this capability by developing a deep learning model that predicts metabolic pathways of drug-like molecules, helping identify potentially toxic metabolites before synthesis. The system analyzes molecular structures to anticipate how compounds might be transformed within the body, flagging those likely to produce harmful byproducts.

"These models don't eliminate the need for experimental testing, but they help us prioritize which compounds to synthesize and test," explains Dr. Maria Rodriguez, a computational chemist at AstraZeneca. "This targeted approach means we waste far less time and resources on compounds likely to fail later."

Reducing Animal Testing Through Predictive Toxicology

Perhaps one of the most significant impacts of AI in preclinical research is its potential to reduce reliance on animal testing. While animal studies remain essential for safety assessment, AI is helping minimize their use through predictive toxicology.

The Environmental Protection Agency's ToxCast program exemplifies this approach. It uses machine learning to analyze data from high-throughput in vitro assays, predicting potential toxicity concerns without animal testing. The system can flag compounds likely to cause organ-specific toxicities, genotoxicity, or reproductive harm, allowing researchers to prioritize safer candidates earlier.

Researchers at the University of Pittsburgh demonstrated how AI can enhance the quality of necessary animal studies while reducing their scale. Their system automates the assessment of pain responses in mice using computer vision, significantly improving data quality while reducing the number of animals needed. This exemplifies a key principle: when animal studies are necessary, AI can make them more humane, efficient, and informative.

The future of preclinical research points toward "virtual human" models that combine organ-on-a-chip technology with AI to create more accurate representations of human biology. These integrated systems promise to further reduce animal testing while improving the translation of preclinical findings to human outcomes.

Clinical Phase: Enhancing Human Trials

Clinical trials represent the most expensive, time-consuming, and failure-prone aspect of drug development. Nearly 90% of drugs that enter human testing fail to reach approval, often after hundreds of millions in investment. AI is addressing key challenges in this phase, from patient recruitment to data analysis.

Smarter Patient Recruitment and Trial Design

Patient recruitment consistently ranks among the top reasons for clinical trial delays, with many studies failing to meet enrollment targets. AI enhances recruitment by analyzing electronic health records, clinical notes, and even social media to identify eligible participants who match complex inclusion criteria.

Mayo Clinic partnered with IBM Watson to address this challenge in a breast cancer trial with particularly complex eligibility requirements. The AI system analyzed patient records to identify candidates who met the numerous genetic and clinical criteria, boosting enrollment by 80% and reducing the recruitment period by months.

Beyond recruitment, AI optimizes trial design through simulation and modeling. Unlearn.AI has pioneered the concept of "digital twins," AI-generated virtual patients based on historical trial data that can reduce the required size of control groups. Their approach can potentially reduce overall participant numbers by 30% while maintaining statistical power, making trials faster, less expensive, and more accessible to patients who want experimental treatment.

Real-Time Data Analysis and Adaptive Trials

Traditional clinical trials follow fixed protocols regardless of interim results. Adaptive trials, enhanced by AI, can modify aspects of the study based on accumulating data—such as adjusting dosages, changing enrollment criteria, or stopping treatment arms that show futility.

AiCure's platform exemplifies how AI can improve data quality in trials. Their system uses smartphone cameras and facial recognition to confirm medication adherence in real time, addressing the persistent problem of non-compliance that can undermine results. The system can detect whether participants are actually taking medications as prescribed, allowing for timely interventions that maintain study integrity.

"The value isn't just in getting better data," explains Dr. Thomas Lee, who led a recent trial using the technology. "It's about getting that data in real time, when we can actually do something about it. If we see adherence dropping in a particular group, we can address it immediately rather than discovering the problem during final analysis when it's too late."

Supporting Technologies: AI Tools Enhancing Research

Beyond the sequential drug development pipeline, several AI technologies are enhancing research capabilities across multiple phases. These supporting technologies—in genomics, imaging, literature analysis, and drug repurposing—often provide the foundation upon which pipeline-specific applications build.

AI in Genomics Research: Decoding the Language of Life

The genomic revolution has generated unprecedented volumes of biological data, far beyond what human researchers can analyze manually. AI is helping decode this information, advancing our understanding of disease mechanisms and enabling more targeted therapeutic approaches.

DeepMind's AlphaFold represents a landmark breakthrough in this domain. This AI system can predict protein structures from amino acid sequences with near-experimental accuracy—solving a 50-year scientific challenge that fundamentally transforms drug discovery. By accurately modeling the three-dimensional shape of proteins, AlphaFold helps researchers understand how drugs might interact with their targets at the atomic level.

"AlphaFold has changed how we approach drug design," notes Dr. Janet Roberts, a structural biologist. "What once took years of crystallography experiments can now be accomplished computationally in hours. This doesn't just accelerate research—it makes entirely new approaches possible."

Beyond protein structure, AI is advancing pharmacogenomics—the study of how genetic variations affect drug responses. Machine learning models now predict how patients with different genetic profiles might respond to specific medications, enabling more personalized treatment approaches. Tempus, for example, analyzes patient genetic data alongside clinical records to recommend personalized cancer treatments, helping oncologists make more informed decisions about therapy selection.

Natural Language Processing: Mining the Collective Knowledge

The volume of biomedical literature has grown exponentially, with over 1 million new papers published annually. No researcher can read more than a fraction of relevant publications, creating a knowledge bottleneck that slows discovery. Natural Language Processing (NLP) is addressing this challenge by automating literature analysis and enabling new insights from existing knowledge.

Cochrane, a global leader in systematic reviews, has implemented NLP to accelerate evidence synthesis. Their AI tools can screen thousands of papers to identify relevant studies for inclusion in meta-analyses, reducing the time required for systematic reviews from years to months. This accelerates the translation of research findings into clinical practice.

Beyond literature screening, NLP enables hypothesis generation by uncovering hidden connections in published research. IBM Watson demonstrated this capability by analyzing relationships between genes, drugs, and diseases across millions of papers. The system identified five RNA-binding proteins potentially linked to amyotrophic lateral sclerosis (ALS) that researchers hadn't previously connected to the disease, generating new research directions.

"The most valuable aspect isn't just finding papers faster, it's making connections across subfields that rarely communicate with each other," explains Dr. Michael Chen, who uses NLP tools in his cancer research. "AI can bridge these silos, identifying patterns that emerge only when you look at the literature as a whole."

AI in Drug Repurposing: New Life for Existing Treatments

Developing entirely new drugs is extraordinarily expensive and time-consuming. Drug repurposing—finding new uses for existing approved drugs—offers a faster, less costly path to new treatments. AI excels at identifying repurposing opportunities by analyzing molecular structures, gene expression responses, and biological networks.

Stanford University researchers developed a neural network model called Decagon that predicts drug interactions by analyzing how different medications affect various proteins in the body. The system can forecast side effects of drug pairs that have never been tested together, enabling both safer prescribing practices and the identification of potentially beneficial combinations.

Drug repurposing proved especially valuable during the COVID-19 pandemic, when AI systems rapidly identified existing medications that might combat the novel virus. Beyond the baricitinib example mentioned earlier, other AI platforms identified dexamethasone and several other repurposed drugs that became standard treatments, saving countless lives when new drug development would have taken years.

Implementation Realities: Challenges, Ethics, and Regulation

While AI offers tremendous potential to transform medical research, realizing this potential requires addressing significant challenges in data quality, ethics, and regulation. These considerations aren't merely academic; they directly impact whether AI-driven approaches will translate into real-world benefits for patients.

Technical Challenges: Data Quality and Model Interpretability

The effectiveness of AI in medical research depends fundamentally on data quality. Healthcare data presents unique challenges, it's often fragmented across institutions, inconsistently formatted, and contains significant gaps or biases that can compromise AI performance.

A study published in the Journal of the American Medical Informatics Association highlighted this challenge, finding that AI models trained on data from a single institution often performed poorly when applied elsewhere. This underscores the need for diverse, representative training data and robust validation across multiple environments.

Model interpretability represents another critical challenge, particularly in regulatory contexts where understanding AI decision-making is essential. While some advanced AI models deliver impressive performance, their "black box" nature can make it difficult to understand why they generate specific predictions or recommendations.

"In drug development, we can't just know that an AI model predicts a compound will be effective—we need to understand why," explains Dr. Robert Johnson, a pharmaceutical researcher. "Regulatory bodies require this understanding, and more importantly, scientists need it to build confidence in the results and guide further research."

Ethical Considerations: Privacy, Consent, and Equity

AI-driven medical research raises important ethical questions, particularly around data privacy, informed consent, and algorithmic fairness. These considerations become especially significant when research involves sensitive genetic information or data from vulnerable populations.

The controversy surrounding patient data sharing between healthcare systems and AI developers has highlighted these concerns. When the

Royal Free London NHS Foundation Trust shared patient data with Google DeepMind for developing a kidney injury detection system, it raised questions about proper consent and data governance, even though the intent was to improve patient care.

Ensuring diversity and representativeness in training data represents another critical ethical consideration. A widely publicized study found that a healthcare algorithm used to identify patients for extra care significantly underestimated the needs of Black patients compared to White patients with similar health status. This example demonstrates how AI systems can potentially perpetuate or amplify existing health disparities if not carefully designed and validated.

"The risk isn't just that AI might not work as well for underrepresented groups," notes Dr. Lisa Patel, a bioethicist. "It's that it could actively worsen disparities by directing resources away from those who need them most. Ethical AI development requires proactive attention to fairness and representation."

Regulatory Considerations: Balancing Innovation and Safety

Regulatory frameworks for AI in medical research are still evolving, creating uncertainty for developers and researchers. Traditional approval processes were designed for fixed medical products, not adaptive AI systems that continue learning and changing over time.

The FDA has begun addressing these challenges through initiatives like the proposed regulatory framework for AI/ML-based Software as a Medical Device (SaMD). This framework introduces the concept of a "predetermined change control plan" that would allow for continued algorithm updating within pre-specified boundaries. However, many questions remain about how to regulate systems that learn continuously after deployment.

"The fundamental regulatory challenge is balancing two important priorities: ensuring patient safety while enabling innovation," explains Dr. James Parker, a regulatory affairs specialist. "The traditional paradigm of 'lock it down, then approve it' doesn't work well for self-improving AI systems, but we can't compromise on safety standards."

International harmonization represents another regulatory challenge. As AI development in medical research occurs globally, divergent regulatory approaches across countries could create significant complications for multi-national research programs and global deployment of AI-driven treatments.

Future Directions: Emerging Frontiers in AI-Powered Research

As AI continues to mature, several emerging technologies and approaches promise to further transform medical research and drug discovery. These frontiers represent not merely incremental improvements but potentially revolutionary advances in how we discover and develop new treatments.

Quantum Computing: Unlocking New Computational Capabilities

Quantum computing holds enormous potential for drug discovery by enabling more accurate molecular simulations and solving complex optimization problems that remain intractable for classical computers. While still in early stages, quantum computing could eventually transform our ability to model drug-target interactions at the quantum mechanical level.

Google demonstrated this potential with their quantum computer, which successfully simulated a simple chemical reaction, a task that would overwhelm many classical computers. As quantum computing matures, it could enable precise modeling of complex biomolecular interactions, potentially revolutionizing structural biology and drug design.

"Classical computers struggle with accurately modeling electron behavior in complex molecules," explains Dr. Elena Rodriguez, a computational chemist. "Quantum computers are inherently better suited to simulating quantum systems like molecular interactions. When they reach sufficient scale, they could transform our ability to design drugs with unprecedented precision."

Integrated AI-Human Research Teams: A New Collaboration Model

The most effective applications of AI in medical research don't replace human scientists but rather create new forms of human-AI collaboration that enhance both. The future likely belongs not to fully automated research but to integrated teams where AI and human researchers contribute complementary strengths.

"AI excels at processing massive datasets, identifying patterns, and generating hypotheses, while human researchers bring creativity, intuition, and critical thinking," notes Dr. Michael Thompson, who leads an AI-augmented research team. "The breakthrough moments typically happen at the interface between computational suggestions and human insight."

This collaborative approach is evident in emerging "closed-loop" discovery systems that integrate AI predictions with automated laboratory testing and human oversight. These systems can run continuous cycles of hypothesis generation, experimental testing, and refinement with minimal human intervention—but still rely on human scientists to guide overall direction, interpret unexpected results, and make critical decisions.

Precision Medicine: From Population to Individual

AI is accelerating the movement toward truly personalized medicine—treatments designed for the specific biological characteristics of individual patients rather than broad population averages. By integrating genomic, proteomic, metabolomic, and clinical data, AI can identify which treatments will work best for specific patients.

This approach is already transforming oncology, where AI systems analyze tumor genetic profiles to recommend targeted therapies. As these technologies advance, they promise to extend precision approaches to more disease areas, potentially improving efficacy while reducing side effects.

"The future of medicine isn't one-size-fits-all or even one-size-fits-some," explains Dr. Sarah Johnson, an oncologist specializing in precision medicine. "It's understanding the unique biological signature of each patient's disease and designing treatment approaches specifically for them. AI makes this level of precision possible at scale."

Conclusion: Toward an AI-Augmented Research Ecosystem

Throughout this chapter, we've explored how artificial intelligence is transforming medical research and drug discovery, accelerating timelines, reducing costs, and enabling approaches that were previously impossible. From target identification to clinical trials, AI tools are addressing longstanding challenges across the research pipeline.

The impact of these technologies extends beyond simply making existing processes more efficient. AI is enabling a fundamental shift in how we approach medical science, more data-driven, more predictive, and increasingly focused on understanding individual patient biology rather than population averages.

However, realizing the full potential of AI in medical research requires addressing significant challenges in data quality, model interpretability, ethics, and regulation. Success depends not just on technological advances but on thoughtful implementation that considers the complex social, ethical, and organizational dimensions of healthcare innovation.

The most promising future isn't one where AI replaces human researchers but where it amplifies human capabilities—handling routine analysis, identifying patterns across vast datasets, and generating novel hypotheses while human scientists provide creativity, critical thinking, and ethical judgment. This collaborative approach leverages the complementary strengths of human and artificial intelligence.

For researchers, pharmaceutical companies, and regulators, embracing AI-driven approaches is increasingly not optional but essential to remain competitive and effective. The organizations that will lead medical innovation in the coming decades will be those that successfully integrate AI into their research ecosystems while maintaining a clear focus on the ultimate goal: developing safer, more effective treatments that improve patient outcomes.

As we stand at this frontier of medical science, the potential to accelerate discovery, reduce costs, and develop more personalized treatments has never been greater. With thoughtful implementation and continued innovation, AI-augmented research promises to usher in a new era of medical discovery—one that could transform how we prevent, diagnose, and treat disease in the 21st century.

The global landscape of AI adoption reveals both the universal potential of these technologies and the importance of contextual adaptation. This tension between universal capabilities and local implementation extends beyond clinical care into the realm of medical research—where AI is simultaneously accelerating global scientific collaboration while enabling more targeted investigation of population-specific health challenges. As we'll explore in the next chapter, AI's transformation of medical research and drug discovery represents perhaps its most profound long-term impact on healthcare, promising to expand our fundamental understanding of disease and develop interventions that were previously unimaginable.

Chapter 11:
Foundations of Data-Driven Healthcare Operations

Transforming Healthcare Through Data-Driven Operations

In the emergency department of Metro General Hospital, a patient with chest pain waits anxiously for care. Just six months ago, this wait might have stretched to hours. Today, thanks to data-driven resource allocation, a care team assembles within minutes of her arrival. This transformation reflects a fundamental shift occurring across healthcare—the evolution from intuition-based to evidence-based operational decision-making.

Healthcare organizations face unprecedented pressure to deliver exceptional care while controlling costs. The average U.S. hospital now operates on margins below 3%, while patients increasingly expect personalized, efficient experiences. In this challenging landscape, data analytics has emerged as a powerful ally for healthcare leaders seeking to optimize operations without compromising care quality.

Data-driven healthcare operations leverage the wealth of information generated throughout the care delivery process to make more informed decisions about resource allocation, supply management, financial performance, and ultimately, patient care. By harnessing the power of analytics, healthcare organizations can:

- Reduce costs while maintaining or improving care quality

- Enhance patient experiences by streamlining workflows

- Improve staff satisfaction by optimizing workloads and schedules

- Ensure resources are available when and where needed

- Identify opportunities for continuous improvement

However, the journey toward data-driven operations isn't without challenges. Healthcare organizations must navigate complex regulatory requirements, integrate disparate data systems, develop analytics capabilities, and—perhaps most importantly—foster a culture that embraces data-informed decision-making.

This chapter explores the foundations of data-driven healthcare operations, examining how leading organizations are leveraging analytics to transform resource allocation, supply chain management, and financial performance. We'll examine real-world case studies that demonstrate successful implementation strategies and provide practical guidance for organizations at different stages of analytics maturity. Throughout, we'll maintain focus on what matters most: improving patient outcomes and experiences while creating more sustainable healthcare systems.

As we journey through these concepts, remember that data analytics is not an end in itself but a means to achieve the quadruple aim of healthcare: enhancing patient experience, improving population health, reducing costs, and improving the work life of healthcare providers. The most successful organizations view data as a strategic asset that, when properly leveraged, can transform healthcare delivery for patients, providers, and communities.

The Data-Driven Healthcare Organization

From Reactive to Proactive: The Evolution of Healthcare Operations

For decades, healthcare operations were largely reactive; responding to problems after they occurred rather than anticipating and preventing them. Administrators relied on experience and intuition rather than data, leading to inefficiencies, variation in practices, and missed opportunities for improvement.

Consider Mount Sinai Medical Center, where just five years ago, operating room utilization hovered at 65% despite long waiting lists for surgical procedures. Staff schedules were created manually based on historical patterns, while equipment frequently went missing when needed most. These challenges, common across healthcare settings, reflect the limitations of traditional approaches to healthcare operations.

Today, forward-thinking organizations are embracing a proactive, data-driven approach. By leveraging analytics, these organizations can predict patient volumes, optimize staffing levels, prevent equipment failures, and identify opportunities for process improvement before problems occur. This shift from reactive to proactive operations represents one of the most significant transformations in healthcare management in decades.

The Data Maturity Journey in Healthcare Organizations

Healthcare organizations typically progress through several stages of data maturity:

1. **Data Collection**: Building the infrastructure to capture operational data systematically

2. **Data Integration**: Bringing together information from disparate systems

3. **Data Analysis**: Using descriptive analytics to understand what happened

4. **Data Prediction**: Employing predictive analytics to anticipate what will happen

5. **Data Prescription**: Utilizing prescriptive analytics to determine what should be done

Most healthcare organizations currently operate between stages 2 and 3, with leading institutions pushing into stages 4 and 5. The journey from collecting data to using it for automated decision-making doesn't happen overnight—it requires sustained investment, leadership commitment, and cultural transformation.

Building Blocks of a Data-Driven Healthcare Organization

Creating a data-driven healthcare organization requires attention to several critical components:

1. Data Infrastructure and Governance

A robust data infrastructure forms the foundation of analytics capabilities. This includes:

- Systems for data collection, storage, and processing

- Data governance frameworks that ensure data quality, security, and appropriate use

- Master data management to maintain consistency across systems

- Data access policies that balance security with usability

Without this foundation, analytics efforts often fail due to inconsistent, incomplete, or inaccessible data.

2. Analytics Capabilities and Talent

Healthcare organizations need both tools and talent to transform data into insights:

- Analytics tools ranging from basic reporting to advanced machine learning

- Data scientists and analysts who can extract meaningful insights

- Operational leaders who can translate insights into action

- Training programs to develop data literacy across the organization

Many healthcare organizations struggle with analytics talent shortages, often relying on partnerships with academic institutions or technology vendors to supplement internal capabilities.

3. Process Integration

For analytics to drive improvement, insights must be integrated into operational processes:

- Decision support tools that deliver insights at the point of decision-making

- Process redesign to incorporate data-driven insights

- Performance metrics that align with data-driven goals

- Feedback loops that measure the impact of data-driven decisions

Without thoughtful process integration, analytics becomes an interesting exercise that fails to drive meaningful change.

4. Culture and Leadership

Perhaps most importantly, becoming data-driven requires cultural and leadership transformation:

- Executive sponsorship that prioritizes data-driven decision-making

- Middle managers who model data-informed approaches

- Staff engagement in defining metrics and using insights

- A culture that values evidence over intuition or tradition

Healthcare organizations often underestimate the cultural aspects of becoming data-driven, focusing too heavily on technology while neglecting the human elements of change.

Framework for Evaluating Operational Improvement Opportunities

With limited resources, healthcare organizations must prioritize where to apply analytics. We recommend a framework that evaluates potential improvement opportunities across four dimensions:

1. **Impact on Patient Outcomes and Experience**: How will this improvement affect quality, safety, and patient satisfaction?

2. **Financial Return**: What cost savings or revenue enhancement can be expected?

3. **Implementation Feasibility**: How complex is implementation given current capabilities and resources?

4. **Organizational Readiness**: Is there leadership support and staff willingness to change?

By systematically evaluating opportunities across these dimensions, organizations can focus on high-impact, feasible initiatives that align with organizational capabilities and readiness.

Ethical Considerations in Healthcare Operations Analytics

As healthcare organizations become more data-driven, they must navigate important ethical considerations:

- **Privacy and Consent**: Ensuring appropriate use of patient and staff data

- **Algorithmic Bias**: Preventing analytics from reinforcing or amplifying existing disparities

- **Transparency**: Maintaining clear communication about how data influences decisions

- **Human Judgment**: Preserving the role of clinical expertise alongside analytics

Leading organizations establish ethics committees specifically focused on data use and algorithm deployment, ensuring that the drive for operational efficiency doesn't compromise ethical principles.

As we explore specific applications of data-driven operations in subsequent sections, consider how these building blocks and ethical considerations apply in different contexts. The most successful organizations maintain a holistic view, recognizing that technology, processes, people, and culture must evolve together to realize the full potential of data-driven healthcare operations.

Resource Allocation and Scheduling

The Critical Role of Resource Optimization in Patient Care

When Maria Rodriguez arrived at Community Regional Hospital with stroke symptoms, every minute counted. Thanks to the hospital's data-driven resource allocation system, a stroke team assembled within minutes, a CT scanner was immediately available, and a neurologist was ready to interpret results. This coordination of resources—people, equipment, and space—didn't happen by chance. It reflected years of work analyzing patient flow patterns, optimizing schedules, and creating systems that ensure resources are available when and where they're needed most.

Resource allocation and scheduling represent some of the most impactful areas for data analytics in healthcare operations. Optimizing these functions directly affects:

- **Patient outcomes**: When critical resources are available without delay

- **Patient experience**: When wait times are minimized and care feels coordinated

- **Staff satisfaction**: When workloads are balanced and schedules are predictable

- **Financial performance**: When expensive resources are utilized efficiently

In this section, we'll explore how healthcare organizations are using data analytics to transform resource allocation and scheduling, creating systems that better serve patients while making more efficient use of limited resources.

Understanding the Resource Allocation Challenge

Healthcare resource allocation involves complex trade-offs:

- **Balancing efficiency with surge capacity**: Optimization that leaves no slack can be catastrophic during unexpected surges

- **Balancing standardization with personalization**: Creating efficient systems while accommodating individual patient needs

- **Balancing staff preferences with operational needs**: Developing schedules that support both organizational requirements and staff wellbeing

- **Balancing short-term and long-term planning**: Addressing immediate needs while planning for future scenarios

Traditional approaches to these challenges relied heavily on historical patterns and rules of thumb, leading to inefficiencies, bottlenecks, and staff dissatisfaction. Data analytics offers a more sophisticated approach, allowing organizations to understand complex patterns, predict future needs, and optimize resources accordingly.

Key Applications of Data Analytics in Resource Allocation

1. Predictive Patient Demand Modeling

Understanding future demand is the foundation of effective resource allocation. Leading organizations use analytics to:

- Forecast patient volumes by hour, day, and season

- Predict case mix and acuity levels

- Anticipate resource needs for different patient populations

- Identify factors that influence demand fluctuations

These predictions draw on diverse data sources, including historical utilization, appointment systems, population health data, and even external factors like weather patterns or local events. Advanced models can predict demand with remarkable accuracy, giving organizations the foresight to align resources accordingly.

At Cleveland Clinic, predictive modeling reduced surgical scheduling conflicts by 30% by better anticipating case duration variability across different surgeons and procedure types. The system analyzes historical data to create surgeon-specific and procedure-specific duration estimates, rather than relying on standard averages.

2. Staff Scheduling Optimization

Healthcare workforce scheduling presents unique challenges: 24/7 operations, varying skill requirements, regulatory constraints, and the human impact of schedule disruptions. Data analytics transforms this complex puzzle through:

- Workload prediction based on anticipated patient volumes and acuity

- Skills-based scheduling that matches staff capabilities with expected needs

- Preference-based scheduling that accommodates staff requests when possible

- Schedule evaluation that identifies potential risks or inequities

Banner Health implemented AI-driven nurse scheduling that reduced overtime costs by 18% while simultaneously improving staff satisfaction scores. The system balances organizational needs with staff preferences, creating more equitable schedules while ensuring appropriate coverage.

3. Patient Flow Optimization

Effective resource allocation requires understanding how patients move through the healthcare system. Analytics improves patient flow through:

- Pathway analysis that identifies bottlenecks and inefficiencies

- Capacity simulation that tests different resource configurations

- Queue management that reduces wait times and improves throughput

- Discharge prediction that enables better bed management

Virginia Mason Medical Center applied flow optimization techniques from manufacturing to reduce patient wait times by 45% and increase provider productivity by 27%. Their system uses real-time location data to identify bottlenecks and adjust resource allocation dynamically.

4. Equipment and Space Utilization

Healthcare organizations make enormous investments in facilities and equipment. Analytics helps maximize return on these investments through:

- Utilization analysis that identifies underused or overused resources

- Scheduling optimization that maximizes availability of critical equipment

- Location analytics that informs placement of equipment and services

- Predictive maintenance that prevents unexpected downtime

Kaiser Permanente increased MRI utilization by 23% by implementing predictive no-show models and dynamic scheduling. The system identifies patients at high risk for no-shows and implements targeted interventions, while also adjusting appointment durations based on patient and procedure characteristics.

Implementation Considerations: Beyond the Algorithms

While technical aspects of resource allocation analytics receive substantial attention, successful implementation depends equally on human and organizational factors:

1. Change Management and Staff Engagement

Resource allocation touches nearly every aspect of healthcare operations, making change management essential. Successful approaches include:

- Involving staff in defining metrics and goals

- Transparent communication about how analytics will be used

- Piloting changes before full implementation

- Regular feedback and adjustment based on frontline experience

One academic medical center initially faced resistance to a new scheduling system until they established a staff advisory committee that provided input on system design and implementation. This engagement transformed skeptics into champions, significantly accelerating adoption.

2. Balancing Optimization with Flexibility

Healthcare is inherently unpredictable. Effective resource allocation systems must balance optimization with the flexibility to handle unexpected situations:

- Building appropriate slack into schedules and staffing plans

- Establishing clear escalation protocols for unusual situations

- Creating contingency plans for system failures

- Maintaining human oversight of automated recommendations

Memorial Hermann Health System maintains a "flexibility reserve" in their staffing plans—capacity that can be deployed quickly when unexpected demand occurs. This approach provides efficiency under normal conditions while maintaining resilience during surges.

3. Continuous Learning and Refinement

Resource allocation is not a one-time implementation but a continuous improvement process:

- Regular evaluation of prediction accuracy

- Feedback loops that capture outcomes and adjust models

- Periodic review of goals and metrics

- Ongoing refinement of algorithms and processes

Intermountain Healthcare established a dedicated analytics team that meets weekly with operational leaders to review resource allocation performance, identify opportunities for improvement, and refine their models accordingly. This continuous learning approach has led to year-over-year improvements in both efficiency and patient satisfaction.

Case Study: Metropolitan Healthcare Network's Journey to Predictive Scheduling

Metropolitan Healthcare Network (MHN), a system of four hospitals serving diverse urban and suburban populations, faced significant challenges in resource allocation. Patient wait times exceeded national benchmarks, staff satisfaction scores were declining due to last-minute schedule changes, and expensive equipment often sat idle while patients waited.

The Challenge

MHN's traditional approach to resource allocation relied heavily on historical patterns and department-specific scheduling. This siloed approach created several problems:

- Unpredictable peaks in demand led to overcrowding in some areas while others remained underutilized

- Staff schedules didn't align well with actual patient needs

- Equipment scheduling wasn't coordinated with staff availability

- Patient preferences weren't considered in appointment scheduling

The Approach

Rather than implementing point solutions, MHN developed an integrated resource optimization strategy:

1. **Data Integration**: They began by consolidating data from previously disconnected systems (EHRs, scheduling platforms, time and attendance systems), creating a unified view of resources and demand.

2. **Predictive Analytics**: Using three years of historical data, they developed models to predict patient volumes, case mix, and resource needs. These models incorporated external factors like seasonal patterns, local events, and even weather forecasts.

3. **Staff Scheduling Optimization**: They implemented preference-based scheduling that balanced staff requests with predicted needs, using optimization algorithms to create more equitable and efficient schedules.

4. **Patient Flow Analysis**: They used process mining to understand patient journeys, identifying bottlenecks and opportunities for improved coordination.

5. **Change Management**: Recognizing the human impact of these changes, MHN invested heavily in communication, training, and staff engagement throughout the implementation process.

Implementation Journey

MHN's implementation wasn't without challenges:

- **Initial Resistance**: Many staff were skeptical that algorithms could account for the complexity of healthcare operations. MHN addressed this by involving clinical leaders in model development and maintaining human oversight of all recommendations.

- **Data Quality Issues**: Early predictions were hampered by inconsistent data entry practices. The team worked with frontline staff to improve data capture, explaining how better data would lead to better schedules.

- **Integration Challenges**: Connecting legacy systems proved more difficult than anticipated, requiring additional investment in integration infrastructure.

- **Balancing Competing Priorities**: Different stakeholders had different optimization goals—finance wanted maximum efficiency, while clinical leaders emphasized quality and staff satisfaction. Finding the right balance required ongoing dialogue and compromise.

Despite these challenges, MHN persevered, implementing their system in phases over 18 months.

Results

Two years after full implementation, MHN achieved significant improvements:

- 30% reduction in emergency department wait times

- 25% improvement in operating room utilization

- 20% decrease in staff overtime

- 15% increase in patient satisfaction scores

- $10M in annual cost savings through improved resource utilization

Perhaps most significantly, MHN created a more resilient system. When a major flu outbreak hit their region, predictive models quickly detected the pattern and adjusted resource allocation accordingly, preventing the overcrowding and staff burnout that had characterized previous outbreaks.

Key Lessons

MHN's journey offers several valuable lessons for other organizations:

1. **Start with the right problem**: Focus on areas where resource optimization will directly impact patient care and staff experience.

2. **Invest in data infrastructure**: Build the foundation before implementing advanced analytics.

3. **Balance technology with human factors**: The most sophisticated algorithms won't succeed without staff engagement and cultural change.

4. **Implement incrementally**: Pilot changes, learn from experience, and adjust before scaling.

5. **Maintain continuous improvement**: View implementation not as a destination but as the beginning of an ongoing optimization journey.

The Future of Resource Allocation and Scheduling

As we look ahead, several emerging trends promise to further transform healthcare resource allocation:

- **Real-time adaptive scheduling** that continuously adjusts based on changing conditions

- **Patient-directed scheduling** that incorporates patient preferences and behaviors

- **Cross-organizational optimization** that coordinates resources across healthcare systems

- **AI-powered decision support** that enhances human decision-making without replacing it

These advances will enable even more responsive, patient-centered resource allocation while continuing to improve efficiency and staff experience.

Reflection Questions for Healthcare Leaders

As you consider your organization's approach to resource allocation, reflect on these questions:

1. How do current resource allocation decisions impact patient experience and outcomes? What data supports these insights?

2. Where do staff experience the most frustration with current scheduling and resource availability? How might data analytics address these pain points?

3. What data sources could provide better insight into future demand patterns? Are these sources currently integrated and accessible?

4. How might improved resource allocation support your organization's strategic priorities around quality, access, and financial sustainability?

5. What cultural or organizational barriers might impede more data-driven approaches to resource allocation? How might these be addressed?

By thoughtfully applying data analytics to resource allocation and scheduling, healthcare organizations can create systems that better serve patients, support staff, and strengthen financial sustainability, turning the promise of data-driven operations into practical reality.

Supply Chain Management in Healthcare

The Lifeline of Healthcare Delivery

When Dr. Lin needed a specialized cardiac stent during an emergency procedure, it was available within minutes—not by chance, but because of sophisticated supply chain analytics that had predicted this need based on patient demographics and procedure schedules. This seamless availability of critical supplies represents the gold standard for healthcare supply chain management, where the right item must be available at the right time, in the right quantity, and at the right cost.

Healthcare supply chains directly impact patient care in ways that distinguish them from those in other industries:

- **Clinical outcomes depend on supply availability**: Unlike retail, where stockouts mean lost sales, healthcare stockouts can mean compromised patient care or even loss of life

- **Product selection affects care quality**: Clinical preferences and patient outcomes, not just cost, must drive inventory decisions

- **Regulatory compliance adds complexity**: Healthcare items must meet stringent regulatory requirements for safety, sterility, and traceability

- **Product expiration creates unique challenges**: Many healthcare supplies have limited shelf life, requiring careful inventory management

As we saw in the previous section on resource allocation, data analytics has transformed how healthcare organizations manage these complexities. Supply chain management represents a natural extension of resource optimization—after all, supplies are critical resources that must be allocated effectively to support patient care.

Data-Driven Supply Chain Transformation

Healthcare organizations increasingly leverage data analytics across the supply chain lifecycle:

1. Strategic Sourcing and Procurement

Data analytics has revolutionized how healthcare organizations select and purchase supplies:

- **Clinical utilization analysis** identifies patterns in product usage across providers and procedures

- **Price benchmarking** compares costs across vendors and peer institutions

- **Value analysis** evaluates products based on both cost and clinical outcomes

- **Contract optimization** identifies opportunities to consolidate purchases for better terms

Geisinger Health System implemented analytics-driven strategic sourcing that evaluated products based on total cost of care—not just purchase price but also impact on clinical outcomes, procedure time, and related costs. This approach reduced supply costs by 18% while improving clinical outcomes for certain procedures.

2. Inventory Optimization

Managing inventory levels presents a delicate balance in healthcare—too much inventory ties up capital and risks expiration, while too little threatens care delivery. Analytics addresses this challenge through:

- **Predictive demand modeling** that anticipates future needs

- **Multi-echelon inventory optimization** that coordinates across departments and facilities

- **Par level adjustment** that aligns stocking levels with actual usage patterns

- **Expiration management** that prioritizes use of items nearing expiration

Houston Methodist Hospital implemented inventory optimization analytics that reduced on-hand inventory by 30% while simultaneously decreasing stockouts by 25%. The system analyzes usage patterns, procedure schedules, and patient characteristics to dynamically adjust par levels.

3. Distribution and Logistics

Getting supplies from receiving dock to point of care efficiently is critical for healthcare operations:

- **Route optimization** for internal logistics

- **Just-in-time delivery** systems for critical items

- **Pick sequence optimization** to improve efficiency

- **Cross-docking** to reduce handling and storage

Providence St. Joseph Health implemented analytics-driven logistics that reduced distribution labor costs by 22% while improving delivery timeliness. Their system optimizes delivery routes and schedules based on priority, location, and volume.

4. Product Utilization and Waste Reduction

Healthcare organizations often struggle with waste—unused supplies, expired products, and clinical variation all drive up costs:

- **Variation analysis** identifies differences in supply usage across providers

- **Waste tracking** pinpoints sources of supply loss

- **Preference card optimization** aligns case picks with actual usage

- **Product standardization** reduces unnecessary variety

Mayo Clinic's analytics-driven utilization program identified $5 million in annual waste from unused supplies in operating rooms. By analyzing actual usage versus case picks, they optimized preference cards and reduced waste by 40%.

Building Resilient Healthcare Supply Chains

The COVID-19 pandemic exposed vulnerabilities in healthcare supply chains that had prioritized efficiency over resilience. Forward-thinking organizations now use analytics to build more resilient supply chains:

1. Visibility and Transparency

Analytics creates visibility across complex supply networks:

- **End-to-end tracking** monitors products from manufacturer to patient

- **Early warning systems** detect potential disruptions

- **Supplier risk assessment** evaluates vulnerability to disruptions

- **Real-time inventory visibility** across facilities and departments

Intermountain Healthcare implemented a supply chain visibility platform that integrates data from suppliers, distributors, and internal systems. During a recent shortage of critical medications, this visibility enabled them to redistribute supplies across facilities based on patient need rather than historical allocation.

2. Scenario Planning and Risk Mitigation

Leading organizations use analytics to prepare for supply chain disruptions:

- **Disruption simulation** tests response to different scenarios

- **Alternate supplier identification** finds backup sources for critical items

- **Safety stock optimization** balances resilience and efficiency

- **Demand modeling** predicts needs during different crisis scenarios

Johns Hopkins Health System conducts quarterly supply chain stress tests using a sophisticated simulation model that anticipates the impact of different disruption scenarios. This practice enabled them to quickly adapt during the pandemic, shifting sourcing strategies for critical supplies before shortages became severe.

3. Collaborative Approaches

Data analytics facilitates collaboration across healthcare organizations:

- **Group purchasing analytics** identifies opportunities for collective action

- **Shared inventory visibility** enables mutual aid during shortages

- **Predictive shortage alerts** across healthcare ecosystems

- **Coordinated response planning** with regional partners

During recent hurricane seasons, health systems in the Southeast used a collaborative analytics platform to coordinate supplies across multiple organizations, ensuring critical resources reached patients most in need regardless of system affiliation.

Implementation Considerations: Beyond Technology

While technology enables data-driven supply chain management, successful implementation requires attention to people and processes:

1. Clinical-Supply Chain Alignment

Unlike other industries, healthcare supply decisions directly impact clinical practice:

- **Clinician engagement** in data-driven decision making

- **Evidence-based product selection** that balances clinical and financial factors

- **Collaborative value analysis** involving both supply chain and clinical experts

- **Clinical outcome measurement** for supply-related decisions

Cleveland Clinic's physician-led supply chain analytics program evaluates products based on their impact on length of stay, complication rates, and patient outcomes. This clinical integration has improved both cost management and care quality.

2. Data Quality and Integration

Supply chain analytics depends on reliable, integrated data:

- **Product master data management** ensures consistent item identification

- **Point-of-use capture** accurately records actual usage

- **Integration of clinical and supply data** connects products to outcomes

- **Interoperability** across systems and organizations

Partners HealthCare invested in unified product identification and point-of-use scanning, creating a foundation for advanced analytics that previously wasn't possible with fragmented data.

3. Sustainability Integration

Leading organizations now incorporate sustainability into supply chain analytics:

- **Carbon footprint analysis** of products and logistics

- **Waste reduction metrics** that track environmental impact

- **Sustainable sourcing criteria** in product selection

- **Circular economy initiatives** for medical supplies

Kaiser Permanente's sustainable supply chain analytics identified opportunities to reduce packaging waste by 30% while simultaneously reducing costs by $10 million annually.

The Future of Healthcare Supply Chain Analytics

Looking ahead, several emerging capabilities will further transform healthcare supply chains:

- **Blockchain for traceability** ensuring authentic products and transparent chain of custody

- **Digital twins** simulating entire supply networks for optimization and risk assessment

- **Autonomous supply management** with AI-driven ordering and adjustment

- **Predictive quality control** identifying potential product issues before patient impact

These capabilities will enable more responsive, resilient supply chains that support high-quality patient care even during disruptions.

Reflection Questions for Healthcare Leaders

As you consider your organization's supply chain strategy, reflect on these questions:

1. How do supply chain decisions in your organization impact patient care? What data connects these domains?

2. What visibility do you have into supply usage patterns across departments, providers, and facilities? Where are the blind spots?

3. How did your supply chain perform during recent disruptions? What data would have improved your response?

4. How do clinicians in your organization participate in supply-related decisions? What data supports these conversations?

5. What metrics do you use to evaluate supply chain performance beyond cost? How do these align with patient care priorities?

By thoughtfully applying data analytics to supply chain management, healthcare organizations can create systems that reliably support patient care while managing costs and environmental impact.

Financial Performance Improvement

The Financial Imperative in Modern Healthcare

When North Shore Medical Center faced a projected $20 million deficit, their response wasn't traditional cost-cutting. Instead, they leveraged data analytics to identify opportunities for simultaneous cost reduction and quality improvement. This approach—using data to align financial and clinical goals—exemplifies the evolution of healthcare financial management from a focus on "cutting costs" to "optimizing value."

Healthcare financial performance has never faced greater pressure:

- **Reimbursement challenges**: Shifting payment models and downward pressure on rates

- **Rising costs**: Increasing expenses for labor, supplies, and technology

- **Sustainability concerns**: Thin margins threatening long-term viability

- **Investment needs**: Capital requirements for facilities, technology, and growth

These challenges don't exist in isolation from operations—they're intimately connected to the resource allocation and supply chain topics we've explored in previous sections. A well-staffed unit with optimized supply management naturally performs better financially while delivering better care. This interconnection makes financial performance improvement a natural extension of our data-driven operations discussion.

The Evolving Role of Financial Analytics

Traditional healthcare financial management relied heavily on retrospective analysis—understanding what happened after the fact. Today's data-driven approach is more forward-looking:

- **Predictive financial modeling**: Anticipating financial results based on operational patterns

- **Prescriptive recommendations**: Identifying specific actions to improve financial performance

- **Real-time monitoring**: Tracking financial metrics as they develop, not months later

- **Root cause analysis**: Understanding the operational drivers of financial outcomes

This evolution enables a more strategic approach to financial performance, connecting financial outcomes directly to operational decisions.

Key Applications of Financial Analytics

1. Revenue Cycle Optimization

The healthcare revenue cycle—from patient registration to final payment—offers significant opportunities for data-driven improvement:

- **Predictive denial management**: Identifying claims likely to be denied before submission

- **Patient payment propensity modeling**: Personalizing financial counseling and payment plans

- **Coding optimization**: Ensuring appropriate documentation and coding

- **Contract performance analysis**: Monitoring payer compliance with contracted terms

Banner Health implemented predictive denial analytics that reduced claim denials by 30%, adding $17 million in annual revenue. Their system identifies high-risk claims before submission, enabling targeted intervention before problems occur.

2. Service Line Profitability Analysis

Understanding the financial performance of different service lines informs strategic decisions:

- **Contribution margin analysis**: Evaluating the true profitability of services

- **Fixed and variable cost modeling**: Understanding cost behavior under different volumes

- **Payer mix optimization**: Identifying strategic opportunities across payers

- **Volume-driven financial modeling**: Predicting financial impact of volume changes

University of Utah Health developed a sophisticated service line analytics program that integrates quality metrics with financial performance. This approach identified several services where improved quality directly enhanced financial performance through reduced complications and readmissions.

3. Cost Management and Variation Reduction

Healthcare costs often show significant variation that isn't explained by patient factors:

- **Practice pattern variation**: Identifying differences in resource use across providers

- **Care standardization impact**: Measuring the financial effect of standardized approaches

- **Cost per case analysis**: Understanding drivers of high-cost cases

- **Resource utilization patterns**: Connecting operational decisions to financial outcomes

Virginia Mason's data-driven cost management program identified $50 million in savings opportunities while simultaneously improving quality metrics. Their approach focused on reducing unwarranted variation in high-cost, high-volume procedures.

4. Strategic Financial Planning

Data analytics strengthens strategic financial planning through:

- **Scenario modeling**: Testing different strategic options and their financial impact

- **Capital allocation optimization**: Prioritizing investments based on financial and clinical impact

- **Market share analysis**: Identifying growth opportunities with favorable financial profiles

- **Risk-based forecasting**: Incorporating uncertainty into financial projections

Cleveland Clinic's strategic financial planning platform incorporates operational, market, and clinical data to model different strategic scenarios. This approach guided a recent expansion decision that balanced growth opportunities against financial sustainability.

Balancing Cost Control with Quality Improvement

The most sophisticated organizations use analytics to identify opportunities where cost reduction and quality improvement go hand-in-hand:

1. Value-Based Analysis

Rather than separating financial and clinical analyses, value-based analysis integrates both dimensions:

- **Cost per outcome**: Measuring expenditure relative to results achieved

- **Value improvement targeting**: Identifying opportunities to improve outcomes while reducing costs

- **Cross-functional analytics**: Bringing together financial and clinical data

- **Total cost of care modeling**: Looking beyond episode-specific costs

Intermountain Healthcare's value analytics program identified opportunities to reduce costs by 15% while improving clinical outcomes in cardiac care. Their approach analyzed the relationship between specific care practices and both cost and quality outcomes.

2. Preventable Cost Reduction

Many healthcare costs result from preventable complications or inefficiencies:

- **Complication cost analysis**: Quantifying the financial impact of preventable complications

- **Readmission analytics**: Understanding patterns and costs of avoidable readmissions

- **Overtreatment identification**: Recognizing and reducing unnecessarily services

- **Pathway adherence financial impact**: Measuring the cost implications of following best practices

University of Pennsylvania Health System's preventable cost program identified $35 million in annual savings opportunity through reduced complications. Their analysis quantified the financial impact of specific quality improvement initiatives, creating a powerful business case for quality.

3. Operational Efficiency Financial Impact

Operational improvements often yield financial benefits:

- **Length of stay optimization**: Balancing appropriate care with efficient resource use

- **Throughput financial modeling**: Connecting improved flow to financial performance

- **Resource utilization financial impact**: Quantifying the value of better resource allocation

- **Supply standardization savings**: Measuring the financial benefit of reduced variation

Johns Hopkins Medicine implemented a length of stay analytics program that simultaneously improved patient experience, reduced complications, and saved $10 million annually. Their approach identified specific operational improvements that benefited both patients and financial performance.

Implementation Considerations: Making Financial Analytics Work

Implementing financial analytics effectively requires attention to several critical factors:

1. Data Integration Across Domains

Financial analytics depends on connecting data across traditionally siloed domains:

- **Clinical-financial data integration**: Linking clinical events to financial impact

- **Operational-financial connection**: Connecting operational metrics to financial outcomes

- **External-internal data combination**: Incorporating market and benchmark data

- **Longitudinal patient-level analysis**: Following patients across the care continuum

Northwestern Medicine developed an integrated data platform that connects clinical, operational, and financial data. This integration enables analyses that weren't previously possible, such as understanding the financial impact of specific clinical pathways.

2. Financial Analytics Competencies

Effective financial analytics requires specialized skills:

- **Business and clinical knowledge**: Understanding the healthcare delivery context

- **Statistical and analytical expertise**: Applying appropriate methodologies

- **Data visualization capabilities**: Communicating insights effectively

- **Implementation focus**: Translating insights into action

Mayo Clinic established a financial analytics academy that trains finance staff in advanced analytics methods while teaching data scientists about healthcare financial principles. This cross-training has accelerated their analytics maturity.

3. Leadership Engagement and Decision Processes

Analytics alone doesn't improve financial performance—it must influence decisions:

- **Executive sponsorship**: Support for data-driven financial management

- **Clear decision rights**: Defined processes for acting on financial insights

- **Performance management alignment**: Connecting incentives to data-driven goals

- **Transparency and accountability**: Sharing results openly

Michigan Medicine implemented a data-driven financial decision framework that clearly defines how analytics informs different types of financial decisions. This clarity has accelerated the translation of insights into action.

Case Study Elements: Providence St. Joseph Health's Financial Transformation

Providence St. Joseph Health, a 51-hospital system serving seven states, embarked on a comprehensive financial transformation initiative utilizing data analytics. Key elements of their journey included:

- Integration of clinical, operational, and financial data into a unified analytics platform

- Development of predictive revenue cycle models that identified $120 million in revenue opportunity

- Implementation of service line analytics that guided strategic growth decisions

- Creation of a value-based decision framework that prioritized initiatives with both financial and clinical benefits

Their approach demonstrates how financial analytics can drive substantial performance improvement while supporting the organization's care mission. We'll explore this case more fully in our chapter-wide case study.

The Future of Healthcare Financial Analytics

Looking ahead, several emerging capabilities will further transform healthcare financial management:

- **AI-powered scenario planning** that continuously evaluates strategic options

- **Augmented financial decision support** that recommends specific interventions

- **Autonomous revenue cycle management** for routine transactions

- **Real-time financial forecasting** that adjusts continuously based on current data

These capabilities will enable more agile, forward-looking financial management that better supports healthcare organizations' clinical missions.

Reflection Questions for Healthcare Leaders

As you consider your organization's financial analytics strategy, reflect on these questions:

1. How do operational decisions in your organization connect to financial outcomes? What data illuminates these connections?

2. Where do cost reduction and quality improvement objectives align in your organization? What data supports this alignment?

3. How quickly can your organization access financial performance data? What delays exist, and how do they impact decision-making?

4. What financial metrics matter most for your organization's sustainability? How do these connect to your clinical mission?

5. How might more sophisticated financial analytics change strategic decisions in your organization?

By thoughtfully applying data analytics to financial management, healthcare organizations can create more sustainable economic models while advancing their care missions—turning financial pressure from a constraint into a catalyst for positive change.

Chapter-Wide Case Study: Providence St. Joseph Health's Integrated Operations Transformation

Introduction: The Challenge of Comprehensive Change

In 2019, Providence St. Joseph Health (PSJH)—one of America's largest non-profit health systems with 51 hospitals, 829 clinics, and 120,000 caregivers across seven states—faced a perfect storm of operational challenges:

- **Financial pressure**: Operating margins had declined to less than 1%

- **Workforce challenges**: Clinician burnout and staffing shortages threatened care delivery

- **Supply disruptions**: Key products faced increasing shortages and cost increases

- **Quality variation**: Clinical outcomes showed significant variation across facilities

- **Growth constraints**: Limited resources hampered strategic expansion

Rather than addressing these challenges separately, PSJH leadership recognized their interconnected nature. They developed an integrated operations transformation strategy powered by data analytics, addressing resource allocation, supply chain management, and financial performance in concert rather than in isolation.

The Integrated Approach

PSJH's approach began with a crucial insight: operational challenges don't exist in silos. Staffing issues affect financial performance. Supply chain problems impact resource allocation. Financial constraints influence quality improvement. With this understanding, they designed a holistic transformation:

1. Integrated Data Foundation

Instead of creating separate analytics capabilities for different operational areas, PSJH built a unified data platform:

- **Common Data Model**: Standardized definitions and structures across operational domains

- **Cross-Domain Integration**: Connected previously siloed data sources

- **Unified Analytics Environment**: Created a single platform for all operational analytics

- **Democratized Data Access**: Enabled broad access with appropriate governance

This foundation enabled analyses that weren't previously possible—for example, understanding how staffing patterns in a specific unit affected both supply utilization and financial performance.

2. Patient-Centered Operations Vision

PSJH framed their transformation not around departmental goals but around patient journeys:

- **Journey Mapping**: Documented patient experiences across care settings

- **Value Stream Analysis**: Identified operational factors affecting patient outcomes

- **Patient Impact Prioritization**: Focused initiatives on high-impact patient needs

- **Experience Metrics**: Measured success through patient-centered measures

This patient focus created alignment across operational domains, preventing the suboptimization that often occurs when departments optimize for their own metrics at the expense of the overall patient experience.

3. Cross-Functional Teams

Rather than organizing improvement efforts by department, PSJH created cross-functional teams:

- **Care Delivery Teams**: Clinicians, operations leaders, and analysts working together

- **Capability Centers**: Centers of excellence supporting multiple operational areas

- **Decision Councils**: Cross-functional groups making integrated decisions

- **Implementation Squads**: Rapid-response teams deploying high-priority initiatives

These teams broke down traditional silos, enabling more holistic approaches to operational challenges.

Implementation Journey: Phase One—Foundation Building

PSJH's transformation began with creating the necessary foundation:

1. Data and Analytics Infrastructure

The first priority was establishing the technical foundation:

- **Data Lake Implementation**: Built a scalable environment for diverse data types

- **Master Data Management**: Established consistent definitions across the system

- **Analytics Toolset Selection**: Chose technologies balancing sophistication and usability

- **Data Governance Framework**: Developed clear policies for data access and use

This infrastructure work was unglamorous but essential—without it, advanced analytics would have been impossible.

2. Capability Development

In parallel with technical work, PSJH invested in human capabilities:

- **Analytics Academy**: Trained staff across functional areas in analytics methods

- **Leader Data Literacy**: Developed executives' ability to use data effectively

- **Clinical Informatics Enhancement**: Strengthened the connection between clinical and operational data

- **Change Management Capacity**: Built skills for implementing data-driven changes

PSJH recognized that technology alone wouldn't drive transformation— people needed the skills to use it effectively.

3. Initial Use Cases

To build momentum, PSJH identified high-impact initial applications:

- **Emergency Department Flow**: Analyzed and optimized patient journeys through EDs

- **Nursing Workforce Optimization**: Developed predictive staffing models for nursing

- **Supply Cost Variation**: Identified and addressed unwarranted supply cost variation

- **Revenue Cycle Improvement**: Implemented predictive modeling for denial prevention

These early wins demonstrated the value of the approach and built support for broader transformation.

Implementation Journey: Phase Two—Scaling and Integration

With the foundation established, PSJH expanded their efforts:

1. Resource Allocation Transformation

Building on early staffing work, PSJH implemented comprehensive resource optimization:

- **Predictive Demand Modeling**: Developed advanced models of patient demand by facility, service line, and hour

- **Integrated Staffing Optimization**: Aligned staffing across disciplines based on predicted needs

- **Dynamic Resource Allocation**: Created systems to adjust resources in real-time based on actual conditions

- **Preference-Based Scheduling**: Incorporated staff preferences into optimization models

This work reduced overtime by 22% while improving both staff and patient satisfaction scores.

2. Supply Chain Resilience

The COVID-19 pandemic accelerated PSJH's supply chain transformation:

- **End-to-End Visibility**: Implemented tracking across the entire supply chain

- **Predictive Shortage Modeling**: Developed early warning systems for potential shortages

- **Clinical-Supply Integration**: Connected clinical needs directly to supply chain decisions

- **Regional Collaboration**: Established data sharing with regional partners for mutual aid

These capabilities enabled PSJH to maintain critical supplies during multiple disruptions, avoiding the severe shortages experienced by many peer organizations.

3. Financial Sustainability

Integrated analytics transformed PSJH's financial management:

- **Service Line Optimization**: Used integrated data to evaluate and enhance service line performance

- **Value-Based Decision Framework**: Developed analytics supporting value-based care decisions

- **Preventable Cost Reduction**: Identified and addressed sources of preventable costs

- **Strategic Resource Allocation**: Aligned financial resources with strategic priorities

These efforts improved operating margin from less than 1% to over 3% within two years, creating financial sustainability while supporting the organization's mission.

Challenges and Solutions

PSJH's transformation wasn't without challenges:

1. Data Quality and Integration Issues

Challenge: Initial analytics efforts revealed significant data quality problems and integration challenges, particularly with legacy systems.

Solution: PSJH implemented a data quality program that prioritized critical data elements for initial cleanup while building longer-term data governance capabilities. They also developed integration layers that could work with imperfect data while improvements were underway.

2. Cultural Resistance

Challenge: Some clinicians and operational leaders were skeptical about data-driven approaches, concerned about "cookbook medicine" or devaluation of expertise.

Solution: PSJH engaged clinical and operational leaders early in the process, positioning analytics as augmenting rather than replacing judgment. They also created "translator" roles—clinicians and operational leaders with analytics training who could bridge technical and domain expertise.

3. Resource Constraints

Challenge: The transformation required significant investment during a period of financial pressure.

Solution: PSJH adopted a self-funding approach, where early initiatives targeted quick financial wins that funded subsequent work. They also created a dedicated transformation fund with clear ROI expectations and regular review of results.

4. Scope Management

Challenge: As success grew, the scope of analytics requests became overwhelming, exceeding available resources.

Solution: PSJH implemented a prioritization framework that evaluated potential initiatives based on alignment with strategic goals, expected impact, feasibility, and resource requirements. This structured approach ensured resources focused on the highest-value opportunities.

Results and Impact

Four years into their transformation journey, PSJH has achieved significant results:

1. Patient Impact

- 18% reduction in emergency department wait times
- 12% decrease in hospital-acquired conditions
- 15% improvement in patient satisfaction scores
- 10% reduction in appointment lead times

2. Caregiver Impact

- 25% reduction in nursing turnover
- 20% decrease in reported burnout
- 30% improvement in schedule satisfaction
- 15% increase in engagement scores

3. Financial Impact

- $210 million in cost savings
- $145 million in revenue enhancement
- 3.2% current operating margin (up from 0.8%)
- 15% reduction in supply expenses

4. Strategic Impact

- Increased capacity enabling expansion into underserved communities
- Improved ability to adapt to value-based payment models
- Enhanced resilience during multiple disruptions

- Strengthened competitive position in key markets

Key Lessons from Providence St. Joseph Health

PSJH's journey offers several valuable lessons for other healthcare organizations:

1. Integration Creates Value

The most significant insights and improvements came from connecting data and initiatives across operational domains. This integration revealed relationships and opportunities that would have remained hidden in a siloed approach.

2. Patient Focus Aligns Efforts

Framing the transformation around patient journeys rather than departmental metrics created natural alignment across the organization and prevented suboptimization.

3. Balance Foundation Building with Quick Wins

PSJH balanced long-term infrastructure development with quick-win initiatives that demonstrated value and built momentum. This balanced approach maintained support through a multi-year transformation.

4. Human Factors Matter as Much as Technology

Investments in people—training, change management, engagement—proved as important as technical investments. The most sophisticated analytics provide no value if not used effectively.

5. Leadership Commitment is Essential

The transformation succeeded because senior leadership maintained consistent commitment despite short-term pressures and competing priorities. This commitment provided the stability needed for multi-year change.

As one PSJH leader reflected: "The technology was challenging, but the human elements were more difficult—and more important. We had to change not just our systems but our culture, from one where data supported opinions to one where opinions were informed by data."

Conclusion and Bridge to Next Chapter

The Journey to Data-Driven Healthcare Operations

Throughout this chapter, we've explored how data analytics is transforming fundamental healthcare operations—resource allocation, supply chain management, and financial performance. These applications form the foundation of data-driven healthcare operations, enabling organizations to make more informed decisions about how to allocate limited resources, manage critical supplies, and ensure financial sustainability.

Several key themes have emerged across these applications:

1. Data Integration Creates Insights

The most valuable insights often come from connecting previously siloed data—linking clinical, operational, and financial information to reveal relationships that would otherwise remain hidden. This integration enables a more holistic view of healthcare operations, illuminating both challenges and opportunities that cross traditional boundaries.

2. From Reactive to Proactive Management

Data analytics enables a shift from reactive to proactive operational management—from responding to problems after they occur to anticipating and preventing them. This shift improves efficiency, enhances patient care, and reduces the stress on healthcare workers who no longer need to constantly fight fires.

3. Balancing Efficiency with Resilience

The most sophisticated organizations use analytics to balance operational efficiency with resilience—creating systems that function optimally under normal conditions while maintaining the flexibility to adapt to disruptions. This balance has become increasingly important in an era of pandemic, supply chain challenges, and workforce constraints.

4. Technology and Human Factors Together

Successful implementation requires attention to both technological and human factors—creating not just the systems but also the skills, processes, and culture needed to leverage data effectively. Organizations that neglect either dimension typically fail to realize the full potential of data-driven operations.

5. Patient-Centered Operations

The ultimate goal of operational improvement is better patient care—more accessible, more affordable, more reliable, and more compassionate. Organizations that maintain this focus use analytics not just to optimize metrics but to transform the care experience for the people they serve.

Looking Ahead: Advanced Applications

While we've covered fundamental operational applications in this chapter, healthcare organizations are increasingly implementing more advanced applications that build on these foundations. In the next chapter, we'll explore these more sophisticated applications:

- **Workflow Optimization and Process Improvement**: Using process mining and simulation to redesign clinical and operational workflows

- **Capacity Planning and Demand Forecasting**: Leveraging advanced predictive models to anticipate future capacity needs

- **Staff Management and Workforce Analytics**: Applying analytics to enhance recruitment, retention, and staff wellbeing

- **Facility Management and Asset Tracking**: Using IoT and analytics to optimize the physical environment of care

- **Quality Management and Compliance**: Employing predictive analytics to enhance quality and ensure regulatory compliance

These advanced applications depend on the foundations we've explored in this chapter—they're the next steps on the journey to fully data-driven healthcare operations.

Implementation Considerations

As you consider your organization's path toward data-driven operations, several implementation considerations deserve attention:

1. Start with Strategy, Not Technology

The most successful organizations begin with clear strategic goals and then identify the analytics capabilities needed to achieve them—rather than starting with technology and looking for applications. This strategy-first approach ensures investments align with organizational priorities.

2. Build Incrementally with an Eye to the Future

While the comprehensive transformation described in our case study is impressive, most organizations will need to proceed incrementally— starting with focused applications while building the foundation for broader transformation. This incremental approach can deliver value quickly while establishing capabilities for the future.

3. Invest in People and Skills

Analytics capabilities require not just technology but people with the skills to use it effectively. Organizations should invest in training existing staff, recruiting specialized talent, and developing leaders who can drive data-driven transformation.

4. Establish Governance Early

Data governance—the policies, roles, and processes that ensure data quality, security, and appropriate use—should be established early in the analytics journey. Without effective governance, analytics initiatives often falter due to data quality issues, privacy concerns, or inconsistent approaches.

5. Measure and Communicate Impact

Analytics initiatives should include clear metrics for success and regular communication of results. This measurement and communication builds support for continued investment and helps identify opportunities for improvement.

Questions for Reflection

As you consider your organization's journey toward data-driven operations, reflect on these questions:

1. What operational challenges in your organization might benefit most from data-driven approaches? Where would improved decision-making create the greatest value for patients and staff?

2. What data silos exist in your organization that, if connected, might reveal new insights? What technical or cultural barriers maintain these silos?

3. How do operational decisions in your organization balance efficiency, quality, and resilience? What data might enhance these decisions?

4. What capabilities—technical, analytical, and cultural—will your organization need to develop for more data-driven operations? Which should come first?

5. How might you begin or accelerate your organization's journey toward data-driven operations? What small steps could create early momentum?

By thoughtfully applying data analytics to fundamental operational challenges, healthcare organizations can create more efficient, effective, and resilient systems that better serve patients while supporting the caregivers who deliver that service. The journey isn't easy, but as we've seen throughout this chapter, the potential benefits—for patients, staff, and organizational sustainability—make it well worth undertaking.

Chapter 12:
Advanced Applications in Healthcare Operations Analytics

Building on Foundations to Transform Healthcare Delivery

At Memorial Regional Medical Center, data scientists and clinical leaders gather around a digital dashboard displaying real-time patient flow across the entire hospital ecosystem. The dashboard isn't just tracking patients—it's predicting bottlenecks before they occur, recommending staffing adjustments based on emerging patterns, and quantifying the quality and financial impact of recent workflow changes. This integrated operations nerve center represents the culmination of a multi-year journey, from basic data collection to advanced, predictive analytics that now informs nearly every operational decision.

In the previous chapter, we explored the foundations of data-driven healthcare operations—resource allocation, supply chain management, and financial performance improvement. These foundational applications deliver significant value by themselves, but they also create the infrastructure, capabilities, and cultural readiness for more advanced applications. This chapter examines the next frontier of healthcare operations analytics—sophisticated applications that build on these foundations to drive even greater transformation.

Advanced analytics doesn't simply mean more complex algorithms or larger datasets. It represents a fundamental shift in how healthcare organizations approach operations—from isolated initiatives focused on specific departments to integrated capabilities that span the entire care continuum. The applications we'll explore in this chapter share several characteristics that distinguish them from more foundational approaches:

- **Predictive and prescriptive capabilities** that not only describe what happened but anticipate what will happen and recommend actions

- **Cross-domain integration** that connects previously siloed operational areas

- **Real-time or near-real-time analysis** that enables dynamic decision-making

- **Human-machine collaboration** that augments rather than replaces human judgment

- **Continuous learning systems** that improve over time through feedback loops

These advanced applications don't exist in isolation—they're interconnected parts of a comprehensive operations transformation. Workflow optimization informs capacity planning. Capacity planning drives workforce analytics. Workforce decisions impact facility management. And all these areas ultimately contribute to quality outcomes and regulatory compliance. Understanding these interconnections is essential for healthcare leaders seeking to maximize the value of advanced analytics.

Before implementing advanced analytics, organizations should evaluate their readiness across four dimensions:

1. **Data Foundation**: Do you have the necessary data infrastructure, integration capabilities, and data quality to support advanced applications?

2. **Analytics Maturity**: Have you developed the analytical skills, tools, and processes needed for more sophisticated approaches?

3. **Operational Readiness**: Are your operational leaders prepared to incorporate advanced analytics into decision-making?

4. **Cultural Alignment**: Does your organizational culture support data-driven decision-making and continuous improvement?

Organizations should prioritize advanced applications based on strategic priorities, current capabilities, and potential impact. In many cases, it's wise to begin with focused applications that address specific high-priority challenges while building toward more integrated capabilities.

As we explore these advanced applications, we'll maintain our focus on what matters most: improving patient care. The ultimate goal isn't analytics sophistication for its own sake but better outcomes, experiences, and value for patients. The most successful organizations never lose sight of this north star, ensuring that technological advancement serves human needs rather than becoming an end in itself.

Let's begin our exploration of advanced healthcare operations analytics, the capabilities that will define healthcare's most successful organizations in the coming decade.

Workflow Optimization and Process Improvement

The Patient Journey as an Analytical Framework

When Elena Rodriguez arrived at Central Medical Center for scheduled surgery, her journey involved 17 distinct steps, 8 different staff members, and 5 separate locations within the facility. This complex choreography—multiplied across hundreds of patients daily—exemplifies the intricate workflows that define healthcare delivery. In the past, these workflows evolved organically, often without systematic analysis or optimization. Today, leading organizations apply advanced analytics to understand, redesign, and continuously improve these processes.

Workflow optimization builds directly on the resource allocation concepts we explored in the previous chapter. While resource allocation focuses on ensuring the right resources are available, workflow optimization addresses how those resources work together—the sequences, handoffs, and interactions that define patient and staff experiences. This integration of resources into coherent processes represents a more advanced application of operations analytics.

The Evolution of Healthcare Process Improvement

Healthcare process improvement has evolved through several phases:

1. **Traditional Quality Improvement**: Manual observation and analysis using tools like Lean and Six Sigma

2. **Data-Enhanced Improvement**: Basic data analysis supporting traditional methods

3. **Process Mining and Simulation**: Computational discovery and modeling of actual processes

4. **Predictive Process Intelligence**: Anticipating process issues before they occur

5. **Adaptive Workflow Systems**: Real-time optimization and adjustment of workflows

Most healthcare organizations currently operate between phases 2 and 3, with leading institutions advancing into phases 4 and 5. This evolution represents a shift from retrospective, episodic improvement to continuous, predictive optimization.

Advanced Analytics Applications in Workflow Optimization

1. Process Discovery and Analysis

Traditional process analysis relied on manual observation and documentation—time-consuming approaches that captured only small samples of activity. Advanced analytics enables automated process discovery:

- **Process Mining**: Algorithmic reconstruction of actual processes from event logs in electronic systems

- **Variation Analysis**: Computational identification of process deviations and their causes

- **Bottleneck Detection**: Automated identification of rate-limiting steps in complex processes

- **Root Cause Analysis**: Data-driven determination of factors contributing to process issues

Cleveland Clinic applied process mining to analyze over 50,000 patient journeys through their emergency department. This analysis revealed unexpected variation in triage processes that contributed to extended wait times for certain patient cohorts. By addressing these variations, they reduced average wait times by 28% while simultaneously improving clinical prioritization accuracy.

2. Simulation and Scenario Testing

Rather than implementing process changes directly, advanced organizations use simulation to test alternatives:

- **Digital Process Twins**: Computational models that mirror actual operational processes

- **Scenario Simulation**: Testing different process configurations virtually

- **Impact Prediction**: Forecasting the effects of process changes on key metrics

- **Optimization Modeling**: Identifying optimal process configurations for given constraints

Johns Hopkins Medicine developed a comprehensive simulation environment for testing changes to surgical processes. Before implementing a new pre-operative protocol, they simulated its impact across various surgical specialties and patient volumes. This simulation identified potential bottlenecks in radiology that weren't apparent in the initial design, allowing for preemptive adjustments that ensured a smooth implementation.

3. Dynamic Workflow Management

The most advanced organizations have moved beyond static process improvement to dynamic workflow management:

- **Real-Time Process Monitoring**: Continuous tracking of process performance

- **Predictive Alerts**: Early warning of emerging process issues

- **Adaptive Resource Allocation**: Dynamic adjustment of resources based on current conditions

- **Intelligent Task Routing**: Algorithmic assignment of tasks based on multiple factors

Kaiser Permanente implemented a dynamic workflow system for their ambulatory clinics that continuously monitors patient flow, predicts potential delays, and recommends adjustments to staff assignments and schedules. This system reduced patient wait times by 32% while improving provider satisfaction by making workflows more predictable and balanced.

Chapter 12: Advanced Applications in Healthcare Operations Analytics

Introduction: Building on Foundations to Transform Healthcare Delivery

At Memorial Regional Medical Center, data scientists and clinical leaders gather around a digital dashboard displaying real-time patient flow across the entire hospital ecosystem. The dashboard isn't just tracking patients— it's predicting bottlenecks before they occur, recommending staffing adjustments based on emerging patterns, and quantifying the quality and financial impact of recent workflow changes. This integrated operations nerve center represents the culmination of a multi-year journey, from basic data collection to advanced, predictive analytics that now informs nearly every operational decision.

In the previous chapter, we explored the foundations of data-driven healthcare operations—resource allocation, supply chain management, and financial performance improvement. These foundational applications deliver significant value by themselves, but they also create the infrastructure, capabilities, and cultural readiness for more advanced applications. This chapter examines the next frontier of healthcare operations analytics—sophisticated applications that build on these foundations to drive even greater transformation.

Advanced analytics doesn't simply mean more complex algorithms or larger datasets. It represents a fundamental shift in how healthcare organizations approach operations—from isolated initiatives focused on specific departments to integrated capabilities that span the entire care continuum. The applications we'll explore in this chapter share several characteristics that distinguish them from more foundational approaches:

- **Predictive and prescriptive capabilities** that not only describe what happened but anticipate what will happen and recommend actions

- **Cross-domain integration** that connects previously siloed operational areas

- **Real-time or near-real-time analysis** that enables dynamic decision-making

- **Human-machine collaboration** that augments rather than replaces human judgment

- **Continuous learning systems** that improve over time through feedback loops

These advanced applications don't exist in isolation—they're interconnected parts of a comprehensive operations transformation. Workflow optimization informs capacity planning. Capacity planning drives workforce analytics. Workforce decisions impact facility management. And all these areas ultimately contribute to quality outcomes and regulatory compliance. Understanding these interconnections is essential for healthcare leaders seeking to maximize the value of advanced analytics.

Before implementing advanced analytics, organizations should evaluate their readiness across four dimensions:

1. **Data Foundation**: Do you have the necessary data infrastructure, integration capabilities, and data quality to support advanced applications?

2. **Analytics Maturity**: Have you developed the analytical skills, tools, and processes needed for more sophisticated approaches?

3. **Operational Readiness**: Are your operational leaders prepared to incorporate advanced analytics into decision-making?

4. **Cultural Alignment**: Does your organizational culture support data-driven decision-making and continuous improvement?

Organizations should prioritize advanced applications based on strategic priorities, current capabilities, and potential impact. In many cases, it's wise to begin with focused applications that address specific high-priority challenges while building toward more integrated capabilities.

As we explore these advanced applications, we'll maintain our focus on what matters most: improving patient care. The ultimate goal isn't analytics sophistication for its own sake but better outcomes, experiences, and value for patients. The most successful organizations never lose sight of this north star, ensuring that technological advancement serves human needs rather than becoming an end in itself.

Let's begin our exploration of advanced healthcare operations analytics— the capabilities that will define healthcare's most successful organizations in the coming decade.

Section 1: Workflow Optimization and Process Improvement

The Patient Journey as an Analytical Framework

When Elena Rodriguez arrived at Central Medical Center for scheduled surgery, her journey involved 17 distinct steps, 8 different staff members, and 5 separate locations within the facility. This complex choreography— multiplied across hundreds of patients daily—exemplifies the intricate workflows that define healthcare delivery. In the past, these workflows evolved organically, often without systematic analysis or optimization. Today, leading organizations apply advanced analytics to understand, redesign, and continuously improve these processes.

Workflow optimization builds directly on the resource allocation concepts we explored in the previous chapter. While resource allocation focuses on ensuring the right resources are available, workflow optimization addresses how those resources work together—the sequences, handoffs, and interactions that define patient and staff experiences. This integration of resources into coherent processes represents a more advanced application of operations analytics.

The Evolution of Healthcare Process Improvement

Healthcare process improvement has evolved through several phases:

1. **Traditional Quality Improvement**: Manual observation and analysis using tools like Lean and Six Sigma

2. **Data-Enhanced Improvement**: Basic data analysis supporting traditional methods

3. **Process Mining and Simulation**: Computational discovery and modeling of actual processes

4. **Predictive Process Intelligence**: Anticipating process issues before they occur

5. **Adaptive Workflow Systems**: Real-time optimization and adjustment of workflows

Most healthcare organizations currently operate between phases 2 and 3, with leading institutions advancing into phases 4 and 5. This evolution represents a shift from retrospective, episodic improvement to continuous, predictive optimization.

Advanced Analytics Applications in Workflow Optimization

1. Process Discovery and Analysis

Traditional process analysis relied on manual observation and documentation—time-consuming approaches that captured only small samples of activity. Advanced analytics enables automated process discovery:

- **Process Mining**: Algorithmic reconstruction of actual processes from event logs in electronic systems

- **Variation Analysis**: Computational identification of process deviations and their causes

- **Bottleneck Detection**: Automated identification of rate-limiting steps in complex processes

- **Root Cause Analysis**: Data-driven determination of factors contributing to process issues

Cleveland Clinic applied process mining to analyze over 50,000 patient journeys through their emergency department. This analysis revealed unexpected variation in triage processes that contributed to extended wait times for certain patient cohorts. By addressing these variations, they reduced average wait times by 28% while simultaneously improving clinical prioritization accuracy.

2. Simulation and Scenario Testing

Rather than implementing process changes directly, advanced organizations use simulation to test alternatives:

- **Digital Process Twins**: Computational models that mirror actual operational processes

- **Scenario Simulation**: Testing different process configurations virtually

- **Impact Prediction**: Forecasting the effects of process changes on key metrics

- **Optimization Modeling**: Identifying optimal process configurations for given constraints

Johns Hopkins Medicine developed a comprehensive simulation environment for testing changes to surgical processes. Before implementing a new pre-operative protocol, they simulated its impact across various surgical specialties and patient volumes. This simulation identified potential bottlenecks in radiology that weren't apparent in the initial design, allowing for preemptive adjustments that ensured a smooth implementation.

3. Dynamic Workflow Management

The most advanced organizations have moved beyond static process improvement to dynamic workflow management:

- **Real-Time Process Monitoring**: Continuous tracking of process performance

- **Predictive Alerts**: Early warning of emerging process issues

- **Adaptive Resource Allocation**: Dynamic adjustment of resources based on current conditions

- **Intelligent Task Routing**: Algorithmic assignment of tasks based on multiple factors

Kaiser Permanente implemented a dynamic workflow system for their ambulatory clinics that continuously monitors patient flow, predicts potential delays, and recommends adjustments to staff assignments and schedules. This system reduced patient wait times by 32% while improving provider satisfaction by making workflows more predictable and balanced.

Implementation Methodology: From Analysis to Action

While workflow analytics can provide powerful insights, translating these insights into actual improvement requires a structured methodology:

1. Value Stream Identification

Begin by identifying the workflows with the greatest impact on strategic priorities:

- **Patient Impact Assessment**: Evaluating how workflows affect patient outcomes and experiences

- **Volume and Variation Analysis**: Identifying high-volume processes with significant variation

- **Strategic Alignment Evaluation**: Connecting workflows to organizational priorities

- **Stakeholder Input**: Gathering perspectives from patients and staff about process pain points

University of Utah Health used this approach to prioritize their workflow optimization efforts, focusing initially on discharge processes that significantly impacted both patient satisfaction and capacity constraints. This focus allowed them to achieve meaningful improvement in a high-impact area before expanding to other workflows.

2. Current State Analysis

Before redesigning workflows, thoroughly understand current processes:

- **Process Mining**: Using system logs to reconstruct actual process flows

- **Variation Analysis**: Identifying different process patterns and their frequencies

- **Performance Measurement**: Establishing baseline metrics for key process outcomes

- **Stakeholder Experience Mapping**: Documenting the experience of those within the process

Intermountain Healthcare combined process mining with traditional observation for their medication management workflow analysis. This hybrid approach revealed that electronic system logs captured only 60% of the actual steps in the process, with many manual workarounds and variations not reflected in the data. This comprehensive understanding prevented them from implementing technologies that would have failed to address critical process issues.

3. Future State Design

Design improved workflows balancing standardization with appropriate flexibility:

- **Evidence-Based Design**: Incorporating proven best practices from literature and peers

- **Simulation Testing**: Modeling proposed changes before implementation

- **Stakeholder Co-Design**: Involving patients and staff in redesign efforts

- **Flexibility Planning**: Identifying where variation is appropriate and beneficial

Virginia Mason Medical Center used simulation modeling to test eight different configurations of their new oncology care workflow before implementation. This testing revealed that the initially preferred design would actually increase wait times under common demand scenarios, leading to significant redesign before deployment.

4. Implementation Planning

Develop comprehensive implementation strategies:

- **Phased Rollout Design**: Planning staged implementation to manage risk

- **Training and Support Planning**: Preparing stakeholders for new workflows

- **Technology Configuration**: Aligning systems with new process designs

- **Metric Development**: Establishing measures to track implementation success

Partners HealthCare developed a sophisticated implementation planning tool for workflow changes that incorporates analytics-based predictions of adoption challenges. The tool analyzes factors like stakeholder readiness, process complexity, and technology dependencies to generate customized implementation plans for different departments and roles.

5. Continuous Improvement

Establish mechanisms for ongoing optimization:

- **Real-Time Monitoring**: Tracking key performance indicators continuously

- **Anomaly Detection**: Identifying unexpected process deviations

- **Feedback Integration**: Capturing and analyzing stakeholder feedback

- **Iterative Refinement**: Making ongoing adjustments based on performance data

Mayo Clinic implemented a continuous improvement system for their clinic workflows that analyzes performance data daily and suggests refinements weekly. This approach has enabled them to achieve sustained improvement rather than the temporary gains often seen with traditional process improvement methods.

Balancing Standardization with Clinical Autonomy

One of the most significant challenges in healthcare workflow optimization is balancing standardization with appropriate clinical autonomy. Advanced analytics can actually enhance this balance rather than threatening it:

1. Evidence-Based Variation

Rather than eliminating all variation, sophisticated approaches distinguish between beneficial and problematic variation:

- **Outcome-Linked Variation Analysis**: Connecting process variations to patient outcomes

- **Appropriate Variation Identification**: Recognizing where clinical judgment should drive decisions

- **Standard Work with Decision Points**: Creating processes with explicit decision nodes for clinical judgment

- **Learning from Positive Deviance**: Identifying variations that produce better-than-expected outcomes

Geisinger Health System's workflow analytics program specifically identifies "positive deviants"—clinicians whose process variations consistently produce superior outcomes. Rather than enforcing rigid standardization, they study these variations to understand what might be incorporated into standard workflows.

2. Shared Decision Frameworks

Advanced workflow systems can support clinical decision-making rather than constraining it:

- **Clinical Decision Support Integration**: Providing relevant information at decision points

- **Cognitive Workflow Analysis**: Understanding the mental processes behind clinical decisions

- **Collaborative Filtering**: Suggesting approaches based on similar clinical scenarios

- **Explanation-Based Systems**: Providing rationales for workflow recommendations

University of Pennsylvania Health System implemented a collaborative decision support system for complex care planning that suggests workflow variations based on patient characteristics while providing clinicians with the evidence behind these suggestions. This approach improved adherence to evidence-based practices while preserving appropriate clinical autonomy.

3. Clinician Engagement in Design

The most successful workflow optimization initiatives deeply engage clinicians:

- **Clinician-Led Design Teams**: Ensuring clinical leadership of workflow initiatives

- **Usability Testing with Clinicians**: Validating designs with actual users

- **Clinical Impact Forecasting**: Predicting how changes will affect clinical practice

- **Ongoing Clinical Feedback Loops**: Continuously incorporating clinician insights

Cleveland Clinic established a Physician Informatics Council that evaluates all proposed workflow changes for their impact on clinical practice. This oversight ensures that efficiency gains don't come at the expense of clinical effectiveness or provider experience.

Practical Guidance for Healthcare Leaders

For organizations seeking to advance their workflow optimization capabilities, consider this practical guidance:

1. Start with End-to-End Patient Journeys

Rather than optimizing isolated departmental processes, focus on complete patient journeys:

- **Journey Mapping**: Document the entire patient experience across departments

- **Handoff Analysis**: Pay special attention to transitions between departments

- **Outcome Linkage**: Connect process metrics to patient outcomes

- **Experience Integration**: Incorporate patient perspectives in all analyses

Organizations that optimize only within departments often create "locally optimal, globally suboptimal" processes that improve metrics in one area while creating problems elsewhere. Journey-focused optimization prevents this pitfall.

2. Invest in Visualization and Communication

The most sophisticated analytics provide little value if stakeholders can't understand the insights:

- **Interactive Process Visualizations**: Create intuitive representations of complex processes

- **Role-Based Dashboards**: Tailor information to different stakeholders' needs

- **Narrative Development**: Frame data in compelling stories that drive action

- **Simulation Animations**: Use visual simulations to communicate potential changes

Mayo Clinic found that adoption of workflow changes increased by over 40% when they used interactive visualizations rather than traditional process documentation to communicate with stakeholders.

3. Balance Quick Wins with Transformational Change

Effective workflow optimization programs include both short-term improvements and longer-term transformation:

- **Rapid Improvement Cycles**: Implement high-impact, low-complexity changes quickly

- **Foundation Building**: Simultaneously develop capabilities for more complex changes

- **Value Realization Tracking**: Measure and communicate the impact of improvements

- **Capability Development**: Use each project to build organizational skills

Johns Hopkins Medicine maintains a portfolio of workflow initiatives that balances "quick win" projects (completion in 60-90 days) with transformational projects (12-18 months) to maintain momentum while building toward significant change.

4. Address Technology and Human Factors Together

Successful workflow optimization requires attention to both technological and human dimensions:

- **Sociotechnical System Design**: Consider technology and human factors simultaneously

- **Change Impact Assessment**: Evaluate how changes affect different stakeholders

- **Cognitive Load Analysis**: Ensure changes don't overwhelm cognitive capacity

- **Adoption Barrier Identification**: Proactively address potential resistance

Providence St. Joseph Health incorporates "day in the life" simulations for stakeholders before implementing new workflows. These simulations uncover potential adoption barriers that analytics alone might miss, enabling preemptive adjustments.

The Future of Workflow Optimization

Looking ahead, several emerging capabilities will further transform healthcare workflow optimization:

- **Ambient Intelligence**: Environmental sensing that automatically captures workflow data without manual entry

- **Intelligent Process Automation**: Systems that autonomously optimize routine processes

- **Federated Learning**: Cross-organizational workflow learning while preserving data privacy

- **Natural Language Interfaces**: Voice-based interaction with workflow systems

These advances will make workflow optimization more accessible, comprehensive, and integrated into daily operations rather than existing as a separate improvement activity.

Reflection Questions for Healthcare Leaders

As you consider your workflow optimization strategy, reflect on these questions:

1. How do current workflows impact patient and staff experiences? What data illuminates these impacts?

2. Where does process variation in your organization reflect appropriate clinical judgment versus unwarranted deviation?

3. How might more sophisticated workflow analytics change the way improvement initiatives are prioritized and designed in your organization?

4. What capabilities—technical and human—will your organization need to develop for advanced workflow optimization?

5. How can you balance standardization with appropriate autonomy in your clinical processes?

By thoughtfully applying advanced analytics to workflow optimization, healthcare organizations can create processes that simultaneously improve efficiency, enhance clinical outcomes, and elevate human experiences: for both patients and providers.

Capacity Planning and Demand Forecasting

From Reactive to Proactive Capacity Management

During the winter surge of 2023, while many hospitals scrambled to find beds for an influx of respiratory patients, Northwell Health was ready. Their advanced capacity planning system had predicted the surge weeks in advance based on multiple data streams: ED visit patterns, testing data, regional epidemiological signals, and historical seasonal trends. This foresight allowed them to adjust staffing, modify elective schedules, and prepare surge spaces before the crisis hit, avoiding the last-minute scramble that characterized many peer institutions.

This scenario illustrates the evolution from reactive to proactive capacity management—an evolution enabled by advanced analytics. While the resource allocation approaches discussed in the previous chapter help optimize existing capacity, advanced capacity planning focuses on predicting future needs and developing strategies to meet them. This predictive orientation represents a more sophisticated application of operations analytics.

Capacity planning connects directly to the workflow optimization we just explored. Optimized workflows increase effective capacity without additional resources, while capacity constraints shape workflow design. These interconnections highlight the integrated nature of advanced operations analytics.

Dimensions of Healthcare Capacity

Healthcare capacity planning spans multiple dimensions:

1. **Physical Capacity**: Beds, rooms, and physical infrastructure

2. **Human Capacity**: Clinical and non-clinical staffing

3. **Equipment Capacity**: Diagnostic and therapeutic technologies

4. **Time Capacity**: Scheduling and availability

5. **Virtual Capacity**: Telehealth and digital care capabilities

Advanced analytics enables integrated planning across these dimensions rather than the siloed approaches that characterized traditional capacity management.

Advanced Analytics Applications in Capacity Planning

1. Multi-Factor Demand Forecasting

Traditional demand forecasting relied heavily on historical patterns and simple trends. Advanced approaches incorporate multiple factors:

- **Multi-variable Modeling**: Incorporating diverse predictive factors beyond historical utilization

- **External Data Integration**: Including community factors like demographics, disease prevalence, and social determinants

- **Signal Detection**: Identifying early indicators of demand shifts

- **Uncertainty Quantification**: Expressing predictions as probability distributions rather than point estimates

Cleveland Clinic's demand forecasting model incorporates over 200 variables—including traditional utilization metrics, population health data, scheduled procedures, provider productivity, and even weather patterns. This comprehensive approach improved forecast accuracy by 40% compared to their previous method.

2. Dynamic Capacity Modeling

Rather than treating capacity as fixed, advanced analytics enables dynamic modeling:

- **Flexible Capacity Simulation**: Modeling different capacity configurations based on demand scenarios

- **Capacity Elasticity Analysis**: Identifying where and how capacity can flex to meet changing needs

- **Rate-Limiting Factor Identification**: Pinpointing the constraining elements in capacity systems

- **Virtual and Physical Capacity Integration**: Modeling how digital capabilities can complement physical resources

Stanford Health Care developed a capacity elasticity model that identifies how different services can expand or contract based on demand fluctuations. This model guided their COVID-19 response, enabling them to increase ICU capacity by 73% while maintaining essential services.

3. Scenario Planning and Stress Testing

Advanced organizations use analytics to prepare for a range of possible futures:

- **Scenario Generation**: Developing plausible future scenarios based on multiple factors

- **Capacity Stress Testing**: Assessing system performance under extreme conditions

- **Recovery Planning**: Modeling the return to normal operations after disruptions

- **Resilience Analysis**: Identifying vulnerabilities in capacity systems

Mayo Clinic conducts quarterly capacity stress tests that simulate multiple scenarios, from disease outbreaks to infrastructure failures to major community events. These exercises have identified critical vulnerabilities that would have remained hidden in standard planning processes.

Regional Health System Planning

Healthcare capacity increasingly requires coordination beyond individual organizations:

1. Regional Demand Forecasting

Advanced analytics enables planning at community and regional levels:

- **Population Health Modeling**: Predicting community healthcare needs based on demographic and health status data

- **Care Migration Analysis**: Tracking how patients move between facilities and systems

- **Service Distribution Optimization**: Modeling optimal distribution of services across a region

- **Equity Impact Assessment**: Evaluating how capacity decisions affect healthcare access across different populations

The Maryland Health Services Cost Review Commission implemented a regional capacity planning system that analyzes needs across the entire state. This approach identified opportunities to reduce duplicative investments while addressing care gaps in underserved communities.

2. Collaborative Capacity Management

Analytics facilitates coordination across organizations:

- **Shared Early Warning Systems**: Collective monitoring of demand signals

- **Cross-System Load Balancing**: Coordinating patient distribution during high-demand periods

- **Mutual Aid Modeling**: Planning resource sharing during emergencies

- **Coordinated Expansion Planning**: Aligning capacity investments across systems

During recent natural disasters, health systems in Louisiana used a collaborative analytics platform to coordinate patient transfers and resource sharing. This coordination maintained care access despite significant facility damage and enabled more rapid recovery.

3. Public-Private Planning Integration

Advanced capacity planning bridges public and private healthcare resources:

- **Integrated Capacity Tracking**: Monitoring both public and private resources

- **Emergency Response Modeling**: Simulating coordinated responses to public health emergencies

- **Resource Allocation Algorithms**: Optimizing distribution of limited resources

- **Cross-Sector Impact Analysis**: Evaluating how healthcare capacity affects and is affected by other sectors

The Northwest Healthcare Response Network developed an integrated capacity management system that coordinates 35 hospitals and numerous public health agencies. This system proved invaluable during COVID-19, enabling coordinated resource distribution that matched patient needs with available capacity.

Implementation Considerations for Advanced Capacity Planning

Implementing sophisticated capacity planning requires attention to several critical factors:

1. Data Integration and Quality

Effective capacity planning depends on diverse, high-quality data:

- **Multi-source Data Integration**: Combining internal and external data sources

- **Data Latency Reduction**: Minimizing delays in data availability

- **Data Quality Management**: Ensuring accuracy and completeness

- **Metadata Management**: Maintaining clear definitions and provenance

Partners HealthCare invested in a data integration platform specifically for capacity planning that reduced data latency from weeks to hours while dramatically improving quality. This foundation enabled much more responsive planning and adjustment.

2. Modeling and Analytical Approaches

Capacity planning requires sophisticated analytical methods:

- **Time Series Analysis**: Advanced techniques for detecting patterns in temporal data

- **Machine Learning for Prediction**: Algorithms that identify complex relationships in demand drivers

- **Discrete Event Simulation**: Modeling capacity systems with appropriate randomness

- **Optimization Algorithms**: Identifying optimal capacity configurations under constraints

University of California San Francisco Medical Center developed a hybrid modeling approach that combines machine learning for demand prediction with discrete event simulation for capacity planning. This combination improved prediction accuracy while enabling realistic modeling of operational constraints.

3. Decision Support Integration

Analytics must integrate into planning and operational processes:

- **Executive Dashboards**: Providing strategic capacity insights for leadership

- **Operational Decision Support**: Translating forecasts into actionable recommendations

- **Alert and Notification Systems**: Communicating capacity risks proactively

- **Feedback Loops**: Capturing actual outcomes to improve future forecasts

Cleveland Clinic implemented a tiered decision support structure that provides different capacity insights for strategic planning (3-5 years), tactical planning (3-18 months), and operational management (daily-weekly). This structure ensures the right information reaches the right decision-makers at the right time.

4. Governance and Accountability

Effective capacity planning requires clear governance:

- **Capacity Planning Oversight**: Establishing responsibility for planning processes

- **Cross-Functional Collaboration**: Ensuring coordination across departments

- **Forecast Accuracy Monitoring**: Tracking and improving prediction performance

- **Decision Accountability**: Clarifying who makes capacity decisions based on analytics

Geisinger Health System established a Capacity Planning Council with representation from clinical, operational, and financial leadership. This governance structure has enabled more coherent planning and clearer accountability for capacity decisions.

Practical Guidance for Healthcare Leaders

For organizations seeking to enhance their capacity planning capabilities, consider this practical guidance:

1. Start with Strategic Alignment

Before investing in advanced analytics, clarify how capacity planning supports strategic goals:

- **Strategic Capacity Requirements**: Define what capacity will be needed to achieve strategic objectives

- **Planning Horizon Alignment**: Match planning timeframes to strategic timeframes

- **Investment Prioritization**: Focus analytical capabilities on strategically important capacity dimensions

- **Metric Development**: Establish measures that connect capacity decisions to strategic outcomes

Memorial Sloan Kettering Cancer Center aligned their capacity planning initiative explicitly with their strategic goal of reducing time-to-treatment for new cancer patients. This alignment focused analytics development and ensured executive support.

2. Build Incrementally with Early Wins

Develop capabilities through a phased approach:

- **Forecasting Accuracy Baseline**: Establish current performance to demonstrate improvement

- **Focused Initial Applications**: Apply new capabilities to high-priority capacity challenges

- **Value Demonstration**: Measure and communicate the impact of improved planning

- **Capability Expansion**: Gradually extend to additional capacity dimensions

Kaiser Permanente began their advanced capacity planning journey with a focused application to operating room utilization—a high-value, clearly defined problem. This initial success built credibility for more ambitious applications.

3. Integrate with Operational Planning

Connect capacity insights to operational decisions:

- **Planning Process Integration**: Embed capacity analytics in existing planning cycles

- **Decision Protocol Development**: Create clear processes for acting on capacity insights

- **Cross-functional Communication**: Ensure insights reach all relevant stakeholders

- **Scenario Response Planning**: Prepare operational responses to different capacity scenarios

Children's Hospital of Philadelphia developed a capacity alert system that initiates specific operational protocols when forecasts predict capacity constraints. This system has reduced crisis management by enabling proactive operational adjustments.

4. Balance Precision with Interpretability

Ensure analytical sophistication doesn't sacrifice understandability:

- **Transparent Modeling**: Use approaches that stakeholders can comprehend

- **Assumption Clarity**: Make planning assumptions explicit and adjustable

- **Visualization for Understanding**: Present complex capacity data in intuitive formats

- **Scenario Storytelling**: Frame potential futures in narrative terms

Stanford Health redesigned their capacity planning reports after realizing that operational leaders struggled to interpret probabilistic forecasts. Their revised approach presents scenarios as narratives with clear decision implications, significantly improving utilization of the analytics.

Case Study Elements: Regional Capacity Coordination in Minnesota

Health systems in Minnesota developed a collaborative capacity planning approach that demonstrates advanced analytics in action. Key elements included:

- Integration of data across competing health systems while preserving appropriate privacy

- Development of a shared demand forecasting model that improved prediction accuracy for all participants

- Implementation of a load-balancing algorithm that optimized patient distribution during capacity constraints

- Creation of a joint capacity investment framework that reduced duplicative resources while improving access

This collaboration demonstrates how advanced analytics can facilitate regional planning beyond individual organizational boundaries. We'll explore this case more fully in our chapter-wide case study.

The Future of Capacity Planning Analytics

Looking ahead, several emerging capabilities will further transform healthcare capacity planning:

- **Digital Twin Simulation**: Complete virtual replicas of healthcare delivery systems for planning

- **Autonomous Capacity Adjustment**: AI-driven systems that implement capacity changes based on forecasts

- **Cross-Industry Integrated Planning**: Coordination with adjacent sectors like transportation and housing

- **Personalized Demand Forecasting**: Predicting individual patient needs and preferences

These advances will enable more responsive, precise capacity planning that better serves both routine needs and unexpected events.

Reflection Questions for Healthcare Leaders

As you consider your capacity planning strategy, reflect on these questions:

1. How accurate are your current demand forecasts? What factors might improve their precision?

2. How does capacity planning in your organization connect to strategic priorities? What would strengthen this connection?

3. What capacity dimensions present the greatest challenges in your organization? How might advanced analytics address these challenges?

4. What regional coordination currently exists for capacity planning? Where might greater collaboration create value?

5. How resilient are your capacity systems to unexpected disruptions? What stress testing might reveal vulnerabilities?

By applying advanced analytics to capacity planning, healthcare organizations can move from reactive scrambling to proactive preparation—ensuring the right resources are available to meet patient needs while optimizing investment and improving resilience.

Staff Management and Workforce Analytics

The Human Element in Healthcare Operations

When Memorial Hospital implemented a new staffing model based on advanced analytics, something unexpected happened. Not only did patient outcomes improve as predicted, but nurse turnover dropped by 28% in six months. Exit interviews revealed a common theme: nurses felt their workloads had become more manageable and predictable, and they could spend more time on meaningful patient care. This experience illustrates a crucial insight about healthcare operations—staff wellbeing and operational performance are intimately connected.

Healthcare remains fundamentally human work. While technology and analytics transform many aspects of operations, the people who deliver care represent both the largest expense and the most critical resource in healthcare organizations. Staff management analytics has evolved from basic scheduling and productivity metrics to sophisticated approaches that optimize the workforce while enhancing wellbeing.

This section builds directly on the capacity planning concepts we just explored. Staff represents a critical capacity dimension, often the constraining factor in healthcare delivery. Staff management analytics extends capacity planning by focusing specifically on the human element, with particular attention to wellbeing alongside efficiency.

The Evolution of Workforce Analytics in Healthcare

Healthcare workforce analytics has progressed through several stages:

1. **Basic Productivity Measurement**: Simple ratios of staff to workload

2. **Staffing and Scheduling Optimization**: Analytics-driven staff allocation

3. **Workforce Planning and Forecasting**: Predictive models of staffing needs

4. **Performance and Engagement Analytics**: Data-driven approaches to staff development

5. **Wellbeing and Resilience Optimization**: Analytics that balance efficiency with sustainability

Most organizations currently operate in stages 2-3, with leading institutions advancing into stages 4-5. This evolution reflects a shift from viewing staff primarily as a cost to be minimized toward recognizing them as a strategic asset to be optimized and sustained.

Advanced Analytics Applications in Staff Management

1. Predictive Workforce Planning

Beyond basic staffing ratios, advanced analytics enables sophisticated workforce planning:

- **Multi-factor Staffing Models**: Incorporating patient acuity, care complexity, and other factors beyond census

- **Skills-Based Planning**: Ensuring the right skill mix for patient needs

- **Lead Indicator Monitoring**: Identifying early signals of staffing challenges

- **Scenario-Based Planning**: Preparing for different possible staffing futures

Cleveland Clinic implemented a predictive staffing model that incorporates over 30 variables to determine optimal staffing levels. This model reduced both understaffing and overstaffing events by more than 40%, improving both care quality and cost management.

2. Dynamic Staff Allocation

Rather than static staffing plans, advanced analytics enables responsive allocation:

- **Real-Time Workload Monitoring**: Tracking actual versus predicted workload

- **Adaptive Assignment Algorithms**: Adjusting staff assignments based on changing conditions

- **Cross-Training Optimization**: Identifying where flexible roles create the greatest value

- **Team Composition Analysis**: Determining optimal team configurations for different scenarios

Stanford Health Care implemented a dynamic nurse allocation system that continuously monitors workload and adjusts assignments throughout shifts. This approach reduced workload variation by 35% while improving continuity of care.

3. Wellbeing and Burnout Prevention

The most sophisticated organizations use analytics to maintain workforce sustainability:

- **Burnout Risk Prediction**: Identifying individuals and groups at high risk

- **Workload Impact Modeling**: Quantifying how operational decisions affect staff wellbeing

- **Recovery Analysis**: Ensuring adequate recovery time between intensive work periods

- **Engagement Factor Identification**: Determining what workplace elements drive engagement

Providence St. Joseph Health developed a wellbeing analytics platform that integrates workload data, schedule patterns, and engagement indicators to predict burnout risk. This system has guided interventions that reduced nursing turnover by 23% while improving patient satisfaction.

4. Career Path and Talent Development

Advanced analytics informs long-term workforce development:

- **Skills Gap Analysis**: Identifying future capability needs versus current capabilities

- **Career Trajectory Modeling**: Predicting career development patterns and needs

- **Learning Impact Analysis**: Measuring the effectiveness of development investments

- **Succession Planning Analytics**: Data-driven identification of future leaders

Kaiser Permanente's talent analytics program identifies emerging clinical leaders based on a sophisticated model that considers clinical outcomes, peer collaboration patterns, and patient feedback. This approach has improved leadership selection compared to traditional methods.

Ethical Considerations and Privacy Concerns

Workforce analytics raises important ethical questions that organizations must address:

1. Privacy and Consent

Staff data requires careful handling:

- **Transparent Purpose Communication**: Clearly explaining how data will be used

- **Consent Management**: Ensuring appropriate consent for data use

- **De-identification Practices**: Protecting individual privacy in analyses

- **Access Control**: Limiting who can view sensitive workforce data

Mayo Clinic established a workforce data governance council that includes staff representatives from different roles and levels. This council reviews all proposed workforce analytics to ensure privacy protection and ethical use.

2. Algorithmic Fairness

Analytics systems can inadvertently perpetuate or amplify biases:

- **Bias Detection**: Identifying and addressing algorithmic bias

- **Diverse Input Data**: Ensuring training data represents workforce diversity

- **Outcome Equity Monitoring**: Tracking how analytics affects different staff groups

- **Transparency in Methods**: Making analytical approaches understandable to stakeholders

University of Pennsylvania Health System conducts regular equity audits of their workforce analytics systems, testing for differential impacts across demographic groups and adjusting algorithms when disparities are identified.

3. Balancing Efficiency and Humanity

Perhaps most fundamentally, workforce analytics must balance operational goals with human needs:

- **Multi-dimensional Optimization**: Considering wellbeing alongside efficiency

- **Staff Input Integration**: Incorporating frontline perspectives in analytics design

- **Flexibility Preservation**: Maintaining room for human judgment and adaptation

- **Purpose Connection**: Ensuring analytics supports meaningful work rather than mechanizing it

Johns Hopkins Medicine developed a balanced scorecard for their workforce analytics program that gives equal weight to operational metrics, staff wellbeing measures, and patient outcomes. This balanced approach prevents optimization of any single dimension at the expense of others.

Implementation Guidance for Healthcare Leaders

Implementing advanced workforce analytics requires thoughtful leadership:

1. Begin with Trust Building

Staff may reasonably be concerned about how workforce data will be used:

- **Inclusive Governance**: Involve staff in designing analytics approaches

- **Clear Value Communication**: Articulate how analytics will benefit both organization and staff

- **Transparent Reporting**: Share results openly with those affected

- **Feedback Integration**: Adjust approaches based on staff input

Partners HealthCare began their workforce analytics journey with a series of staff forums where leaders explicitly committed to principles of fair and beneficial use. This foundation of trust enabled much broader adoption than peer organizations achieved.

2. Connect to Organizational Values

Workforce analytics should visibly reflect organizational values:

- **Mission Alignment**: Ensure analytics approaches support organizational mission

- **Value Expression**: Design systems that embody stated values

- **Cultural Consistency**: Align analytics with desired organizational culture

- **Purpose Reinforcement**: Use analytics to strengthen connection to purpose

Cleveland Clinic frames their workforce analytics program explicitly as an expression of their value of "caregivers first"—using data to create a more supportive and sustainable work environment rather than simply driving efficiency.

3. Start with High-Impact Applications

Build momentum through focused initial applications:

- **Pain Point Identification**: Address recognized workforce challenges

- **Rapid Value Demonstration**: Generate early wins that demonstrate value

- **Staff-Identified Priorities**: Focus on issues staff identify as important

- **Balanced Benefit Creation**: Ensure benefits flow to staff as well as organization

Intermountain Healthcare launched their advanced workforce analytics program with a focus on reducing administrative burden, a priority consistently identified in staff surveys. This focus generated immediate goodwill while delivering organizational benefits.

4. Develop Analytical Literacy

Build capacity to use workforce insights effectively:

- **Leader Education**: Develop leaders' ability to interpret and apply analytics

- **Staff Analytical Skills**: Build basic data literacy among all staff

- **Decision Support Design**: Create intuitive tools that translate analytics into action

- **Use Case Libraries**: Build repositories of successful workforce analytics applications

Mayo Clinic created a workforce analytics academy that trains leaders across disciplines in using workforce data effectively. This investment in analytical literacy has dramatically improved the translation of insights into action compared to peer institutions that focused solely on analytical systems.

Leadership Implications: Moving Beyond Metrics to Meaning

Advanced workforce analytics has profound implications for healthcare leadership:

1. From Control to Enablement

Traditional workforce management focused on control and compliance. Advanced analytics enables a shift toward enablement:

- **Decision Support vs. Direction**: Providing insights that inform rather than dictate decisions

- **Frontline Empowerment**: Equipping staff with analytics to guide their own work

- **Collaborative Improvement**: Using data to facilitate staff-led enhancement

- **Purpose Connection**: Leveraging analytics to strengthen connection to mission

Cleveland Clinic's nurse staffing system evolved from a centralized assignment approach to a collaborative platform where nurses use analytics to develop their own assignment plans. This evolution improved both operational outcomes and staff satisfaction.

2. From Standardization to Personalization

Rather than treating all staff identically, advanced analytics enables appropriate personalization:

- **Individual Workload Adaptation**: Adjusting assignments based on individual capabilities and circumstances

- **Personalized Development**: Tailoring growth opportunities to individual needs

- **Work Pattern Flexibility**: Accommodating diverse preferences where possible

- **Life Stage Consideration**: Adapting expectations across career stages

Stanford Health Care implemented a personalized scheduling system that considers individual preferences, life circumstances, and career stage. This approach has significantly improved retention of both early-career and late-career nurses who previously left due to inflexible scheduling.

3. From Reactive to Proactive Support

Advanced analytics enables leaders to provide support before problems emerge:

- **Early Intervention**: Addressing challenges before they affect performance or wellbeing

- **Proactive Resource Allocation**: Providing additional support based on predicted needs

- **Preventive Wellbeing Practices**: Implementing measures to maintain resilience

- **Strategic Development**: Building capabilities ahead of anticipated needs

Intermountain Healthcare's leadership development analytics identifies emerging leaders 18-24 months before traditional succession planning would recognize them. This foresight enables earlier development investment, creating a more robust leadership pipeline.

4. From Measurement to Meaning

Perhaps most importantly, advanced workforce analytics can help leaders focus on what truly matters:

- **Outcome Orientation**: Focusing on results rather than activities

- **Value Alignment**: Ensuring metrics reflect organizational values

- **Purpose Connection**: Using data to strengthen connection to mission

- **Holistic Assessment**: Considering wellbeing alongside performance

University of California San Francisco Medical Center redesigned their physician performance dashboard to highlight patient impact measures rather than productivity metrics. This shift improved physician engagement while maintaining financial performance.

The Future of Healthcare Workforce Analytics

Looking ahead, several emerging capabilities will further transform workforce analytics:

- **Augmented Work Design**: AI-assisted redesign of roles and responsibilities

- **Cognitive Demand Modeling**: Sophisticated assessment of mental workload

- **Team Effectiveness Prediction**: Advanced modeling of team dynamics and performance

- **Wellness-Centered Scheduling**: Systems that optimize for wellbeing alongside operational needs

These advances promise a future where workforce analytics creates more sustainable, satisfying healthcare work that simultaneously improves operational performance and human experience.

Reflection Questions for Healthcare Leaders

As you consider your workforce analytics strategy, reflect on these questions:

1. How do current workforce metrics in your organization balance operational and wellbeing considerations? What might a more balanced approach include?

2. What signals might provide early warning of workforce challenges in your organization? How could these be systematically monitored?

3. How do staff in your organization perceive workforce analytics? What might increase trust in data-driven approaches?

4. What ethical guardrails does your organization have for workforce analytics? How might these be strengthened?

5. How might advanced workforce analytics change leadership practices in your organization? What capabilities would leaders need to develop?

By thoughtfully applying advanced analytics to workforce management, healthcare organizations can create more sustainable, satisfying work environments that simultaneously improve operational performance, staff wellbeing, and patient care. The most successful organizations recognize that in healthcare, taking care of those who provide care is not just ethically right but operationally essential.

Facility Management and Asset Tracking

The Physical Environment as a Strategic Asset

When the new patient tower opened at University Medical Center, something remarkable happened. Patient satisfaction scores rose 18% compared to the old facility, despite the same staff delivering the same clinical care. Meanwhile, operational efficiency improved, nurses walked 30% fewer steps per shift, supply costs decreased by 12%, and equipment utilization rates increased by 25%. These improvements didn't happen by chance. They resulted from sophisticated analytics that optimized the facility design, equipment placement, and workflow integration.

Healthcare facilities and equipment represent massive investments—often billions of dollars for a major medical center. These physical assets profoundly affect both patient experiences and operational efficiency. Advanced analytics transforms how organizations design, manage, and optimize these investments, moving from reactive maintenance to proactive optimization.

This section builds directly on previous topics—facility design shapes workflows, buildings house capacity, and the physical environment significantly impacts staff experience. Facility and asset analytics represents the integration of operational optimization into the physical environment of care.

The Evolution of Facility Analytics in Healthcare

Healthcare facility management has progressed through several stages:

1. **Basic Maintenance Management**: Focusing on building systems and repairs

2. **Regulatory Compliance Tracking**: Ensuring adherence to safety and accreditation requirements

3. **Operational Cost Management**: Optimizing facility-related expenses

4. **Experience-Centered Design**: Creating environments that enhance patient and staff experiences

5. **Integrated Performance Optimization**: Using facilities to drive broader operational goals

Most organizations currently operate in stages 2-3, with leading institutions advancing into stages 4-5. This evolution reflects a shift from viewing facilities primarily as cost centers toward recognizing them as strategic assets that enable exceptional care delivery.

Advanced Analytics Applications in Facility Management

1. Experience-Centered Design Analytics

Leading organizations use analytics to create environments that enhance human experiences:

- **Movement Pattern Analysis**: Studying how people navigate and use spaces

- **Environmental Factor Modeling**: Quantifying how design elements affect experience

- **Sensory Experience Assessment**: Measuring the sensory impact of environments

- **Therapeutic Design Evaluation**: Assessing how environments contribute to healing

Mayo Clinic's Center for Innovation uses sophisticated analytics to study how facility design affects both patient and staff experiences. Their analysis of sound patterns in different unit designs led to acoustic modifications that improved patient sleep quality by 28% and reduced staff cognitive errors by 14%.

2. Operational Integration Analytics

Advanced analytics connects facility management to broader operational goals:

- **Workflow-Centered Space Utilization**: Aligning facility use with optimal workflows

- **Capacity-Operation Alignment**: Ensuring facilities support capacity goals

- **Staff Impact Assessment**: Measuring how facility factors affect workforce performance

- **Care Model Integration**: Designing spaces that enable innovative care models

Cleveland Clinic used simulation modeling to test how different emergency department layouts would affect operational metrics. This analysis led to a redesign that improved throughput by 20% while enhancing both patient and staff satisfaction.

3. Smart Building Systems

Analytics-driven building systems create more responsive environments:

- **Predictive Environmental Control**: Anticipating and adjusting environmental conditions

- **Demand-Based System Management**: Optimizing building systems based on actual usage

- **Anomaly Detection**: Identifying unusual patterns that may indicate problems

- **Energy Optimization**: Balancing efficiency with comfort and clinical needs

Johns Hopkins Hospital implemented a machine learning system that predicts and adjusts environmental conditions based on historical patterns, current occupancy, and external factors. This system reduced energy costs by 23% while improving environmental comfort scores.

4. Advanced Asset Management

Beyond basic tracking, advanced analytics optimizes equipment utilization:

- **Utilization Pattern Analysis**: Identifying how equipment is actually used

- **Predictive Maintenance**: Anticipating maintenance needs before failures

- **Clinical-Operational Integration**: Connecting equipment management to clinical needs

- **Total Cost of Ownership Optimization**: Balancing acquisition, maintenance, and operational costs

UCSF Medical Center's advanced asset management system analyzes utilization patterns for high-value equipment, identifying opportunities to reduce fleet size while improving availability. This approach saved over $12 million in capital costs while reducing clinical delays.

Integration with Clinical Workflows

The most sophisticated facility analytics directly supports clinical work:

1. Workflow-Centered Design

Rather than designing and then adapting workflows to them, leading organizations use analytics to create environments optimized for specific workflows:

- **Care Process Modeling**: Analyzing clinical workflows to inform design

- **Simulation-Based Design Testing**: Evaluating facility designs using workflow simulations

- **Adaptability Assessment**: Ensuring spaces can evolve with changing care models

- **Multi-disciplinary Integration**: Creating environments that support team-based care

Stanford Healthcare's "workflow-first" design approach for their new hospital involved detailed modeling of over 300 clinical processes before finalizing architectural plans. This approach created spaces that demonstrably enhance clinical efficiency while improving both patient and provider experiences.

2. Environmental Factors in Clinical Outcomes

Advanced analytics quantifies how facility elements affect clinical results:

- **Environment-Outcome Correlation**: Analyzing relationships between design factors and patient outcomes

- **Infection Control Analytics**: Identifying facility features that affect infection rates

- **Safety Enhancement Design**: Creating environments that reduce error risk

- **Recovery-Promoting Features**: Identifying elements that accelerate healing

The Center for Health Design's analytics program has quantified the impact of specific design elements on clinical outcomes across multiple facilities. Their analysis found that rooms with certain natural light characteristics were associated with 22% shorter lengths of stay for some conditions, controlling for clinical factors.

3. Real-Time Location Intelligence

Location analytics creates new possibilities for care delivery:

- **Patient Flow Optimization**: Using location data to improve movement through facilities

- **Team Coordination Enhancement**: Facilitating more efficient staff collaboration

- **Resource Proximity Analysis**: Ensuring critical resources are optimally located

- **Safety and Security Improvement**: Using location data to enhance protection

Geisinger Health System implemented a real-time location system that improved trauma team assembly time by 37% by optimizing staff and equipment positioning and creating location-aware alerting systems.

Practical Implementation Guidance

Implementing advanced facility analytics requires practical approaches:

1. Start with High-Impact Areas

Focus initial efforts where facility factors significantly affect outcomes:

- **Critical Pathway Analysis**: Identifying where facility elements impact crucial processes

- **Pain Point Assessment**: Addressing known facility-related challenges

- **High-Volume Area Focus**: Optimizing spaces used most frequently

- **Renovation Planning Integration**: Incorporating analytics into planned changes

Memorial Sloan Kettering Cancer Center began their facility analytics program by focusing on chemotherapy treatment areas—high-volume spaces where environmental factors significantly affect patient experience. This focused approach delivered meaningful improvements before expanding to other areas.

2. Build Cross-Functional Collaboration

Effective facility analytics requires collaboration across traditionally separate domains:

- **Clinical-Facilities Partnerships**: Connecting clinical and facilities expertise

- **IT-Facilities Integration**: Bringing together technology and physical infrastructure

- **Operations-Design Collaboration**: Linking operational and architectural perspectives

- **Patient Experience-Facilities Alignment**: Connecting experience design with physical space

Cleveland Clinic established a Facilities Clinical Council that pairs facilities engineers with clinicians to identify and solve challenges at the intersection of physical environment and care delivery. This partnership has generated innovations that neither group could have developed independently.

3. Implement Modular, Scalable Approaches

Build capabilities that can grow over time:

- **Targeted IoT Deployment**: Starting with high-value sensor applications

- **Scalable Data Architecture**: Creating systems that can expand gradually

- **Proof-of-Concept Testing**: Validating approaches before broad implementation

- **Incremental Sophistication**: Beginning with basic analytics before advancing to more complex methods

Kaiser Permanente implemented a modular approach to facility analytics, beginning with environmental monitoring in clinical areas before expanding to comprehensive systems. This approach delivered early value while building toward more sophisticated capabilities.

4. Focus on Actionable Insights

Ensure analytics leads to practical improvements:

- **Decision Support Integration**: Connecting insights to facility-related decisions

- **Operational Protocol Development**: Creating standard responses to analytics insights

- **User-Friendly Visualization**: Making facility data accessible to non-technical users

- **Feedback Loop Creation**: Capturing the impact of facility changes for continuous improvement

New York-Presbyterian Hospital developed a facility analytics dashboard specifically designed for unit managers, translating complex data into actionable recommendations. This approach significantly increased the implementation of analytics-driven improvements compared to more technical presentations.

The Future of Healthcare Facility Analytics

Looking ahead, several emerging capabilities will further transform facility management:

- **Autonomous Building Systems**: Self-optimizing environments that adapt to changing conditions

- **Digital Twins**: Complete virtual replicas of facilities for simulation and testing

- **Augmented Reality Facility Management**: Visualization of systems and data within physical spaces

- **Biophilic Analytics**: Quantifying how natural elements affect healthcare outcomes

These advances promise increasingly responsive, healing environments that actively contribute to care delivery rather than simply housing it.

Reflection Questions for Healthcare Leaders

As you consider your facility analytics strategy, reflect on these questions:

1. How do your facilities enhance or hinder optimal workflows? What data might illuminate these relationships?

2. What facility-related factors most affect patient and staff experiences in your organization? How are these measured and monitored?

3. How might more sophisticated facility analytics change capital investment decisions in your organization?

4. What collaboration currently exists between clinical, operational, and facilities teams in your organization? How might this be enhanced?

5. What environmental factors in your facilities might be affecting clinical outcomes? How could these be better understood?

By thoughtfully applying advanced analytics to facility management, healthcare organizations can create environments that actively contribute to exceptional care—spaces that enhance healing, support efficient operations, and elevate human experiences for both patients and staff.

Quality Management and Compliance

The Culmination of Operational Excellence

When Elizabeth Chen was admitted to University Hospital with severe sepsis, a remarkable system sprang into action. Analytics had identified her as high-risk before symptoms fully manifested, the sepsis protocol was immediately initiated, appropriate antibiotics were administered within 37 minutes of arrival, and her care team received real-time guidance based on her specific risk factors. The result: Elizabeth recovered fully, avoiding the ICU entirely. This outcome wasn't luck, it represented the culmination of years of work integrating advanced quality analytics into every aspect of operations.

Quality and safety represent the ultimate purpose of healthcare operations. While the previous sections explored operational areas that support care delivery, quality management focuses directly on care outcomes and experiences. Advanced analytics transforms quality management from retrospective review to predictive intervention, creating systems that actively prevent harm and promote excellence.

This section represents the integration point for all previous topics—resource allocation, workflow optimization, capacity planning, workforce management, and facility design all ultimately serve quality care delivery. Advanced quality analytics draws on and integrates these operational domains to drive exceptional outcomes.

The Evolution of Quality Analytics in Healthcare

Healthcare quality management has progressed through several stages:

1. **Retrospective Review**: Analyzing adverse events after they occur

2. **Metric Monitoring**: Tracking quality indicators and thresholds

3. **Predictive Risk Detection**: Identifying potential quality issues before harm occurs

4. **Prescriptive Intervention**: Recommending specific actions to prevent harm

5. **Learning Health Systems**: Creating organizations that continuously improve through systematic learning

Most organizations currently operate in stages 2-3, with leading institutions advancing into stages 4-5. This evolution reflects a shift from reactive quality management toward proactive quality optimization—a shift enabled by advanced analytics.

Advanced Analytics Applications in Quality Management

1. Predictive Safety Analytics

Beyond tracking past events, advanced analytics anticipates and prevents harm:

- **Predictive Risk Modeling**: Identifying patients at risk for complications or adverse events

- **Real-Time Safety Monitoring**: Continuously analyzing data for emerging safety threats

- **Intervention Impact Prediction**: Forecasting the likely effectiveness of safety interventions

- **Near-Miss Pattern Recognition**: Detecting patterns in near-miss events to prevent future harm

HCA Healthcare developed a predictive algorithm for sepsis that identifies patients at risk up to 6 hours before clinical signs would typically trigger intervention. This system has reduced sepsis mortality by 30% across their hospitals.

2. Quality Variation Reduction

Advanced analytics identifies and addresses unwarranted variation:

- **Care Pattern Analysis**: Detecting variations in practice across providers and settings

- **Outcome-Linked Variation Assessment**: Determining which variations affect outcomes

- **Appropriate Standardization Identification**: Recognizing where standardization would improve quality

- **Beneficial Variation Preservation**: Maintaining variations that appropriately address patient differences

Intermountain Healthcare's advanced variation analytics identified patterns in diabetic care that were associated with significantly different outcomes. By reducing unwarranted variation while preserving appropriate personalization, they improved glycemic control in their diabetic population by 23%.

3. Learning Health System Implementation

The most sophisticated organizations implement systems that learn continuously:

- **Systematic Outcome Analysis**: Continuously evaluating the results of care processes

- **Rapid Cycle Improvement**: Implementing and testing changes quickly based on data

- **Knowledge Dissemination Systems**: Efficiently sharing insights across the organization

- **Organizational Learning Measurement**: Assessing how effectively the organization learns

Geisinger Health System implemented a learning health system platform that captures outcomes data, analyzes patterns, generates improvement hypotheses, tests interventions, and disseminates successful practices.

This system has accelerated their improvement cycle time by 65% compared to traditional approaches.

4. Integrated Compliance Management

Advanced analytics transforms regulatory compliance from burden to value:

- **Predictive Compliance Monitoring**: Identifying potential compliance issues before they occur

- **Automated Documentation Analysis**: Ensuring documentation meets regulatory requirements

- **Regulatory Change Impact Assessment**: Predicting how regulatory changes will affect operations

- **Compliance-Quality Integration**: Aligning compliance activities with quality improvement

Cleveland Clinic developed an integrated compliance analytics system that automatically reviews documentation for regulatory requirements while simultaneously identifying quality improvement opportunities. This approach has reduced compliance workload by 40% while improving quality performance.

Creating a Culture of Continuous Improvement

Advanced quality analytics requires corresponding cultural transformation:

1. From Blame to Systems Thinking

Analytics enables a shift from individual blame to system improvement:

- **Just Culture Implementation**: Using data to distinguish system and individual factors

- **Systemic Factor Identification**: Analyzing patterns to identify underlying causes

- **Blame-Free Reporting Encouragement**: Creating safe spaces for reporting concerns

- **Systems-Based Solution Development**: Designing interventions that address root causes

Johns Hopkins Medicine implemented a "systemic safety" program that uses advanced analytics to identify underlying patterns in safety events. This approach increased safety reporting by 217% while simultaneously reducing serious harm events by 37%.

2. Evidence-Based Improvement

Analytics strengthens the connection between evidence and practice:

- **Knowledge Integration Systems**: Connecting research evidence to point-of-care decisions

- **Practice-Based Evidence Creation**: Generating new evidence from practice patterns

- **Implementation Science Application**: Using data to improve adoption of best practices

- **Outcome-Based Protocol Adjustment**: Refining protocols based on actual outcomes

Mayo Clinic's evidence integration platform combines published research, practice patterns, and outcome data to generate continuously updated care recommendations. This system has improved adherence to evidence-based practices by 42% compared to traditional approaches.

3. Transparency and Accountability

Advanced analytics enables meaningful transparency:

- **Actionable Performance Transparency**: Sharing data in ways that drive improvement

- **Comparative Analysis**: Benchmarking performance against relevant comparators

- **Balanced Accountability Systems**: Creating fair methods for performance evaluation

- **Improvement-Focused Feedback**: Designing performance reports that facilitate improvement

University of Utah Health's transparency initiative shares provider-level quality data internally with rich contextual information that supports improvement. This approach has driven faster quality improvement than either public reporting or non-transparent systems.

4. Patient Partnership

The most advanced quality systems meaningfully involve patients:

- **Patient-Reported Outcomes Integration**: Incorporating patients' assessments of outcomes

- **Experience Analytics**: Analyzing detailed patient experience data

- **Co-Design Facilitation**: Using data to support collaborative design with patients

- **Patient-Centered Measurement**: Developing metrics that matter to patients

Stanford Health Care's patient partnership platform integrates patient-reported data with clinical metrics and uses advanced analytics to identify opportunities for improvement that matter most to patients. This approach has led to improvements that traditional quality systems missed.

Implementation Considerations: Beyond Technology

Implementing advanced quality analytics requires attention to several critical factors:

1. Leadership Commitment and Capability

Quality analytics requires sustained leadership support:

- **Executive Sponsorship**: Visible commitment from senior leaders

- **Resource Allocation**: Adequate investment in analytics capabilities

- **Governance Structures**: Clear oversight and direction

- **Leader Analytical Literacy**: Developing leaders' ability to use quality insights

Partners HealthCare created a Quality Analytics Academy specifically for executives and clinical leaders. This investment in leadership capability significantly improved the organization's ability to translate analytics into improvement.

2. Integration Across Domains

Effective quality analytics connects previously siloed areas:

- **Clinical-Operational Integration**: Linking clinical quality to operational performance

- **Safety-Efficiency Connection**: Balancing safety and efficiency goals

- **Experience-Outcome Alignment**: Connecting patient experience to clinical outcomes

- **Regulatory-Strategic Integration**: Aligning compliance with strategic priorities

Cleveland Clinic's integrated performance platform connects quality, safety, experience, operational, and financial metrics in a unified framework. This integration has enabled more coherent improvement efforts compared to traditional siloed approaches.

3. Meaningful Measurement

Analytics is only as valuable as the metrics it analyzes:

- **Outcome Focus**: Emphasizing results rather than processes where possible

- **Balanced Measurement**: Including multiple dimensions of quality

- **Actionable Metrics**: Selecting measures that can drive improvement

- **Patient-Centered Measurement**: Including what matters most to patients

Intermountain Healthcare revised their quality measurement framework to emphasize outcomes and patient priorities rather than solely regulatory metrics. This shift led to more meaningful improvement efforts and better alignment with patient needs.

4. Data to Action Pathways

Analytics must connect directly to improvement:

- **Decision Support Integration**: Embedding insights into workflow

- **Improvement Method Alignment**: Connecting analytics to structured improvement processes

- **Feedback Loop Design**: Creating cycles of measurement, action, and reassessment

- **Capability Building**: Developing staff skills in using data for improvement

Virginia Mason Medical Center implemented "improvement huddles" that use real-time quality analytics to drive daily improvements. This structured approach to translating data into action has accelerated their improvement timeline compared to traditional quality methods.

Case Study Elements: Memorial Hermann Health System's Journey

Memorial Hermann Health System in Houston implemented an integrated quality analytics program that demonstrates advanced approaches in action. Key elements included:

- Development of a predictive safety system that anticipates risks across multiple domains

- Implementation of a learning health system platform that accelerates improvement cycles

- Creation of a balanced accountability system that drives improvement while maintaining fairness

- Establishment of patient partnership mechanisms that incorporate patient perspectives in quality efforts

This comprehensive approach has reduced serious safety events by 78% over five years while simultaneously improving patient experience and operational efficiency. We'll explore this case more fully in our chapter-wide case study.

The Future of Quality Analytics

Looking ahead, several emerging capabilities will further transform healthcare quality management:

- **AI-Assisted Clinical Decision Support**: Systems that provide real-time guidance based on comprehensive data analysis

- **Continuous Patient Monitoring Analytics**: Using wearable and remote monitoring data to detect quality issues earlier

- **Natural Language Processing for Safety**: Analyzing clinical notes and patient communications for safety signals

- **Precision Quality Improvement**: Tailoring improvement approaches to specific contexts and populations

These advances promise increasingly sophisticated quality systems that prevent harm, promote excellence, and continuously improve based on real-world experience.

Reflection Questions for Healthcare Leaders

As you consider your quality analytics strategy, reflect on these questions:

1. How proactive is your current quality management approach? What might enable more prediction and prevention?

2. How integrated are quality efforts with other operational domains in your organization? What connections might create greater value?

3. How effectively does your organization learn from experience? What systems might accelerate organizational learning?

4. How meaningful are your quality metrics to patients? What might make measurement more patient-centered?

5. How might advanced quality analytics change leadership practices in your organization? What capabilities would leaders need to develop?

By thoughtfully applying advanced analytics to quality management, healthcare organizations can create systems that reliably deliver exceptional care—preventing harm, promoting excellence, and continuously improving based on real-world experience. These capabilities represent the culmination of operational excellence, integrating all aspects of operations to serve healthcare's fundamental purpose: providing the best possible care for every patient.

Integrated Case Study: Minnesota Care Collaborative's Advanced Analytics Journey

Background: A Regional Approach to Healthcare Excellence

The Minnesota Care Collaborative (MCC) formed in 2018 when five independent health systems spanning urban, suburban, and rural communities recognized that their most significant challenges couldn't be solved in isolation. These systems—ranging from a 900-bed academic medical center to a network of critical access hospitals—initially came together to address workforce shortages but soon recognized opportunities for broader collaboration through advanced analytics.

Unlike most healthcare analytics initiatives that focus within organizational boundaries, MCC took a regional approach, recognizing that patients, staff, and resources flow across their systems. This regional perspective created unique opportunities for advanced analytics applications while introducing distinctive challenges around data sharing, governance, and implementation.

Initial Challenges: The Imperative for Advanced Analytics

MCC faced several interconnected challenges that individual organizations struggled to address alone:

- **Workforce constraints**: A regional shortage of healthcare professionals, particularly nurses and specialists

- **Capacity misalignment**: Simultaneous overcrowding and underutilization across facilities

- **Care fragmentation**: Patients receiving uncoordinated care across multiple systems

- **Rural access challenges**: Difficulty maintaining services in lower-population areas

- **Financial sustainability pressures**: Each system faced margin compression and cost challenges

These challenges reflected a fundamental mismatch between healthcare resources and community needs across the region—a mismatch that traditional approaches within organizational boundaries couldn't resolve. The collaborative recognized that advanced analytics across organizational boundaries might offer solutions beyond what any single system could achieve.

Building the Foundation: Cross-System Analytics Infrastructure

The collaborative began by establishing the necessary foundation for advanced analytics:

1. Governance and Trust

MCC created a unique governance structure to support cross-system analytics:

- **Executive Council**: CEOs from each system provided strategic direction

- **Analytics Steering Committee**: Chief Analytics Officers and CMIOs guided technical direction

- **Clinical Councils**: Physician and nursing leaders ensured clinical relevance

- **Data Ethics Committee**: Diverse stakeholders addressed ethical considerations

- **Patient Advisory Group**: Patient representatives guided patient-centered approaches

This multi-level governance created the trust necessary for systems to share sensitive data and implement cross-organizational initiatives.

2. Data Integration Platform

Creating a common data platform across different systems presented significant challenges:

- **Federated Architecture**: Data remained within each system but could be analyzed collectively

- **Common Data Model**: Standardized definitions and structures across systems

- **Privacy-Preserving Analytics**: Methods that protected patient privacy while enabling analysis

- **Identity Resolution**: Approaches to identify when the same patient appeared in multiple systems

- **Distributed Computing**: Analysis could occur across the network without centralizing sensitive data

This infrastructure enabled analyses that weren't previously possible while maintaining appropriate privacy and security.

3. Analytical Capability Development

MCC invested in both technology and human capabilities:

- **Shared Analytics Resources**: Specialists who worked across all systems

- **Center of Excellence Model**: Specific systems led different analytical domains

- **Skill Development Program**: Training to enhance analytics capabilities across all systems

- **Collaborative Development**: Methods for systems to build solutions together

- **Implementation Support Teams**: Resources dedicated to translating insights into action

These capabilities enabled MCC to develop and implement advanced analytics applications that individual systems couldn't have created alone.

Advanced Analytics Applications: An Integrated Approach

Rather than implementing isolated analytics initiatives, MCC developed an integrated suite of capabilities that addressed interconnected challenges:

1. Regional Workflow Optimization

The collaborative implemented advanced workflow analytics across system boundaries:

- **Patient Journey Mapping**: Analyzing how patients moved between systems

- **Cross-System Care Coordination**: Optimizing handoffs between organizations

- **Regional Clinical Pathways**: Developing standardized approaches for key conditions

- **Transition Point Optimization**: Improving interfaces between systems

This work reduced redundant testing by 27%, decreased emergency department revisits after discharge by 34%, and improved patient satisfaction with care transitions by 42%.

2. Collaborative Capacity Management

MCC implemented sophisticated capacity planning across the region:

- **Regional Demand Forecasting**: Predicting resource needs across all systems

- **Load Balancing Algorithms**: Distributing patients optimally based on acuity and capacity

- **Resource Sharing Protocols**: Facilitating equipment and staff sharing during constraints

- **Coordinated Expansion Planning**: Aligning capital investments to serve regional needs

This approach reduced ambulance diversions by 68%, decreased critical care transfer delays by 47%, and improved overall resource utilization by 23%.

3. Workforce Optimization and Wellbeing

The collaborative developed innovative workforce analytics:

- **Regional Staff Planning**: Forecasting workforce needs across all systems

- **Float Pool Optimization**: Creating shared staff resources for surge capacity

- **Burnout Prevention Analytics**: Identifying and addressing burnout factors

- **Cross-System Training Coordination**: Aligning development programs across organizations

These initiatives reduced agency staffing costs by $42 million annually, decreased nursing turnover by 26%, and improved staff engagement scores across all systems.

4. Shared Quality Improvement

MCC implemented a learning health system approach across organizational boundaries:

- **Comparative Effectiveness Analysis**: Identifying which approaches produced the best outcomes

- **Best Practice Dissemination**: Rapidly sharing effective methods across systems

- **Collaborative Improvement Projects**: Addressing quality challenges together

- **Patient-Centered Measurement**: Developing common patient-reported outcome measures

This work reduced mortality for several key conditions by 17-28%, decreased complications by 23%, and improved patient-reported outcomes by 31%.

Implementation Journey: Challenges and Solutions

MCC's implementation journey wasn't without significant challenges:

1. Data Integration Challenges

Integrating data across different systems proved technically difficult:

- **Challenge**: Inconsistent data definitions and structures across systems

- **Solution**: Development of a common data model with explicit mapping from each system's native format

- **Challenge**: Privacy and security concerns about cross-system data sharing

- **Solution**: Implementation of privacy-preserving analytics methods that didn't require direct data sharing

- **Challenge**: Missing data elements critical for certain analyses

- **Solution**: Targeted data quality improvement for high-priority elements

These solutions required significant investment but created the foundation for all subsequent work.

3. Organizational Alignment Difficulties

Aligning multiple independent organizations presented governance challenges:

- **Challenge**: Different strategic priorities across systems

- **Solution**: Identification of "shared pain points" where all systems faced similar challenges

- **Challenge**: Concern about competitive disadvantage through collaboration

- **Solution**: Clear agreements about which areas would involve collaboration versus competition

- **Challenge**: Different risk tolerances for innovation

- **Solution**: Phased implementation allowing systems to adopt at different paces

This careful attention to organizational dynamics proved as important as technical considerations.

3. Implementation Complexity

Moving from analytics to action across organizational boundaries required careful planning:

- **Challenge**: Different operational processes across systems

- **Solution**: Focus on interfaces between systems rather than internal processes

- **Challenge**: Varying levels of analytics maturity

- **Solution**: Capability building to ensure all systems could effectively use insights

- **Challenge**: Resistance to cross-system standardization

- **Solution**: Balancing standardization at interfaces with flexibility within systems

This balanced approach to implementation enabled progress despite organizational differences.

4. Sustainability Concerns

Creating lasting impact required attention to long-term sustainability:

- **Challenge**: Initial grant funding would eventually end

- **Solution**: Development of a shared ROI model demonstrating value to each system

- **Challenge**: Maintaining momentum through leadership changes

- **Solution**: Embedding collaboration in governance structures beyond individual leaders

- **Challenge**: Evolving technology and market conditions

- **Solution**: Regular reassessment of strategic direction and technical approach

This forward-looking approach has enabled MCC to sustain and expand their work over time.

Results and Impact: The Power of Integrated Advanced Analytics

Four years into their journey, MCC has achieved significant results that no single organization could have accomplished alone:

1. Patient Impact

- 22% reduction in mortality for targeted conditions

- 37% decrease in preventable readmissions

- 41% improvement in care coordination metrics

- 28% increase in patient satisfaction with regional care

2. Provider Impact

- 24% reduction in documented burnout

- 31% improvement in provider satisfaction

- 18% decrease in turnover

- 26% increase in time spent with patients

3. Operational Impact

- $87 million in annual savings across all systems

- 34% improvement in resource utilization

- 42% reduction in transfer delays

- 29% decrease in duplicate testing

4. Community Impact

- Maintained rural access points that would otherwise have closed

- Reduced regional health disparities by 18%

- Improved access to specialty care in underserved areas

- Enhanced disaster response capability

These integrated results demonstrate how advanced analytics across domains and organizations can create impact beyond what siloed approaches could achieve.

Key Lessons from Minnesota Care Collaborative

MCC's experience offers several valuable lessons for other healthcare organizations:

1. Think Beyond Organizational Boundaries

The most significant opportunities for advanced analytics may exist at the interfaces between organizations rather than within them. Looking beyond traditional boundaries can reveal solutions to seemingly intractable problems.

2. Integration Creates Value

The greatest impact came from connecting previously separate analytics domains—workflow, capacity, workforce, and quality. This integration revealed relationships and opportunities that would have remained hidden in siloed approaches.

3. Balance Standardization with Flexibility

Successful implementation required standardizing enough for effective collaboration while maintaining flexibility for local adaptation. This balance was key to adoption across diverse organizations.

4. Governance Equals Technology

The collaborative invested as much in governance and trust-building as in technical infrastructure. This balanced approach was essential for translating analytics into action across organizational boundaries.

5. Start with Shared Pain

Focusing initial efforts on challenges that all organizations faced created alignment and momentum. This shared pain approach overcame competitive concerns and built collaborative muscles.

As one MCC leader reflected: "We began thinking we were creating a technical solution to share data. We discovered we were actually building a new model for regional healthcare delivery—one where advanced analytics helps us collectively meet community needs rather than individually optimize our own operations."

Future Directions and Conclusion

The Evolving Landscape of Healthcare Operations Analytics

As we've explored throughout this chapter, advanced analytics is transforming healthcare operations—from workflow optimization to capacity planning, workforce management, facility design, and quality improvement. These applications represent significant advances beyond the foundational capabilities discussed in the previous chapter. But the evolution continues, with several important trends shaping the future landscape:

1. From Episodic to Continuous Analytics

Advanced analytics is increasingly moving from periodic analysis to continuous intelligence:

- **Real-time Data Processing**: Analyzing information as it's generated rather than retrospectively

- **Continuous Learning Systems**: Algorithms that improve automatically based on new data

- **Embedded Analytics**: Intelligence integrated directly into operational systems

- **Proactive Alerting**: Notification of emerging issues before they become problems

These capabilities transform analytics from a separate activity into an integrated aspect of daily operations—creating organizations that continuously sense, learn, and adapt.

2. From Siloed to Ecosystem Analytics

The boundaries of healthcare operations analytics are expanding beyond individual organizations:

- **Cross-Organization Collaboration**: Shared analytics across healthcare entities

- **Supplier-Provider Integration**: Connected analytics across the supply chain

- **Payer-Provider Alignment**: Collaborative analytics across the payment divide

- **Community Integration**: Analytics that incorporate broader social and environmental factors

This ecosystem approach recognizes that healthcare operations exist within complex networks where optimization across boundaries creates greater value than optimization within them.

3. From Human-Directed to Augmented Intelligence

The relationship between humans and analytics is evolving:

- **Human-AI Collaboration**: Systems that combine human and artificial intelligence

- **Cognitive Automation**: Automation of complex cognitive tasks

- **Decision Augmentation**: Systems that enhance rather than replace human judgment

- **Ethical Oversight**: Human guidance of AI-driven systems

This evolution moves beyond simplistic notions of "AI replacing humans" toward sophisticated partnerships that leverage the strengths of both.

4. From Operational to Transformational Analytics

Analytics is increasingly driving fundamental business model innovation:

- **New Care Models**: Analytics enabling novel approaches to care delivery

- **Digital-Physical Integration**: Seamless connection between virtual and in-person care

- **Precision Operations**: Customized operational approaches for different populations

- **Value-Based Optimization**: Analytics specifically designed for value-based care models

These applications move analytics from improving existing operations to enabling entirely new approaches to healthcare delivery.

A Maturity Roadmap for Healthcare Organizations

Healthcare organizations vary widely in their analytics maturity. The following roadmap offers guidance for organizations at different stages:

Stage 1: Foundation Building (0-12 months)

Organizations beginning their advanced analytics journey should focus on creating the necessary foundation:

- **Data Integration**: Connect data across key operational systems

- **Governance Development**: Establish structures for data management

- **Analytical Talent Acquisition**: Build core analytics capabilities

- **Use Case Identification**: Select high-impact initial applications

- **Cultural Preparation**: Begin shifting toward data-driven decision making

Success at this stage creates the capabilities needed for more advanced applications.

Stage 2: Domain Optimization (12-24 months)

With foundation in place, organizations can implement domain-specific advanced analytics:

- **Workflow Analytics**: Optimize processes within departments

- **Predictive Staffing**: Implement advanced workforce planning

- **Capacity Modeling**: Develop more sophisticated capacity management

- **Quality Prediction**: Begin moving toward predictive quality approaches

- **Facility Optimization**: Enhance physical environment management

These applications deliver substantial value while building capabilities for integration.

Stage 3: Cross-Domain Integration (24-36 months)

More mature organizations can begin connecting previously separate domains:

- **Integrated Operations Centers**: Create unified operational intelligence

- **Cross-domain Decision Support**: Connect insights across functional areas

- **Scenario Planning Systems**: Develop comprehensive planning capabilities

- **Learning Health System Implementation**: Establish systematic improvement

- **Experience-Operations Integration**: Connect experience and operational metrics

This integration reveals relationships and opportunities that remain hidden in siloed approaches.

Stage 4: Ecosystem Advancement (36+ months)

The most sophisticated organizations extend analytics beyond traditional boundaries:

- **Regional Collaboration**: Implement cross-organization analytics

- **Community Integration**: Connect healthcare operations to community factors

- **Supply Chain Integration**: Extend analytics across the supply network

- **Payer-Provider Alignment**: Collaborate across the payment divide

- **Digital Transformation**: Enable new digitally-powered care models

This expansion recognizes that the greatest opportunities often exist at the interfaces between traditional domains.

Practical Starting Points: Where to Begin

For organizations early in their analytics journey, several practical starting points deserve consideration:

1. Start with Strategic Alignment

Before investing in technology, clarify how advanced analytics will support strategic goals:

- **Strategic Analytics Alignment**: Define how analytics will advance organizational priorities

- **Value Identification**: Clarify expected benefits and timeline

- **Capability Assessment**: Honestly evaluate current analytics maturity

- **Executive Alignment**: Ensure leadership understanding and support

- **Resource Commitment**: Secure necessary investment for sustainability

This strategic foundation prevents analytics initiatives from becoming technical exercises disconnected from organizational priorities.

2. Invest in Foundational Capabilities

Build the technical, human, and process capabilities that enable advanced analytics:

- **Data Architecture**: Create infrastructure that supports advanced applications

- **Analytical Talent**: Develop or acquire necessary expertise

- **Governance Structures**: Establish clear data management practices

- **Change Management Capacity**: Build ability to implement analytics-driven changes

- **Ethical Frameworks**: Develop principles for responsible analytics use

These foundational investments may seem less exciting than advanced applications but are essential for sustainable success.

3. Select High-Impact Initial Applications

Choose early applications carefully to build momentum:

- **Pain Point Focus**: Address recognized operational challenges

- **Quick Win Potential**: Select applications that can deliver value relatively quickly

- **Stakeholder Support**: Ensure key stakeholders support the initial focus

- **Foundation Building**: Use initial applications to develop broader capabilities

- **Value Demonstration**: Establish clear metrics to show impact

Well-chosen initial applications build credibility and support for more ambitious efforts.

4. Balance Technology with Human Factors

Pay equal attention to technical and human dimensions:

- **User-Centered Design**: Create analytics that work for actual users

- **Implementation Planning**: Develop comprehensive approaches to change

- **Skill Development**: Build capabilities to use advanced analytics

- **Cultural Evolution**: Cultivate data-driven decision making

- **Leadership Development**: Prepare leaders to lead analytically

Organizations that neglect these human factors often develop sophisticated analytics that fail to drive actual improvement.

The Vision: Healthcare Operations Transformed

As we conclude this exploration of advanced healthcare operations analytics, let's envision what healthcare delivery could look like when these capabilities reach their full potential:

Imagine a healthcare system where:

- **Patients experience seamless, coordinated care** that anticipates their needs and preferences

- **Clinicians practice at the top of their licenses**, supported by systems that reduce administrative burden and enhance clinical decision making

- **Staff work in sustainable, satisfying environments** that balance efficiency with wellbeing

- **Resources flow dynamically to meet changing needs**, ensuring optimal use without waste

- **Facilities actively contribute to healing** through environments optimized for both clinical and human needs

- **Quality continuously improves** through systems that learn from every patient encounter

- **Communities receive care aligned with their unique needs** through analytics that understand population patterns

- **Innovation flourishes** as analytics reveals new possibilities for care delivery

This vision represents not just incremental improvement but fundamental transformation—healthcare operations reimagined through the power of advanced analytics.

A Call to Action: The Journey Ahead

Achieving this vision won't be easy. It requires sustained investment, cultural change, new capabilities, and collaborative approaches that transcend traditional boundaries. But the potential rewards—better patient care, more sustainable operations, improved staff experience, and enhanced community health—make the journey worthwhile.

As you reflect on your organization's path toward advanced operations analytics, consider these questions:

1. What operational challenges in your organization might benefit most from advanced analytics? Where would sophisticated insights create the greatest value for patients and staff?

2. What capabilities—technical, analytical, cultural, and leadership—will your organization need to develop for advanced operations analytics? Where are the most critical gaps?

3. How might advanced analytics change relationships within and beyond your organization? What new collaborations might become possible?

4. What ethical considerations should guide your analytics journey? How will you ensure that technology serves human needs rather than the reverse?

5. What first steps could your organization take to begin or accelerate its journey toward advanced operations analytics?

By thoughtfully pursuing advanced healthcare operations analytics, organizations can create systems that simultaneously improve quality, enhance experiences, increase efficiency, and promote sustainability. This balanced optimization—so difficult with traditional approaches—becomes possible through the integrated intelligence that advanced analytics provides.

The healthcare organizations that thrive in the coming decade will be those that effectively harness these capabilities—not as technical exercises but as catalysts for transformation in service of their fundamental mission: providing the best possible care for the communities they serve.

The advanced operational applications we've explored demonstrate AI's remarkable potential to enhance healthcare efficiency, quality, and accessibility. Yet these powerful capabilities bring equally significant responsibilities. As AI systems increasingly influence critical aspects of healthcare delivery—from resource allocation to clinical workflows—ensuring they operate ethically becomes paramount. In the next chapter, we'll examine the ethical frameworks and regulatory approaches that must guide AI implementation, ensuring these technologies remain aligned with healthcare's fundamental values of beneficence, non-maleficence, autonomy, and justice. This ethical dimension isn't separate from operational considerations but rather the essential foundation that makes technological advancement truly beneficial.

Chapter 13:
Ethical Considerations, Privacy and the Regulatory Landscape

The Critical Intersection of AI, Ethics, and Healthcare

Artificial intelligence is radically transforming healthcare, promising to enhance diagnostic accuracy, enable personalized treatments, and improve healthcare delivery efficiency. Yet these powerful technologies also raise profound ethical questions that strike at the heart of medicine's fundamental values. How do we safeguard patient privacy when AI demands unprecedented access to sensitive health data? How can we ensure these systems deliver fair and equitable care across diverse populations? Who bears responsibility when AI-assisted decisions lead to harm?

The stakes in healthcare AI ethics are exceptionally high. Unlike many other AI applications, healthcare implementations can directly impact human life and wellbeing, amplifying both the potential benefits and risks. The intimate nature of health data and the vulnerability of patients create unique ethical imperatives that distinguish healthcare AI from applications in other domains.

At its core, the ethical implementation of AI in healthcare involves balancing several critical tensions:

- Innovation versus safety: accelerating beneficial AI advances while protecting patients from harm

- Data utilization versus privacy: leveraging valuable health data while respecting confidentiality

- Automation versus human judgment: augmenting clinical expertise without diminishing professional discretion

- Global development versus local values: creating international standards while respecting cultural differences

These tensions play out across multiple dimensions: from the technical challenges of algorithm design and data governance to the human elements of patient-provider relationships and clinical decision-making; from organizational implementation to national regulation and global governance.

This chapter explores this complex landscape, providing a structured examination of key ethical considerations, privacy challenges, and regulatory approaches for AI in healthcare. We begin by examining core ethical principles as they apply to healthcare AI, then explore data privacy and security issues unique to this context. We examine how AI reshapes patient-provider relationships, analyze diverse regulatory frameworks across global regions, and address critical questions of liability and responsibility. The chapter also offers practical guidance for implementing ethical AI governance in healthcare organizations and concludes by examining emerging challenges and future directions.

By understanding and proactively addressing these ethical dimensions, we can work toward a future where AI enhances healthcare in ways that are not just technologically sophisticated, but ethically sound, upholding the values of beneficence, non-maleficence, autonomy, justice, and human dignity that lie at the heart of healthcare itself.

Core Ethical Principles for AI in Healthcare

The integration of AI into healthcare necessitates a thoughtful application of established ethical principles to new technological contexts. While these principles remain foundational to healthcare ethics, AI introduces novel challenges in their interpretation and implementation.

Beneficence and Non-maleficence

AI systems in healthcare must be designed primarily to benefit patients and minimize harm. This requires rigorous validation of AI algorithms across diverse populations and clinical settings before deployment. Unlike traditional medical interventions, AI systems can scale rapidly, potentially magnifying both benefits and harms. Organizations must implement robust monitoring systems to detect and address unexpected adverse outcomes, especially as AI systems continue to learn and evolve in clinical environments.

Autonomy and Informed Consent

Patient autonomy faces new challenges in the AI era. Meaningful informed consent requires that patients understand how AI influences their care—a difficult task given the complexity and opacity of many AI systems. Healthcare providers must develop clear, accessible ways to explain AI's role in diagnosis, treatment recommendations, and prognosis without overwhelming patients with technical details. Additionally, traditional one-time consent models may be insufficient for AI systems that continuously learn and adapt; more dynamic, ongoing consent processes may be necessary.

Justice, Equity, and Fairness

AI systems risk perpetuating or amplifying existing healthcare disparities if not carefully designed and implemented. Algorithmic bias can emerge when training data underrepresent certain populations or contain historical patterns of discrimination. Ensuring fairness requires diverse training data, regular bias audits across different demographic groups, and careful consideration of how seemingly neutral data points might serve as proxies for protected characteristics. Healthcare organizations must also address the "digital divide" by ensuring equitable access to AI-enhanced care regardless of patients' technological literacy or resources.

Transparency and Explainability

The "black box" nature of many advanced AI systems presents significant challenges in healthcare, where understanding the rationale behind decisions is crucial for both clinical and ethical reasons. While perfect explainability may not always be achievable, AI systems in healthcare should provide appropriate levels of transparency based on risk and context. Clinicians need sufficient understanding of how AI generates its recommendations to exercise their professional judgment, while patients deserve clear explanations of how AI influenced their care.

Accountability and Responsibility

Clear frameworks for accountability are essential when healthcare decisions involve AI systems. These frameworks must delineate responsibilities among various stakeholders—including healthcare providers, technology developers, healthcare institutions, and regulators. Documentation of AI-assisted decisions should be robust enough to support retrospective review when adverse events occur. As AI systems become more autonomous, traditional liability models may need to evolve, potentially including concepts like "algorithmic negligence" or shared responsibility between human and machine decision-makers.

By thoughtfully applying these core ethical principles to AI in healthcare, we can harness the tremendous potential of these technologies while safeguarding the human values at the heart of medicine. This requires ongoing dialogue among clinicians, technologists, ethicists, policymakers, and patients as AI capabilities and applications continue to evolve.

Data Privacy and Security in the AI Era

Healthcare AI systems require unprecedented access to sensitive patient information, creating unique privacy and security challenges that extend beyond traditional healthcare data protections.

Unique Privacy Challenges of Healthcare AI

AI in healthcare intensifies privacy concerns in several ways. These systems often require massive datasets to train effectively, increasing the scale of potential data exposure. They can also discover non-obvious correlations between seemingly unrelated data points, potentially revealing sensitive information even from partial data. Additionally, the longitudinal nature of healthcare AI—tracking patients over time—creates detailed profiles that pose heightened privacy risks. As healthcare integrates consumer technologies and social determinants of health, the boundary between medical and non-medical data blurs, complicating privacy protections.

Critical Security Considerations for AI Systems

Healthcare AI systems face specialized security vulnerabilities beyond traditional cybersecurity concerns. Adversarial attacks can manipulate AI outputs by subtly altering inputs—sometimes in ways imperceptible to humans—potentially leading to misdiagnoses or inappropriate treatments. Data poisoning attacks, where malicious actors corrupt training data, can compromise system integrity from the outset. Model inversion attacks may enable bad actors to reconstruct private training data from the model itself. These threats require security approaches specifically designed for AI systems.

Privacy-Preserving Techniques for AI Development

Several approaches can enhance privacy while maintaining data utility:

De-identification and Anonymization: Traditional approaches remove direct identifiers from data, but AI's ability to connect disparate data points increases re-identification risks. Even "anonymous" datasets can become identifiable when combined with other information or processed by sophisticated algorithms.

Federated Learning: This emerging approach keeps data decentralized, training AI models across multiple sites without transferring raw patient data. The model travels to the data rather than vice versa, substantially reducing privacy risks while enabling collaboration across institutions and regions.

Differential Privacy: This mathematical framework adds precisely calibrated noise to data or analyses, providing provable privacy guarantees while preserving statistical validity. It offers particular promise for healthcare AI by enabling analysis of sensitive data while mathematically limiting privacy risks.

Synthetic Data: AI-generated synthetic datasets that statistically mimic real patient data without corresponding to actual individuals can provide training material while eliminating direct privacy concerns.

Balancing Data Utility with Privacy Protection

The tension between data access and privacy protection represents a central challenge in healthcare AI. Overly restrictive privacy measures can hamper AI performance and potentially limit patient benefits, while inadequate protections risk serious privacy violations. Finding this balance requires:

1. Contextual privacy frameworks that adjust protections based on data sensitivity and use case

2. Ongoing stakeholder engagement to align privacy approaches with patient and provider values

3. Regular reassessment as technologies evolve and new privacy risks emerge

Case Study: Privacy-Protective Imaging AI

A multinational effort to develop an AI system for detecting diabetic retinopathy illustrates effective privacy-protective implementation. The collaboration used federated learning to train the algorithm across five countries with varying privacy regulations. The approach kept sensitive patient images within their original institutions while allowing the AI model to learn from diverse populations. Differential privacy techniques were applied to model updates, preventing potential reconstruction of patient data. The resulting system demonstrated both high diagnostic accuracy and robust privacy protection, receiving regulatory approval across multiple jurisdictions while maintaining public trust.

By implementing these advanced privacy and security approaches, healthcare organizations can harness AI's transformative potential while fulfilling their fundamental obligation to protect patient confidentiality.

The Patient-Provider Relationship in AI-Augmented Healthcare

The integration of AI into healthcare fundamentally transforms the sacred relationship between patients and providers—a relationship built on trust, empathy, and human connection that has been at the heart of medicine for millennia.

Transforming Dynamics of Care Delivery

AI technologies are reshaping clinical workflows and interactions in multiple ways. They can automate routine administrative tasks, potentially freeing clinicians to focus more on patient care. They offer unprecedented access to specialized expertise in resource-limited settings. And they can empower patients with information previously accessible only to medical professionals, potentially shifting the knowledge balance in clinical encounters. These changes require thoughtful adaptation from both providers and patients to preserve effective therapeutic relationships.

Balancing AI Recommendations with Human Judgment

When AI systems and human clinicians collaborate in patient care, complex questions arise about how to navigate differences in judgment. Clinicians may face challenging decisions when AI recommendations contradict their clinical instincts. Providers must cultivate appropriate skepticism toward AI outputs while leveraging their unique human capabilities—contextual understanding, ethical reasoning, and empathic connection—that AI cannot replicate. Healthcare organizations must develop clear protocols for clinicians to question, override, or supplement AI recommendations when appropriate.

Trust and Transparency with Patients

Patient trust is essential for effective healthcare and must be carefully maintained as AI enters the clinical relationship. Patients may reasonably question whether AI systems understand their unique circumstances or share their values. They may worry about privacy, bias, or dehumanization of their care. Building trust requires transparency about AI's role, limitations, and potential benefits, explained in accessible language that helps patients make informed decisions about their care.

Communicating AI's Role in Diagnosis and Treatment

Healthcare providers face the challenge of explaining AI's involvement in clinical decisions without overwhelming patients with technical details. This requires developing clear frameworks for disclosure that match the level of AI involvement with appropriate explanation. Providers must be prepared to discuss both the benefits AI brings to diagnosis or treatment planning and its limitations. The goal is informed engagement rather than passive acceptance of technology-mediated care.

Maintaining the Human Element in Technology-Mediated Care

As AI assumes more clinical functions, preserving the irreplaceable human elements of healthcare becomes essential. Empathy, compassion, and personal connection remain central to healing relationships and cannot be delegated to algorithms. Healthcare organizations must design AI implementations that enhance rather than diminish these human aspects of care. This means creating space for meaningful personal interaction, ensuring technology remains in service to the therapeutic relationship rather than dominating it.

Case Study: Primary Care AI Assistant that Strengthens Relationships

A primary care practice implemented an AI system designed specifically to enhance patient-provider relationships with remarkable results. The system transcribes and analyzes clinic visits in real-time, drafting clinical notes and highlighting potential follow-up items. This frees physicians to maintain eye contact and active listening rather than focusing on documentation during appointments. The AI also generates personalized, physician-reviewed follow-up materials for patients, reinforcing key points from their visit. Importantly, the system was designed with input from both patients and providers, focusing on augmenting rather than replacing human connection. After implementation, the practice saw improvements in both patient satisfaction scores and provider well-being measures, demonstrating how thoughtfully designed AI can strengthen rather than undermine therapeutic relationships.

The successful integration of AI into healthcare ultimately depends on designing systems that respect and enhance the essential human connection at the heart of medicine. By addressing these relational aspects of healthcare AI with the same rigor applied to technical performance, we can create a future where technology strengthens rather than diminishes the healing relationship between patients and providers.

The Global Regulatory Landscape

The regulation of AI in healthcare is evolving rapidly across different regions, reflecting varying cultural values, healthcare systems, and governance philosophies. Understanding these different approaches is crucial for organizations developing or deploying healthcare AI globally.

Comparative Analysis of Major Regulatory Approaches

United States: Innovation-Focused Oversight

The U.S. approach emphasizes balancing innovation with patient safety through risk-based regulation. The FDA has developed a framework for AI/ML-based Software as a Medical Device (SaMD) that acknowledges the unique challenges of regulating continuously learning systems. This framework introduces the concept of a "predetermined change control plan" that allows for certain algorithmic modifications without requiring full regulatory review. HIPAA continues to govern patient data privacy, though it was not designed with AI applications in mind. This regulatory approach generally enables rapid innovation while providing baseline patient protections.

European Union: Rights-Based Comprehensive Regulation

The EU has adopted a more comprehensive, rights-centered approach. The General Data Protection Regulation (GDPR) significantly impacts healthcare AI through its provisions on algorithmic decision-making, data minimization, and the "right to explanation." The proposed EU AI Act classifies most healthcare AI applications as "high-risk," requiring rigorous pre-market assessment, robust documentation, and ongoing monitoring. This approach prioritizes patient rights and safety, potentially at the cost of slowing innovation, but creates a strong framework for trustworthy AI.

China: Development-Oriented Approach

China has pursued an approach that promotes rapid AI development while maintaining central oversight. Recent regulations create specialized pathways for AI medical devices with streamlined approval processes. China's vast population and centralized healthcare data resources provide advantages for AI development, while its regulatory system emphasizes national strategic objectives. Privacy protections exist but generally subordinate individual rights to collective benefits and development goals.

Other Significant Regional Frameworks

Canada has pioneered impact assessment approaches for algorithmic systems. Japan has developed a "human-centered" AI framework emphasizing social harmony. India's emerging approach focuses on leveraging AI to address healthcare access challenges while balancing limited regulatory resources. These diverse frameworks offer alternative models that reflect different societal values and healthcare priorities.

Cross-Border Challenges and Harmonization Efforts

The global nature of AI development creates significant challenges for regulatory compliance across jurisdictions. Data localization requirements in some regions conflict with the need for diverse training data. Varying standards for explainability, validation, and privacy protection create complex compliance landscapes for global deployments.

International efforts to address these challenges include the International Medical Device Regulators Forum's work on SaMD principles and the OECD's AI Policy Observatory. The WHO has developed guidance on ethics and governance of AI for health to promote globally applicable principles. Despite these efforts, substantial regulatory divergence persists, creating compliance burdens that can disadvantage smaller organizations and potentially limit patient access to beneficial technologies.

Cultural and Social Factors Influencing AI Regulation

Regulatory approaches reflect deeper cultural values and social contexts. Societies with stronger collectivist orientations may accept broader data use for public benefit, while those emphasizing individual rights prioritize personal control over data. Cultural attitudes toward authority and expertise influence acceptance of AI in clinical decision-making. Societal trust in healthcare institutions, technology companies, and government shapes public expectations for regulatory oversight.

Healthcare system structures also impact regulatory approaches. Single-payer systems may focus on population-level benefits and cost-effectiveness, while market-based systems may emphasize individual choice and innovation. These factors must be considered when developing globally deployable AI healthcare solutions.

Case Study: Multi-Regional Deployment of an AI Diagnostic System

A diagnostic AI system for detecting diabetic retinopathy illustrates successful navigation of diverse regulatory environments. The developer created a core algorithm with modular components that could be adapted to different regulatory requirements. For the EU market, they enhanced explainability features and implemented GDPR-compliant data handling. For U.S. deployment, they focused on clinical validation studies meeting FDA requirements. In China, they partnered with local institutions to conduct region-specific validation and secure regulatory approval.

Rather than building separate systems for each market, the company developed a compliance framework that identified core regulatory requirements across regions alongside market-specific adaptations. This approach balanced the efficiency of a global platform with the necessity of respecting local regulatory requirements, ultimately achieving successful deployment across multiple jurisdictions while maintaining the system's clinical effectiveness.

The global regulatory landscape for healthcare AI will continue to evolve as technologies advance and real-world evidence accumulates. Organizations developing these technologies must engage proactively with regulatory frameworks across regions, contributing to the ongoing dialogue between innovation and oversight that will shape the future of AI in healthcare.

Liability and Responsibility in AI-Driven Healthcare

The integration of AI into healthcare creates complex questions about responsibility and liability when things go wrong. Traditional liability frameworks were not designed for scenarios where algorithms influence or make medical decisions, creating uncertainty for all stakeholders.

Determining Liability in AI-Assisted Decisions

When adverse events occur involving AI-assisted healthcare, liability questions become multifaceted. Unlike traditional medical errors, AI-related adverse events may involve multiple parties: healthcare providers, technology developers, healthcare institutions, and potentially data providers. The "black box" nature of many advanced AI systems complicates liability determination by making it difficult to trace exactly how decisions were reached.

Current legal frameworks generally focus on human actors, leaving uncertainty about liability when AI systems contribute to medical errors. Several models are emerging to address this gap:

1. **Provider-focused liability**: Places primary responsibility on healthcare professionals who use AI tools, treating them as responsible for validating AI recommendations.

2. **Shared liability**: Distributes responsibility across the human-AI ecosystem based on each actor's role and the degree of autonomy granted to the AI system.

3. **AI-specific liability**: Emerging frameworks that recognize the unique nature of AI systems and create specialized liability standards.

4. **Enterprise liability**: Places responsibility at the institutional level rather than on individual providers, recognizing the systemic nature of AI implementation.

Malpractice Considerations in the AI Context

AI creates new dimensions of potential malpractice. Providers may face liability for inappropriate reliance on AI recommendations, but also potentially for failing to use available AI tools that would have prevented harm. The standard of care, a central concept in malpractice—is evolving rapidly as AI adoption increases, creating ambiguity about what constitutes reasonable practice.

Documentation of clinical reasoning when overriding or following AI recommendations becomes critically important for malpractice defense. Healthcare organizations must develop clear guidelines on when and how providers should question AI outputs to protect both patients and clinicians.

Manufacturer Responsibility for AI Medical Devices

Manufacturers of AI healthcare products face evolving liability considerations. Product liability law typically focuses on design defects, manufacturing defects, and failure to warn. AI systems raise novel questions in each category:

- When is an algorithmic error considered a design defect?

- How do liability frameworks apply to continuously learning systems that evolve after deployment?

- What level of transparency and disclosure is required to fulfill the duty to warn?

Regulatory bodies are developing new frameworks to address these questions. The FDA's "predetermined change control plan" approach represents one effort to clarify manufacturer responsibilities for AI systems that learn and change over time.

Insurance and Risk Management Approaches

New insurance models are emerging to address AI-related healthcare risks. These include:

- Enhanced medical malpractice coverage specifically addressing AI-assisted care

- Technology errors and omissions policies for AI developers

- Cyber liability insurance covering AI-related data breaches

- Specialized AI liability coverage bridging traditional insurance gaps

Risk management strategies include robust documentation of AI decision processes, regular algorithmic audits, clear protocols for human oversight, and comprehensive incident reporting systems.

Case Study: Resolving Liability in an Oncology AI System Error

A major teaching hospital implemented an AI system to assist oncologists in treatment planning. When the system recommended an inappropriate chemotherapy regimen for a patient with multiple comorbidities, the treating oncologist followed the recommendation without thoroughly reviewing the patient's complex medical history. The patient suffered serious complications.

The subsequent liability investigation revealed multiple contributing factors: the AI system had been trained primarily on data from patients without significant comorbidities; the user interface highlighted the recommendation without adequately displaying its confidence level; hospital protocols did not clearly define when physicians should override AI recommendations; and the oncologist received insufficient training on the system's limitations.

The resolution distributed responsibility across multiple parties. The hospital accepted enterprise liability for inadequate implementation protocols. The AI developer updated the system to better handle patients with comorbidities and modified the interface to clearly indicate confidence levels. The hospital implemented more rigorous training requirements and clearer override protocols. The insurance company worked with all parties to develop a claims framework that recognized the shared responsibility while ensuring the patient received appropriate compensation.

This case illustrates the complex, multi-stakeholder nature of AI liability in healthcare and demonstrates how forward-thinking policies can address these challenges while supporting continued innovation. As AI becomes more deeply integrated into healthcare, developing clear, fair liability frameworks will be essential to ensure patient protection while enabling beneficial technological advancement.

Implementing Ethical AI Governance in Healthcare Organizations

While ethical principles and regulatory requirements provide essential frameworks, translating these into effective organizational practices requires deliberate governance structures. Healthcare organizations need practical approaches to ensure AI systems uphold ethical standards throughout their lifecycle.

Developing Organizational AI Ethics Policies

Effective AI ethics policies establish clear boundaries and expectations for AI use within healthcare organizations. These policies should:

- Articulate specific ethical principles aligned with the organization's mission and values

- Define scope and limitations for AI applications, with special attention to high-risk uses

- Establish data governance standards specific to AI development and deployment

- Create transparency requirements for AI systems at different risk levels

- Delineate clear lines of accountability for AI-related decisions

Ethics policies should be developed through inclusive processes involving diverse perspectives—clinical, technical, administrative, and patient representatives. They should remain living documents, regularly reviewed and updated as technologies and practices evolve.

Ethical AI Review Processes and Oversight Mechanisms

Healthcare organizations need structured review mechanisms to evaluate AI systems before and during deployment. Key elements include:

1. **Ethics Review Committees**: Multidisciplinary bodies that evaluate proposed AI applications, similar to IRBs for research but focused on operational AI implementation.

2. **Risk Assessment Frameworks**: Structured approaches to categorize AI applications based on potential impact, determining appropriate levels of oversight.

3. **Algorithmic Impact Assessments**: Systematic evaluations of AI systems for potential unintended consequences, with particular attention to impacts on vulnerable populations.

4. **Continuous Monitoring Systems**: Processes for ongoing evaluation of deployed AI, including performance audits, bias assessments, and feedback mechanisms.

These oversight mechanisms should operate with appropriate authority to delay or modify AI implementations that present ethical concerns, while remaining streamlined enough to support beneficial innovation.

Training Healthcare Professionals in AI Ethics

Healthcare professionals need specific training to navigate the ethical dimensions of AI technologies:

- Foundational understanding of AI capabilities and limitations

- Skills to recognize potential algorithmic bias and appropriate responses

- Frameworks for obtaining informed consent for AI-assisted care

- Guidelines for balancing AI recommendations with clinical judgment

- Practical approaches to explaining AI's role to patients

Training should be role-specific, with clinicians, administrators, and technical teams receiving education tailored to their responsibilities. AI ethics education should be integrated into both formal curricula and continuing education, evolving as technologies advance.

Patient and Stakeholder Engagement Strategies

Ethical AI governance requires meaningful engagement with patients and other stakeholders. Effective strategies include:

- Patient advisory boards focused on AI implementation

- Transparent communication about AI use in clinical settings

- Accessible mechanisms for patients to provide feedback on AI-assisted care

- Regular public forums to discuss organizational AI policies

- Collaborative partnerships with community organizations representing diverse patient populations

Engagement should be substantive rather than symbolic, with patient and community input genuinely influencing AI governance decisions.

Case Study: Integrated Ethics Governance at Academic Medical Center

A large academic medical center successfully implemented comprehensive AI ethics governance through a tiered approach. The organization established an AI Ethics Council with representation from clinical departments, data science, ethics, legal counsel, and patient advocates. This council developed organizational AI ethics principles and policies through a year-long collaborative process.

For implementation, they created a three-tier review process. Low-risk applications (primarily administrative AI) underwent streamlined review focusing on data security and accuracy. Moderate-risk clinical applications (decision support tools with human oversight) received more comprehensive ethics review, including bias testing and explainability requirements. High-risk applications (autonomous diagnostic systems or treatment recommendations) underwent rigorous review including clinical validation, fairness assessments, and ongoing monitoring protocols.

To build capacity, the organization developed a certificate program in AI ethics for clinicians and administrators, ultimately training over 500 staff. They established a patient AI advisory board that meets quarterly to provide feedback on policies and implementation.

The governance system has successfully evaluated more than 30 AI applications, approving most while requiring modifications to address ethical concerns in several cases. The framework has become a model for other healthcare systems, demonstrating how robust ethical governance can enable responsible AI innovation while maintaining trust and accountability.

Implementing ethical AI governance requires significant organizational commitment but is essential for responsible deployment of these powerful technologies in healthcare. By establishing clear policies, robust review processes, comprehensive training, and meaningful stakeholder engagement, healthcare organizations can create environments where AI enhances care while upholding core ethical values.

Future Directions and Emerging Challenges

As AI continues to advance, new applications are emerging that push ethical and regulatory boundaries in unprecedented ways. These frontier technologies present novel challenges that current frameworks may be ill-equipped to address.

AI in Genomics and Precision Medicine

The convergence of AI with genomics and precision medicine creates powerful capabilities for personalized healthcare while raising profound ethical questions. AI systems can identify patterns in genetic data that humans cannot perceive, potentially revolutionizing disease prediction and treatment selection. However, these applications present distinctive challenges:

- **Intergenerational Privacy**: Genetic data inherently reveals information about biological relatives, complicating traditional individual consent models.

- **Predictive Uncertainty**: AI-generated predictions about future disease risk based on genetic data carry significant uncertainty, raising questions about disclosure of potentially anxiety-inducing information.

- **Equity in Precision Medicine**: Many genomic databases overrepresent European populations, potentially creating precision medicine approaches that work better for some groups than others.

Healthcare organizations and regulators must develop frameworks that balance the transformative potential of AI-powered precision medicine with these novel risks, ensuring benefits are equitably distributed and individual rights protected.

Brain-Computer Interfaces and Neural Technologies

The integration of AI with neural technologies represents perhaps the most intimate frontier in healthcare technology. Direct interfaces between human brains and AI systems—from non-invasive EEG headsets to implanted devices—raise unprecedented questions:

- **Neural Privacy**: Should there be special protections for brain data beyond those for other health information?

- **Cognitive Liberty**: How do we protect individuals' right to mental self-determination when AI can potentially influence neural activity?

- **Identity and Agency**: How might these technologies affect our conception of human identity and autonomous decision-making?

As therapeutic applications expand from treating severe neurological conditions to enhancing normal cognitive function, the boundary between medical and non-medical uses blurs, challenging existing regulatory frameworks based on clear disease categories.

Autonomous AI Systems in Critical Care

Critical care environments—where decisions must be made rapidly with incomplete information—are becoming testing grounds for increasingly autonomous AI systems. These applications hold tremendous promise for improving patient outcomes but raise difficult questions:

- **Appropriate Autonomy Levels**: What degree of independent decision-making should AI systems have in life-critical situations?

- **Human-AI Collaboration**: How should responsibility be balanced when decisions emerge from human-AI teams?

- **Crisis Ethics**: How should AI systems prioritize competing values during emergencies when ideal solutions are impossible?

As these systems become more capable, healthcare organizations must determine not just what AI can do, but what it should do, especially in high-stakes clinical environments.

Evolving Regulatory Models for Adaptive AI

Traditional regulatory approaches—designed for stable products with predictable behaviors—are increasingly inadequate for AI systems that continuously learn and adapt. New regulatory models are emerging to address this challenge:

- **Pre-Certification Models**: Focusing on developer quality processes rather than specific product versions

- **Continuous Monitoring Frameworks**: Implementing real-world performance surveillance throughout the product lifecycle

- **Outcome-Based Regulation**: Shifting from process requirements to measurable safety and efficacy outcomes

These approaches represent promising directions, but significant work remains to create regulatory frameworks that effectively balance innovation with safety for adaptive AI systems.

International Collaboration on Global Standards

As healthcare AI becomes increasingly global, international organizations are assuming greater importance in developing shared ethical frameworks and technical standards:

- The World Health Organization has developed ethics guidelines for AI in health, emphasizing human autonomy, equity, and explainability

- The International Organization for Standardization is creating technical standards for AI in healthcare applications

- The Global Partnership on AI is facilitating multi-stakeholder collaboration on responsible AI governance

Despite these efforts, tensions remain between the benefits of global harmonization and respect for cultural differences in values and priorities. Finding the right balance between universal principles and contextual implementation will remain a central challenge.

These emerging frontiers in healthcare AI do not merely extend existing ethical questions—they raise fundamentally new ones that will require innovative thinking and multidisciplinary collaboration. By anticipating these challenges and developing proactive approaches, we can help ensure that even the most advanced AI applications in healthcare remain aligned with human values and needs.

The Path Forward

The integration of AI into healthcare represents one of the most promising and challenging technological transformations of our time. Throughout this chapter, we have explored the complex ethical considerations, privacy challenges, and evolving regulatory landscape that shape this transformation. As we look to the future, several key principles emerge as essential guideposts for responsible advancement.

At the core of ethical AI in healthcare lies respect for human dignity and autonomy, commitment to fairness and equity, transparency appropriate to context, and clear accountability structures. These principles must be operationalized through robust governance frameworks, privacy-protecting technical approaches, and regulatory systems that balance innovation with safety.

Actionable Recommendations for Key Stakeholders

For AI Developers and Technology Companies:

- Implement "ethics by design" approaches that incorporate ethical considerations from the earliest stages of development

- Invest in privacy-preserving techniques like federated learning and differential privacy

- Develop explainable AI systems appropriate for healthcare contexts

- Engage diverse stakeholders, including patients, throughout the development process

- Establish rigorous testing protocols for bias and safety across diverse populations

For Healthcare Providers and Institutions:

- Develop comprehensive AI ethics policies and governance structures

- Implement tiered review processes based on the risk level of different AI applications

- Provide targeted training for clinicians on effectively working with AI systems

- Create clear protocols for balancing AI recommendations with clinical judgment

- Engage patients meaningfully in AI governance and implementation decisions

For Policymakers and Regulators:

- Develop adaptive regulatory frameworks appropriate for continuously learning systems

- Foster international collaboration while respecting cultural and contextual differences

- Balance innovation and safety through risk-based approaches

- Invest in regulatory capacity building to match the pace of technological advancement

- Create incentives for responsible AI development and implementation

For Patients and the Public:

- Advocate for transparency in how AI is used in healthcare settings

- Engage with healthcare organizations in shaping AI policies and practices

- Develop AI literacy to make informed decisions about AI-assisted care

- Participate in appropriate data sharing for AI advancement while understanding privacy rights

- Hold institutions accountable for ethical AI implementation

The Imperative of Ongoing Dialogue and Adaptation

The ethical and regulatory landscape for AI in healthcare will continue to evolve as technologies advance and new applications emerge. This evolution demands ongoing, inclusive dialogue among all stakeholders. Static frameworks will quickly become obsolete as AI capabilities grow and new ethical challenges arise.

This dialogue must be truly multidisciplinary, bringing together technical experts, healthcare professionals, ethicists, patients, policymakers, and the broader public. It must also be global in scope while remaining attentive to cultural contexts and diverse healthcare systems. The goal should not be rigid consensus but rather a dynamic, evolving understanding that can adapt to technological change while remaining anchored in core human values.

Vision for Ethical AI in Healthcare

The future of AI in healthcare holds tremendous promise: diagnostic systems that can detect disease earlier and more accurately than human clinicians alone; treatment approaches personalized to individual characteristics; administrative efficiencies that redirect resources to direct patient care; and unprecedented insights into disease mechanisms and prevention strategies.

Realizing this promise requires more than technical innovation—it demands ethical frameworks, governance structures, and regulatory approaches that ensure these powerful technologies serve human needs and values. By proactively addressing the complex ethical dimensions of healthcare AI, we can work toward a future where these technologies augment human capabilities while preserving the fundamentally human dimensions of healing.

The path forward requires balancing seemingly competing values: innovation with safety, efficiency with equity, personalization with privacy. By navigating these tensions thoughtfully, we can harness AI's transformative potential while ensuring it remains in service to the fundamental purpose of healthcare: improving human wellbeing with compassion, respect, and justice.

Chapter 14: Forging the Future of Healthcare with Data and AI

The Journey So Far

Throughout this book, we've traversed the expansive landscape of artificial intelligence and data analytics in healthcare, exploring how these technologies are fundamentally transforming medicine from reactive to proactive, from standardized to personalized, and from intuition-driven to evidence-based. From the early expert systems of the 1960s to today's sophisticated deep learning models, we've witnessed an extraordinary evolution in our capacity to harness computational power for healing.

We began by examining the foundations of healthcare data, understanding the complex tapestry of clinical, administrative, genomic, and patient-generated information that forms the bedrock of data-driven healthcare. We explored how AI has revolutionized clinical diagnosis and treatment planning, enabling earlier detection of disease and more personalized therapeutic approaches. We investigated how machine learning and advanced analytics are optimizing healthcare operations, from resource allocation and supply chain management to workforce optimization and facility design.

Throughout this journey, we've encountered not just technological innovations but also profound ethical questions about privacy, equity, transparency, and the changing nature of the patient-provider relationship. We've examined diverse regulatory frameworks across global regions and considered how healthcare organizations can implement responsible AI governance.

Converging Themes: The New Paradigm of Healthcare

As we reflect on the various applications and implications of AI in healthcare, several unifying themes emerge that point toward a new paradigm in medicine:

From Episodic to Continuous Care

Traditional healthcare has been primarily episodic: focused on discrete encounters when patients are ill. AI and connected technologies are enabling a fundamental shift toward continuous care, where health monitoring extends beyond clinical settings into daily life. Wearable devices, remote sensors, and AI analytics create an ongoing flow of health information, allowing for early intervention before critical thresholds are crossed. This continuous model promises not just better management of chronic conditions but potentially the ability to detect and prevent disease before symptoms manifest.

From Population to Precision

For centuries, medicine has been based on population averages, with treatments designed for the "typical" patient. The integration of AI with genomic medicine, digital biomarkers, and rich patient data is enabling unprecedented precision—treatments tailored not just to broad categories but to the unique biological, behavioral, and environmental factors of individual patients. This precision approach promises greater efficacy with fewer side effects, optimizing both outcomes and resource utilization.

From Reactive to Predictive and Preventive

Perhaps the most profound shift is from healthcare that primarily reacts to illness toward systems that predict and prevent disease. AI's ability to analyze patterns across vast datasets enables identification of subtle risk signals long before traditional clinical manifestations. This predictive capability, combined with increasingly precise intervention strategies, creates the potential for a healthcare system focused on maintaining wellness rather than merely treating illness.

From Siloed to Integrated

Healthcare has traditionally operated in specialist silos, often leading to fragmented care experiences. AI and advanced analytics are helping bridge these divisions, creating integrated views of patients across specialties and settings. This integration extends beyond clinical domains to connect healthcare with social services, community resources, and environmental factors, recognizing health as the product of complex, interrelated systems.

From Exclusive to Democratized Expertise

AI is helping extend specialized medical expertise beyond elite institutions to underserved and remote areas. Through telemedicine, mobile technologies, and AI-powered decision support, high-quality healthcare guidance is becoming accessible to populations previously excluded from the benefits of medical advancement. This democratization of expertise has particular significance for addressing global health inequities.

Challenges on the Horizon

Despite the extraordinary promise of AI and data in healthcare, significant challenges remain that will require thoughtful navigation:

Ensuring Ethical AI Development and Implementation

As AI systems become more deeply embedded in healthcare decisions, ensuring they operate ethically becomes increasingly crucial. The challenge extends beyond technical issues of bias to deeper questions about autonomy, transparency, and the appropriate balance of algorithmic and human judgment. Healthcare organizations must develop robust ethical frameworks and governance structures that can evolve alongside rapidly advancing technologies.

Balancing Innovation with Regulation

The pace of AI innovation often outstrips regulatory frameworks, creating tension between rapid advancement and appropriate oversight. Regulatory approaches must balance encouraging beneficial innovation with ensuring patient safety, data protection, and ethical use. This likely requires more adaptive, risk-based regulatory models that can respond to rapidly evolving technologies while maintaining fundamental principles of safety and effectiveness.

Bridging the Digital Divide

The benefits of AI and data-driven healthcare risk exacerbating existing disparities if not thoughtfully implemented. Digital literacy, access to technology, and representation in training datasets all affect who benefits from these advances. Ensuring equitable access to AI-enhanced healthcare requires deliberate strategies to bridge digital divides, create inclusive datasets, and design technologies that work for diverse populations.

Maintaining Human Connection

As healthcare incorporates more technology, preserving the essential human dimensions of care becomes both more challenging and more important. The art of medicine—empathic communication, therapeutic relationships, and the healing power of human connection—must be enhanced rather than diminished by technology. Success requires designing AI systems that augment human capabilities while creating space for meaningful personal interaction.

Creating Sustainable Economic Models

While AI promises greater efficiency and effectiveness, it also requires significant investment in infrastructure, talent, and organizational change. Creating sustainable economic models for AI in healthcare remains challenging, particularly in resource-constrained settings. New approaches to valuation, reimbursement, and return on investment will be needed to align financial incentives with the potential of these technologies to improve health outcomes.

Charting the Path Forward

As we look to the future, several principles can guide the continued integration of AI and data into healthcare:

Human-Centered Design

The design of AI systems should begin not with technological capabilities but with human needs—of patients, clinicians, and communities. Human-centered design approaches engage stakeholders throughout development, ensuring technologies enhance rather than disrupt the healthcare experience. This requires deep understanding of clinical workflows, patient journeys, and the social contexts in which healthcare occurs.

Collaborative Intelligence

The most powerful applications of AI in healthcare will leverage the complementary strengths of human and artificial intelligence. Humans bring contextual understanding, ethical reasoning, empathy, and creativity; AI offers pattern recognition, consistency, and the ability to process vast information quickly. Frameworks for effective human-AI collaboration, with appropriate division of responsibilities, will be essential for realizing the full potential of both.

Continuous Learning Systems

Healthcare organizations must evolve from static structures to dynamic learning systems—continuously gathering data, generating insights, testing improvements, and adapting based on outcomes. AI can facilitate this evolution by automating data analysis, identifying improvement opportunities, and helping evaluate the impact of changes. This creates a virtuous cycle where each patient interaction contributes to future improvement.

Global Collaboration with Local Adaptation

Many healthcare challenges transcend national boundaries, requiring collaborative approaches to AI development and implementation. Shared standards, open research, and cross-border data sharing (with appropriate privacy protections) can accelerate progress. Simultaneously, AI applications must be adaptable to local healthcare systems, cultural contexts, and resource constraints rather than imposing a one-size-fits-all model.

Trust Through Transparency and Engagement

Public trust is essential for realizing the potential of AI in healthcare. Building this trust requires transparency about how AI systems work, what data they use, and how they influence decisions. It also demands meaningful engagement with patients and communities in shaping how these technologies are deployed. Without trust, even the most sophisticated AI systems will fail to achieve their potential impact.

A Vision for the Future

As we conclude this exploration, let us envision a future where AI and data analytics have helped transform healthcare in fundamental ways:

Imagine a healthcare system where diseases are routinely detected at their earliest, most treatable stages—where subtle patterns in laboratory values, vital signs, and behavior trigger preventive interventions before serious illness develops. Where treatments are precisely tailored to each patient's unique biology, preferences, and life circumstances, maximizing effectiveness while minimizing side effects.

Envision clinical environments where administrative burdens have been largely automated, allowing healthcare professionals to focus their time and attention on the aspects of care that most require human judgment, creativity, and compassion. Where AI systems continuously monitor for potential errors or oversights, creating multiple layers of safety for both patients and providers.

Picture a world where healthcare resources flow to where they're most needed, guided by sophisticated analytics that balance current demands with anticipated needs. Where global health challenges are addressed through collaborative intelligence networks that combine human expertise with artificial intelligence, accelerating research and democratizing access to medical knowledge.

Imagine healthcare that extends seamlessly beyond clinical settings into communities and daily life, supported by ambient intelligence that promotes wellness while respecting privacy and autonomy. Where individuals are empowered partners in their health management, with access to AI-enhanced tools that translate complex medical information into actionable insights.

This future is neither inevitable nor impossible—it will be shaped by the choices we make today in how we develop, regulate, and implement these powerful technologies. By thoughtfully addressing the technical, ethical, and human dimensions of AI in healthcare, we can work toward a future where data and artificial intelligence serve their highest purpose: improving health, alleviating suffering, and extending the quality and duration of human life.

The journey has only begun, and much work remains. But the convergence of data science, artificial intelligence, and healthcare has created unprecedented opportunities to transform how we prevent, diagnose, and treat disease. By approaching these opportunities with wisdom, creativity, and a commitment to human values, we can forge a future of healthcare that is more precise, proactive, personalized, and accessible than ever before, truly transforming treatment for generations to come.

About the Author

With over 15 years of experience driving successful marketing and account management strategies across the healthcare, pharmaceutical, and consumer goods sectors, Ryan Bauer specializes in transforming complex challenges into growth opportunities. Ryan's expertise lies in building and leading high-performing teams, growing multimillion-dollar accounts, fostering long-term client relationships, and delivering data-driven innovative solutions that consistently exceed expectations.

As a widely sought-after writer and speaker, Ryan has presented at several universities, national conferences (SXSW, CES, AdTech, BlogWorld, etc.), and hundreds of other events. Ryan's presentations offer insightful, educational content to businesses and organizations on marketing campaign development. Ryan is the author of two books: Authentic Consumer Experiences: Build Your Brand, Drive Demand, and Create Endless Opportunities with Experiential Marketing and Transforming Treatment, and New Pathways to Lifesaving Care with Data and AI.